WHITE

NOISE

BALLROOMS

STEPHEN BARBER

WHITE
NOISE
BALLROOMS

DIAPHANES

1.

FUTURA NIGHTS,
OCTOBER 1978

Now the dead will no longer be buried, now this spectral city will become the site for execrations and lamentations, now time itself will disintegrate and void itself, now human bodies will expectorate fury and envision their own transformation or negation, now infinite and untold catastrophes are imminently on their way—ready to cross the bridge over the river Aire and engulf us all—in this winter of discontent, just beginning at this dead-of-night instant before midnight, North-Sea ice-particles already crackling in the air and the last summer long-over, the final moment of my seventeenth birthday, so we have to go, the devil is at our heels... And now we're running at full-tilt through the centre of the city, across the square beneath the Purbeck-marble edifice of the Queen's Hotel, down towards the dark arches under the railway tracks, the illuminated sky shaking, the air fissured with beating cacophony, the ground underfoot trembling.

As we pass through those long, sloping tunnels, their arched brick walls streaming with water, the trembling intensifies. Beyond the far side of the tunnels, in near-darkness, a chaotic straggle of bodies extends towards us along the narrow pavement at the base of an immense, abandoned building, seven hundred figures or so—elated and exhilarated, simultaneously downcast and accursed—girls in fishnet tights and ripped silk dresses, scarlet-lipsticked mouths and bleached or jet-black hair, boys in ancient black-leather motorcycle-jackets or heavy overcoats and hand-inscribed razored t-shirts, all emitting their own vocal strata of noise against the monstrous bursts from that building's interior. And against the facade, there also stand resolutely isolated, shadow-hidden figures, in silence, alone, near-embedded into that building's soot-encrusted, scarred surface, shards of broken brick against split-lipped and hooded faces, disjointed from that straggle of bodies.

At exactly midnight, the paint-peeled oak gates of that now-derelict tramshed—its vast interior space once teeming with steel carriages ready to head on electrified lines for the city's peripheries, and now emptied-out for over twenty years—are due to be prised open, and the Futura festival will begin at that instant. It will not end for exactly forty-eight hours. Many of the crowd carry tattered blankets in the expectation that there could be sleep to be had in the unknown world inside the tramshed facades, others carry nothing but a plastic-sheathed entrance-card with a stencilled image of a ghost figure in a 1930s suit, face gone beneath his hat. There has never before been such a festival here in the North, only one-off nights of oblivion at punk-rock venues sited—alongside polluted rivers that stream with naphthalene detrita or industrial zones of coal-tar residues—on the cities' discarded edges, occupying the decrepit nightclubs, dancehalls or ballrooms whose proprietors despair of finding other bookings. Our location is at the heart of the city's aberrations.

Through the cacophony-beaten, worn-down facades of the century-old tramshed, the noise is diminishing, reduced now to sequences of sudden, split-second electronic wails. Whoever is testing the sound-system now decides that its malfunctioning is irreparable, or has reached the acoustic threshold at which it can be sure to irreparably damage all listeners' ears. Only the dementia and psychosis propelled night-screaming of the inmates of the High Royds Asylum for the Insane, the sub-city for the mad on the exposed hills to the north-west of this city, could compete with those last wailings, before the tramshed's interior abruptly falls silent. We are going inside, and will not emerge until our bodies have been exposed to experimental treatments or unprecedented ordeals, as with those subjected tonight to the High Royds inmates' bodies. The surrounding city is falling silent, too—the bars closed over an hour ago and the final drinkers pass by on the street's opposite side without speaking, casting disbelieving glances at the dishevelled line of figures. Already, another two hundred bodies have amassed behind us.

Nobody here in the zigzagging line loves this city, or this country: England. The name of this festival is cast in sardonic irony: any future was curtailed and annulled, before our lives began. The Second World War ended only thirty-three years ago, our fathers are still obsessed with it or wounded by it, and tracts of every industrial city of the North remain wastelanded by its aerial bombings. We despise our distant fathers and our nerve-shredded mothers are hidden. We already belong to the markets, slaughterhouses and corporations of this city, our lives and bodies set to be gutted-out and discarded by them, unless we elude and refuse them. The blinded government of England, Callaghan's government, is almost ready to fall. A bad time is coming, far worse than ever before, only the span of this coming winter away: Thatcher is coming, and the devil is already here, to see and touch, in this darkened, fallen-apart city. Serial-killing is here, gang-warfare is here. Along with the entity of noise we are about to confront, moments from now, a tramshed-facade away, our only intimate attachment is to our own violent exhilaration, and its instantaneous combustions and conjunctions with other bodies.

It's midnight, and those bodies around us are growing restless. Everyone falls quiet for a moment, as the seized-up hinges of the gates gradually pivot-open to create a narrow aperture. A short, hunchbacked man with a black beard emerges, limps out on clubbed feet into the middle of the street, Swinegate, glacially appraises the line of bodies, as though they are gathered there solely for purposes of slaughter or prostitution, expires a reluctant breath, looks up into the stars of that endless moonlit night above the city, then nods to himself, gives a minuscule hand-

7

gesture for the gates to be wide-opened and stands to the far side of them, glancing with definitive disinterest at the hand-gripped entrance-cards. Even those isolated figures enmeshed in the tramshed's blackened facade detach themselves, and are irresistibly sieved inside with everyone else. The accelerating line of bodies fractures, and we follow the rusted tracks that emerge from the tramshed gates, ready to enter a lightless void already seething with disorientated bodies. As we leave behind the surrounding city, it appears to respire again, as though a great malediction is lifting.

Inside this cold and abandoned tramshed—which its momentary proprietors, to conceal its denudation, have called the 'Queen's Hall', as though in derision of the queen of England whose reign's twenty-five-year jubilee took place a year ago, or else to intimate that this hall is the infernal twin of the lavish Queen's Hotel, in which every inhabitant of this city dreams of spending at least one night of their lives, on the far side of the dark arches—an atmosphere of acute fear soon comes alive. In the two decades since the trams were scrapped, no work of renovation was ever undertaken here, and the slate floors are still slick with a screen of oil, thickest between the steel tracks, where engineers spent decades on their backs at work on the trams' undercarriages. The overhead power lines are gone, but the corroded gantries that supported those lines remain, and above them, an immense void of soot-constellated air stretches to the ceiling, far above us. The blackened interior walls of this tramshed hold an ineradicable coating of century-accumulated work-sweat, cacophony, cigarette-tar and benzene, generated by relentless, intense activity, now overlayered with the haunted aura of that activity's abandonment. With the sudden heat-influx of a thousand young bodies into the hall, that coating is already pulsing back into life and emitting a dense toxic stench.

No lights have been switched on in the hall, and all that can be glimpsed of its interior is revealed by the burning ends of cigarettes. The mass of bodies, propelled into the hall through their own velocity, now begin to panic, as though they have been led into a chamber designed solely for their slaughter. A sizzling of malfunctioned electricity traverses the space overhead as a scattering of fluorescent tubes fixed to the overhead gantries are turned on, casting a vertical light down upon the accumulated bodies. Exposed, we scrutinise one another, eye to eye and face to face: an audience of the dead. A scream of feedback turns all eyes to one corner of the hall, close to the entrance, where the hunchbacked promoter—whose hands have just activated the lighting by pulling down a lever—now clutches a microphone, ready to introduce the Futura festival. He even has a few notes ready. But the microphone will not stop screaming, his first muttered words are inaudible, and after ten seconds of downcast fury, he throws the microphone to the ground and gestures a crossed X with both arms in renunciation, as though the festival is finished before its first moment.

The fluorescent tubes glow down on the bodies below, but above them, the tramshed vault seeps upwards into an engulfing darkness that hangs above us. Another thousand bodies have entered the hall's now-sealed doors: it has reached its maximum capacity. The lighting reveals the contours of a platform constructed in scaffolding across the entire far end of the hall, with precarious columns of amplifiers stacked at either side and extending up to the level of the gantries. The entity of noise could manifest itself at any moment, but for now, silence holds its ground as the amassed bodies still stare at one another, at the precipice between terror and elation. Everyone is standing and nobody knows what to do. For the next forty-seven hours, our bodies in that space will be compelled to conjure and inhabit a short-lived sub-city of madness and fear, barricaded by the tramshed walls but aberrantly deep in the heart of that great infernal city of serial-killing and gang-warfare that stretches from the river Aire valley to the northern hills.

I look around for my friends, Iris and Lily, but they have vanished. Pivoting, I see that a long table close to the hall's entrance has been stacked with cans of beer in golden-coloured containers, still affixed to one another with plastic, and I slip through the petrified bodies to reach it. The beer's fee is hand-inscribed on grease-proof paper and taped askew to the wall behind the table, which conceals many hundreds more cans. There will be nothing else to drink for the next forty-seven hours other than rust-tainted water to be collected in your hands from taps and then brought to your tongue and throat. But an excessive glut of amphetamines exists in that hall, and in the shadows alongside the table, entrepreneurs are already distributing handfuls of blue tablets from pharmaceutical bags. Indifferent to the distribution zone of alcohol and amphetamines, the promoter stands alone against the wall as I approach the table, and catches my eye. I know him by sight from many nights at his punk-rock club, the Fuck Club or 'F' Club, which he runs two times each week. He gestures dismissively into space and tells me, 'I rented this hall for almost nothing. And the beer, I took the ferry from Hull and drove to Denmark to collect it myself: it cost almost nothing. I'll have a festival like this in every city of the North next October. Fuck all this, take no fucking notice of this fucking shambles—this is only the beginning. I wanted it to be like 1969, to start with readings by J.G. Ballard, Philip K. Dick, even Gysin. But I'm stuck with a bottom-of-the-bill mad Nazi from fucking Macclesfield.' I look into his disabused eyes. 'You're building an empire, John,' I say, caustically. 'Yes, an empire,' he agrees. 'I'll put you on at the F Club at the end of January, if you want—the new venue, just along Swinegate, by the river. That gives you a few months to get cracking.' I walk away.

As I thread my way through the bodies, the lights are switched back off and an originating outburst of cacophony projects itself from the still-empty platform at the far end of the hall, immediately convulsing the interior surfaces of the tramshed so that fragments of plaster and brick fall from the walls and a miasma of displaced dust plummets from the ceiling onto those bodies below. At that same instant, the faces of Iris and Lily abruptly reappear and each takes one of my hands to lead me through

the crowd towards the platform from which that cacophony is erupting, their faces glowing... Iris has taken two
precious nights off from her trainee nurse's night-shifts
at High Royds where she doses the most vocally delirious
and demented inmates with cocktails of morphine and
chloral hydrate, and watches over their deaths. She usually works at the St. James hospital here in this city but has
been assigned a hard winter of training out at High Royds,
and started only last month. As we ran through the city
tonight, she told me a famous new patient with terminal
glossolaliac dementia arrived the previous night at High
Royds—Eddie Waring, a former television sports-commen-
tator—and she showed me the covertly copied key to the
dispensary from which ingredients are mixed that transport the demented into oblivion. Some nights when she
has no shift, I take the train to a near-derelict town to the
south-west of this city, walk along the Calder river valley
then through a disused railway tunnel that pierces a sheer
hillside, and climb the embankment on the far side to the
terrace house of frozen air and tiny rooms that she shares
with other trainee nurses. Until now, I know nothing of
Lily other than her deep silence and that the skin of her
glowing face is so pallid, illuminating our way through the
convulsing bodies towards the hall's source of cacophony,
that she could be a ghost, or makes me think compulsively
of ghosts—among them, that of my older sister, who died
immediately after her birth, in the bedroom of another
frozen house on this city's peripheries, before I was born,
and lost her life to become another ghost among the innumerable population of this city's maddened, bewildered
spectres. Dead or alive, that population are all equally in
danger of the devil that this city holds within it, all in
danger of its serial-killing, its gang-warfare, its terror and
its horror. There will be no difference, between the bodies
of the dead and the living, in this city.

Four figures are now on the platform, and the outburst of
cacophony which led the population of this hall to move
to its far end, breaking that crowd's bewildered silence
and making their voices cry out in expectation, abruptly

fades out from the precarious columns of speakers stacked at either side of the platform, as though it had been generated of its own accord as a last-gasp residue of the sonic tests that were heard beyond the tramshed walls, as far away as the central square of this city, whose pavements they momentarily convulsed. The four figures on the platform appear unsure what to do, looking at one another in nerve-shredded hesitancy, in the same way that the bodies newly pinioned in the tramshed looked each other in the eyes, an hour earlier. The space around and above those four figures is black and immense, reeking of benzene and toxic residues, petrified and near-solidified in the air after the building's two decades of abandonment, and down below, two thousand or so pressed-together figures form a volatile layer on the ground, hissing and shrieking in anticipation. The four figures exposed on that platform are dressed as though they've arrived for work in a hardware store, and everyone in the hall can sense that, in a split-second, they will either flee the platform, pushing through the crowd and out via the doors into the night air, or else they will begin to perform.

One of the figures approaches the microphone on its stand placed at the edge of the platform, and speaks five offhand words, in a voice of the North: 'Welcome to the atrocity exhibition.' We have gone nowhere, we are already here, transfixed and adhered to the ground, our vision jammed, but our eyes can be unscreened. Instantly, the living entity of noise materialises in that hall. The gantries above us begin to shake in repetition with the beat, and the sound speakers on either side of the platform are seisming too, the propulsions of noise visible as they exit the torn meshed coverings of those speakers. Iris and Lily have led me by either hand—the crowd seemed to rip as we manoeuvred our way through it—almost to the point at which those amassed bodies end, and the platform begins, extending ten feet into the air, and we are occasionally transported backwards and forwards as other bodies infiltrate the crowd from either side. A heat generated by those bodies' gratings-together is now gradually rising up into the tramshed's cold air, in the first fragile tendrils of corporeal condensation that intertwine with the spiralling ascents of cigarette smoke.

The singer's body is solely illuminated from behind by a sequence of lights placed on floor-level at the back of the platform and projected obliquely upwards towards him, and apart from the moments when he approaches the microphone, his face is part-hidden by those vertical trails of cigarette smoke and rising sweat. But when he pierces that curtain of smoke and evaporating body-fluids, we can see his raw, young face, eyes wide, hair and forehead streaming with his own sweat already dripping now onto the front of a C&A shirt of shining nylon fabric, half-tucked into work-trousers. His voice is so drowned in noise that, even singing with such velocity that his throat's tendons are pitched against his skin, it seems he is only murmuring to himself, cast into eyes-wide-open hallucination.

I look from side to side and see that, from the edges, that crowd is already dispersing, heading back towards the alcohol and amphetamine zone, or else to lean in lassitude against the coal-tar surfaced tramshed walls, which are reverberating from the repeated pounding of noise from the platform's speakers, as though blown into minuscule concave and convex deviations with each assault. After a few moments' silence, the noise begins again, this time more frenetic, and now, accentuated above the drone of instruments that accompanies it, for the first time we hear the singer's voice clearly, as he grips the microphone and holds his mouth close to it. His voice roars and echoes through the hall, to the far wall and back again and up beyond the gantries into the voids above them, and also directly into the bodies and arteries and bones of the amassed crowd below. That voice is still immersed in hallucination, but at the same time is dreaming the city at night and its compulsions, exhilarations, elations, abysses.

In peripheral vision, my eyes still focused on the lines of bodies fixed to the tramshed's shaking exterior walls, I realise that the singer has started dancing, while the other three figures are intent on perpetrating an immersing noise for that dance. The singer has taken a step or two back from the microphone, and moves in malfunctioned convulsion, arms flailing as though they need to undertake an intricate sequence of disjointed aberrations in order finally to perform the simplest gesture, fists pumping, knees buckled upwards while his feet keep pounding the wooden floor of the platform. His face too is awrily dancing, somewhere in the zone between psychosis and uncontrollable epileptic propulsion, pupils almost gone, skin streaming with sweat, neck pivoted backwards. When he moves back to the microphone and starts to sing again, I look around at the crowd. I can see many faces weeping and overcome, tears pouring from their eyes, naked shoulders shaking, and other faces are laughing, beside themselves, in the hilarity of desperation and in the vision of a transformed body that is outlandish. It's a theory of the body that will never cohere, has no liveable history, and can only be annulled. Those weeping, laughing faces have witnessed something irreparable. Iris has been standing so close behind me that I can feel the heat pulsing from her body, and when the song abruptly finishes and only wavering jolts of feedback crisscross the voided air, she laughs and whispers in my ear, 'I could just have stayed at High Royds tonight, and seen that there,' but she is weeping too.

Twenty minutes later, it's evident that the singer is drained beyond endurance and barely able to keep on his feet. Between songs, he grips the microphone stand to support himself, eyes closed, but each time the cacophony reaches its driving intensity, he is compelled to dance again and is moving further and further into a terrain of seizure. Between two songs, he lights a cigarette and sits on one of the amplifiers at the back of the platform, putting his fingers to his forehead, but then moves back to the microphone as the percussion for another song kicks in, and starts to sing, then tilts backwards, instantaneously unconscious, arms flailing again but now totally beyond intention, and collapses on his side, the cigarette thrown from his fingers, his limbs still performing spasmodic movements but with an aura of such deep exhaustion that the gestures barely traverse any space, rapidly diminishing into stasis. His bloodless face on the ground appears relieved, blissful in its unconsciousness. The other three figures, who up to now have seemed oblivious, focused only on their cacophony and disinclined to stop playing, raggedly fall silent and set aside their instruments. Two of them pick up the singer, one behind the knees, the other by the shoulders, adeptly, as though they have done this before, and carry him outstretched across the platform, then down steps into darkness. The third figure carefully wipes some fluid from the platform floor beside the microphone with a cloth, glares at the audience and tosses the cloth aside, then rapidly crosses to the steps and is also immersed into darkness.

After the four figures are gone and the platform is emptied, the amplifiers still leak a detritus of noise. I look around for Iris and Lily, but they have vanished again. Everyone in the crowd around me appears distraught and unsure where they are, wrenched and shaking as though they've just experienced a calamity or cataclysm. My throat is dry, and I walk towards the exit of the tramshed, ready to leave. When I reach the bolted oak doors, the promoter stops me with a resolute hand on my forearm and a clubbed booted foot on my own boot. He looks distraught, too: 'Fuck, I put them on at the wrong end of the bill. Next year... But never mind, the devil's been here, in his fucking tracksuit, watching from the back—he took a look at that idiot's dance for a few seconds, then he was fucking gone again. But nobody else is leaving. Just go down that corridor over there and get yourself a bottle, if you're thirsty. I got a deal on four hundred from the Ukrainian market in Chapeltown.' He firmly turns me around and directs me back into the crowd. I say nothing. The night is only starting. On the far side of the amassed bodies, a long, unsupervised corridor leads to a dead-end crammed with bottles of Ukrainian vodka arranged on shelves beside an old work-bench. Off to one side of the corridor, I pass the festival dressing-room. Inside, the four figures who left the platform a few minutes ago are sitting huddled together, the singer now returned to consciousness, shirt and trousers soaked in sweat. Those four figures are beside themselves with laughter.

I lean against the worn brick wall of the corridor as the laughter continues in the room off to the side. It sounds that one of the four figures is being insistently taunted by the other three, but the singer's deep voice is one of the taunting voices, and he is not the victim. Then the figures burst out of the dressing-room, still in the same clothes in which they performed, brush past me at speed, jostling one another, still laughing, the singer's face blanched and dripping with cold sweat, heading towards the end of the corridor and away through the still-reeling crowd to the tramshed gates, momentarily unbolted for them while the promoter reluctantly hands them their fee, and they will exit this hall for the drive in a frozen van along the emptied-out acetylene glare of the M62 motorway, out of this devil's city, rising high among the dark peaks of the Pennine mountains and then descending across the moors where the North's slaughtered children have been buried for over a decade now, to enter another city.

I twist the cap of the bottle taken from the stack at the corridor's dead-end, and look at the label. It reads only: 'Kolos Company of Ukraine, Chapeltown LS7', on a background of blue and yellow. Among the untold streets of back-to-back terrace houses of that district to the north-east of this city's centre, many of them left still-gutted and pulverised from war-era aerial bombing, a distillery in the backyard of a bakery produces strong vodka for the population of that district who fled their own cities of famine and obliterating conflict, and gathered instead in this city during the chaos of displacement after the end of the Second World War, to live here in nostalgia for their own razed cities, now rebuilt and reassigned to other populations. I upend the bottle and swallow a mouthful of the burning liquid, then another.

At the far end of the tramshed, another four figures climb the steps onto the platform. Even though it ended definitively with the singer's fall into unconsciousness, the Futura festival is now ready to begin again. Through the dazed crowd, their eyes still transfixed by what they witnessed on that platform fifteen minutes ago, I walk beside the opposing tramshed walls to those that run along Swinegate, heading in the direction of the platform, but stop after a few steps. In the silence before the next eruption of cacophony, I can faintly hear channels of water coursing vertically down the exterior side of the tramshed walls, which connect with the immense subterranean chambers constructed as workshops and foundries when the adjoining railway viaducts were built in the 1860s, reached from the tunnel under the train tracks by minuscule hatches pierced into the dark arches. The workshops have been disused for many decades, and now the detrita of the city live within those chambers, as negated traces of human life—the mad who resist being transported to the High Royds lunatic asylum on the city's periphery, the destitute and the homeless, the alcoholics and the prostitutes, and those who resolutely refuse this city and this land, England, and now wait to die. Through the tramshed wall, I can almost hear them gathering against its reverse face, in their own sub-city of the deranged, to listen in to the muted cacophonies, with disinterest.

After further mouthfuls of vodka, I lean my back directly against the wall, and feel the chill that traverses it from the chambers on the reverse side. I can see that the four figures on the platform at the far end of the hall are preparing to transmit their cacophony, and I rapidly take more mouthfuls until the bottle is drained and slips out of my hand, the neck snapping from its body of glass as it strikes the slate floor. Then my knees buckle and I slide down the tramshed wall, the shreds of coal-tar embedded into the facade scraping against the skin over my vertebrae, into a position of skewed kneeling. At the moment when the sound speakers begin to emit repeated slabs of sound, so loud that the bones in my eardrums are already protesting, I enter a half-awake alcohol-induced blackout limbo-state, unable to move or close my eyes.

Now time disintegrates, and many hours go by in that darkened tramshed with its own autonomous durations: instead of night and day, there are expanses of pummelling cacophony that appear unending, followed by expanses of silence that also seem endless, until the momentum of cacophony exerts itself again. I can see the shapes of bodies amassed in that tramshed, intermittently cohered into frenzied knots with convulsed limbs and then dispersing again, so that my eyes glimpse the opposing wall of the tramshed, against which other bodies are also leaning, or have fallen. At one point, I see the spectral figure of Lily above me, pointing in the direction of the platform in excitement, as a new cacophony opens up, and exhorting me to stand and witness what will take place. Realising that I will not move, she tries to pull me up by her pale-skinned hand, but I stay affixed to the tramshed wall, in an interzone between the invisible population of the sub-viaduct chambers at my back, and the exhausted population of the tramshed directly ahead, in my malfunctioned field of vision. Then Lily smiles, and vanishes again. At another point, a figure with an entirely black-masked head, two slits for eyes, lifts the serrated neck of the broken vodka bottle to the side of my throat, screams at me, then vanishes too.

By the time I begin to grow lucid again, I feel I have been compulsively imagining or enumerating variants of falls into unconsciousness: that singer's plummet backwards into the disintegrating bliss of his sudden blackout, my own blood-loss haemorrhages in which I tried always to maintain consciousness but realised it was about to slip from me, and the many eyes or faces of people I have seen in this city—run-over by speeding cars, passing out in the hostile streets, or else simply engulfed in ecstasy—whose consciousness veered into its own dissolution. There will be no viable life in this city of gang-warfare and serial-killing without such falls and their releasing of bodies into dreaming. We live in blackouts.

I lever my body back from a concertinaed to vertical position, and open my eyes fully. The drained, broken-in-two bottle is still there beside the base of the wall. My knees are aching, and to activate them I walk over the split slate ground of the tramshed floor to its empty centre. When I turn to face the platform, I realise that the intervals of cacophony and silence have lapsed, and directly against the tramshed's back wall, whitewashed for the occasion, a film is being projected. The surface engulfed by the film image is immense, stretching almost from one side of the tramshed's end to the other, and dispersing upwards into the darkness above the overhead gantries, half film, half void. The soundtrack is channelled directly through the platform's speakers, the film's voices interconnected by spectral trails and spirals of feedback left-over from the performers' cacophonies. Ineradicable traces of the epileptic singer's cries, in his dance convulsions, are now embedded in the fissured walls of that tramshed, and will remain there until its demolition. The film image fills my entire vision. A hooded figure is sliding his way down a slope of coal residue beside an abandoned industrial building after the fall of his body into the surface of a lake, then walks along a highway, the hood pulled back to reveal livid red hair. Then he climbs onto a bench beside a locked television store, to sleep. I recognise the film from seeing it in one of the decrepit film-palaces of this city, two years earlier: *The Man Who Fell to Earth*. The promoter, with his science-fiction and Burroughs obsessions, announced in his handwritten programme for this festival that he would intersperse the cacophonies with projections of films. I look around and realise that, apart from those fallen unconscious while still upright, I am the only figure standing in the entire hall.

Against the blackened benzene-seeping walls of this tramshed, many hundreds of its inhabitants are slumped, body against body, saliva trailing from their lips and pools of urine beneath them. It appears they have been lined against the walls in a coup exacted against this sub-city of the urban deranged and then machine-gunned, but they are sleeping, or unconscious, or in comas. Many thousands of the emptied golden cans are strewn across the ground. Alongside them, in every direction, bodies are awrily splayed on that glacial slate floor, as though they had convulsed there, before freezing into immobility. I could believe that this mass of bodies—two thousand or so, the entire punk-rock population of this city and the adjacent cities of the North—were instead those summarily deported from a city that had been destroyed, now crammed into this space as refugees, as with the bodies of the Ukrainians and Poles who entered this city in bewilderment, their own cities war-razed, thirty or more years ago. I lift the hand of one of the sprawled, his young face aged three decades in one night, and look at his watch, reading time in the glare of the film image. It is now 2am on the second day of the festival: I spent twenty-four hours in my state of unconsciousness.

The only way I can avert a new blackout fall is with a handful of amphetamines, and I walk over to the alcohol and amphetamine zone beside the tramshed's gates. The film is being projected from a rusted gantry twenty feet above the ground, accessed by a ladder welded to the tramshed wall, the reels at the feet of a figure gripping the projector at both sides with the determination to stay awake, the noise of the celluloid traversing the projector echoing in repetition around that end of the tramshed. The entrepreneurs selling amphetamines are also barely awake, their bags negligently dispersed at their ankles, unprotected. Even their sellers disdain to swallow the blue tablets. Such a glut of amphetamines has swamped this city, since last year's winter, that they are now almost worthless as a narcotic commodity—the entire punk-rock population of that city dreams instead of liquids locked in the storerooms of the St. James hospital and the High Royds asylum—and I am alone in taking a handful.

To swallow them at once, and to erase the onset of dehydration now pitching me to the edge of hallucination, I need some water, and walk to the long corridor leading to the toilets, alongside that dead-end dressing-room corridor where the four figures had convulsed with laughter before their escape from this hall. The toilets are housed in an annex to the tramshed. When I enter that vast marble-clad vault, illuminated by dangling lightbulbs attached to the ceiling, a hundred feet above me, the temperature drops by several degrees. I can see small trees growing at roof-top level. These toilets are undivided by sex—they were constructed a century ago solely for the all-male tramshed engineers, never renovated, so they emit a piercing stench all of their own, concentrated from engrained excrement and urine, together with the past two decades' abandon-ment and their sudden reactivation over the past twenty-six hours. The fungal-green and newly graffitied walls stream with incessant vertical floods of water, and the slate floor has subsided in places, as though pounded in a frenzy until it finally splintered, leaving abysses into which the water pours and unalert bodies could readily plummet, to the tramshed's unknown subterranean areas. Several disori-entated figures circle around the annex's floor in states of malediction-spitting delirium, and behind the few intact wooden doors of the cubicles, the gasps and collisions of exhausted, far-gone sex acts resonate up to the ceiling.

After swallowing the handful of blue tablets with tainted, zinc-tasting water at one of the huge bone-china sinks and sluicing my face so that icy drips fall, I turn and see Lily standing beside one of the gaps in the slate floor. She is now wearing a thick dark-coloured full-length greatcoat which she didn't have before and that accentuates her extreme pallor, and smiles, as though she had slyly followed me in here, or had just emerged from one of the cubicles. While everyone in this calamitous sub-city of cacophony looks wrung-out and decades older, Lily perversely appears to have regressed through time, from seventeen back to fif-teen, if she is alive at all. Now I know that, after swallow-ing so many amphetamines, I will want to talk incessantly, but Lily's face will impose silence upon me. When we walk out of the toilet annex and back into the tramshed's main body, we hear the speakers from the far end of the hall emit abrupt bursts of dialogue which echo in abrasure against the wall behind us: '- I think maybe Mr. Newton has had enough.—I think he has.—Ah.' The film is just ending, the drinker's figure slumps in alcoholic uncon-sciousness at an open-air cafe table, a greatcoat identical to the one Lily now wears over his shoulders, his fedora concealing his downturned face, and we watch the film's final seconds until the celluloid unravels and loops down to the floor from the gantry, eluding the hands of the som-nolent projectionist.

Although I know I have to be silent, I say to Lily, 'Let's take a walk outside', and we head for the tramshed's exit gates. The promoter appears to be sleeping too, his eyes half-closed, his hunched back pressed against a splintered wooden chair beside the gates and his thick-soled boots propped on a second chair beneath which a battered tin box with the bar profits is wedged, but when I move to unbolt the gates, he puts his hand on my forearm again and whispers in exasperation, 'Don't go out, there are more films to come—next up is *Barbarella*, then *The Man With The X-Ray Eyes* and some Burroughs cut-up films, *Towers Open Fire*, all that, then the next consignment of beer arrives at dawn and the fucking noise kicks off again at 6am... The Ripper's favourites are on first so he'll be in for that, for sure. I don't understand why everyone has passed-out, we're barely a day into the festival so far. Nobody has any fucking stamina here. I saw you walking around and taking a look at everyone, fucking wired—has anyone died yet?' I shake my head, though it seems to me that the entire population of this tramshed already irrevocably belongs to the dead of this city, then murmur that I will go take a look at the new location of the venue for his punk-rock club, along Swinegate, and he relents with a dismissive, barely-there hand gesture and closes his eyes. I pull the bolts back, the tramshed gates are open, and Lily and I re-enter the night city.

We both take deep breaths of the city's air: dank, dilapidated air—the river close by—but infinitely more breathable than the noxious, deoxygenated air of the walled-in sub-city we have just left behind. That dead-of-night air is far warmer than the frozen air inside. I close the gates behind us, and though they cannot be bolted from outside, the tramshed abruptly appears sealed, the towering brick walls above us enclosing its two thousand collapsed and hallucinating young bodies, transmitting a deep silence through them until I hear the promoter abruptly yelling in fury and the first moments of the *Barbarella* soundtrack slip through the tramshed's gates, followed by the rusted shriek of those gates' bolts being closed. Lily is still smiling to herself, but I can tell she will not want to talk, even though, as the amphetamines kick in, I will have a burning desire to talk and will have to bite my tongue.

The city is deserted, no figures on the pavements, and only a few cars driven by those too obsessional or solitary to sleep, so they must keep driving all through the night, in circuits of the city, followed by occasional police cars, each uniformed driver tracking those circling cars, each uniformed figure in the passenger seat inscribing numbers of parked cars into notebooks which will be catalogued, along with the contents of innumerable other notebooks, logs, recordings, into the great archive of the search for the Yorkshire Ripper, already ongoing for three years now and focused on this city, but still nowhere. The police of this city are derided at every step, and exist in perpetual fury at their failure to locate the Ripper, who has killed nine women so far, across the cities of the North. The aura of serial-killing forms a lethal presence pressed-down over this city and the surrounding cities of the North, so that it infiltrates all of their inhabitants' gestures. In darkness, those cities' streets are almost emptied: women will not go out in fear of being serially-killed, men will not go out for fear of being detained and taken to the cells in the subter-ranean corridors under this city's police stations, or other cells of the cities of the North, and harangued and beaten there for precious data on the Ripper's location. In order to go out into this city in darkness, its inhabitants must possess some irresistible compulsion, for gang-warfare, or alcohol, or punk-rock, or desire, that overrides those fears and casts them into oblivion.

In my peripheral vision, I watch Lily looking upwards at the soot-blackened lavish facades of Swinegate: the hotels and warehouses and bars built over a century ago, even before the tramshed from which we've just escaped, and now almost all derelict in this city's fall. Once, this was one of the great cities of the North, but after this com-ing winter, it will fall still harder: Thatcher is coming, the Ripper will still be here, and the devil is staying with us, too. Occasionally, Lily runs her fingers through her hair, which is almost as white as her face, or over her lips, and I can see that her nails are sharp and split.

After a few seconds' walk along Swinegate, we reach an intersection. To the right is the bridge over the river Aire, and to the left, a wide street leading under the railway viaducts towards the arcades of this city, built as ornate walkways and showrooms for luxuries and technological experiments in the Victorian era, their entrances now mostly boarded-up and barred. At the far side of the intersection, a rundown, emptied-out warehouse occupies the site between the viaduct and the continuation of Swinegate, and the subterranean cellars beneath the building form the site into which the Futura festival's promoter will now relocate his punk-rock club, taking two moribund weekday nights from the hands of the disabused proprietor. Since the winter of last year, the F Club was located out to the north-east of this city's centre, in Chapeltown, and required a nocturnal walk from the city's central square out beyond the brutal twenty-storey glass and aluminium edifice of the St. James hospital, that palace of the dead vacuuming and extinguishing all of the weakened bodies of this city, including those of both my parents, the entire city and its surrounding mountains and flatlands visible from the plate-glass windows of the intensive-care rooms on the top storey, all the way to the cooling towers of the Drax power-station to the south-east and the Pennines to the west, via the hill occupied by the High Royds asylum for the insane and the delirious, approached in all four directions by avenues lined with trees. Whenever I passed by the hospital, on the way to the F Club or back again, on the last winter's nights, the devil was up there, on the twentieth storey, looking out at his domain.

During that winter, and through to the summer which is now ended, the F Club was sited, two nights a week, in an old synagogue, left abandoned when its clientele moved to another district further to the north, the surrounding streets of vacant back-to-back terrace houses then occupied by populations of Ukrainian refugees and Jamaican workers recruited for this city's most unrelenting tasks, across the two decades after the Second World War. In its dereliction, that synagogue's arched upper hall became a Jamaican music club, thudding bass beats into the Chapeltown night air and shaking the adjacent houses, the lower level a Ukrainian restaurant and drinking club. But the streets around that building proved too dangerous even for the F Club's oblivious clientele, and on many nights, leaving the club on foot at 3am, I found myself chased along the otherwise-deserted Chapeltown streets in gang-warfare crossfire, propelling myself a split-second ahead of the gangs' alcohol-laced breath until they gave up in bitter disdain. When I finally stopped and lay reeling on the ground after sprinting headlong down a further street or two, the buildings on either side of me seemed to be col-lapsing on fire around my spinning head. On other occa-sions, when I left the club via the curved stairway's seven marble steps and entered Francis Street, its houses still partly bombed-out and gutted, vigilantes hunting serial-killers from their cars would wind down their windows and ask, 'Are you the Ripper, son?', and if ignored, project bottles to shatter at the ground beneath my feet.

Lily and I now reach the entrance to the cellars on the far side of the intersection, and I bang the side of my fist once on the door, beside which the promoter has already affixed a hand-written poster with forthcoming shows. While the abandoned synagogue in which the F Club was previously located received a name from its Jamaican pro-prietors—the 'Roots' club—these cellars appear nameless. After a moment, a hatch opens, exhausted eyes scrutinise us, and the door opens by a crack. The smell of alcohol and sweat instantly rises up from the staircase leading to the cellar area. An aged man in an immaculate black suit and bowtie gestures towards an enormous open ledger posi-tioned on a card-table, and instructs us, in a Polish accent, 'Please sign in. We're only open until 6am, then everyone has to go.' He notices Lily looking in fascination at his suit. 'You like the suit?—It's from prewar Lvóv. I had it forty years or more already. I used to wear it only on special days, to the cinema, and to concerts in Stryjski park. From the brothers Skladanówsky tailors, on Zamarstynowska street. The fabric is the best, the buttons are Tatra-forest cedarwood. It will last forever. But the city is gone.' He smiles indulgently as Lily runs both hands down over the thick cloth of the lapels, absorbing ghosts, her eyes shining. In a whisper, the aged proprietor asks Lily, 'Are you from Lvóv too?' As the sleeves of her greatcoat retract, I see the still-raw grid of scars traversing the skin of her left wrist.

We sign the ledger and go down. The two low-ceilinged areas at the base of the long staircase are almost in darkness. A bar extends along the left side of the first area, with vodka-bottles scattered around the shelves behind, and a few tables with chairs are arranged on the other side. Four or five absorbed men are playing snooker in the second area, drinking from bottles of Polish beer, and they glance at us only momentarily, with profound disinterest, before returning to their game. That second area angles around into a space not visible from the base of the stairs, and a low wooden platform extends across the far end of that space, each side of its surface semi-collapsed from the weight of sound speakers. The remainder of the platform's surface is deeply incised, as though it has been violently pierced with a stiletto, an infinite number of times. But there is no music tonight, or if there was, it ended many hours ago, and the musicians and their clientele have vanished. Lily smiles with apparent amusement as I return to the bar and she hands me a shotglass of vodka. We will only stay here for a moment longer. I cannot drink it, but I drink it. Her own hand is empty.

The proprietor looks up from his ledger in surprise when we re-emerge after only a few minutes in that club. He sweeps his hand downwards, as though indicating the warehouse's entire subterranean zone, and says, 'If you don't like that one cellar, I have others. They're bricked-up now, but they can soon be opened.' But I have seen what I needed to see, if I take up the offhand proposition of the hunchbacked promoter to inflict a cacophony of my own upon this space, beneath the streets of this city, in three months' time. That promoter must have some fixed preoccupation with this warehouse's cellars to elevate them beyond the other potential sites of his punk-rock club's momentary future: the club located beneath the Majestic cinema on the far side of this city's central square, or the ruined ballroom lodged high on the fifth storey of the Griffin Hotel, a soot-blackened gothic-architecture railway hotel facaded with gargoyles and built in the mid nineteenth century, its corridors of rooms still occupied by the long-term effaced of this city, or even the lavish ballroom located beneath the Queen's Hotel, also built in that era originally as a gothic railway hotel but razed in the 1930s and replaced by a monumental hotel-palace, its marble facades hewn from Dancing Ledge on the Dorset coast, in a style of totalitarian architecture better located in Berlin or Trieste or Bucharest, but now holding the pre-eminent position on the central square of this city and in the dreams of grandeur of its inhabitants. The devil sits most nights in the bar of the Queen's Hotel, carousing with his acolytes, but he drinks no alcohol. And until his recent straitjacketed transportation to the High Royds asylum for the delirious and the demented, Eddie Waring lived for three decades in a suite facing the square. I have never been inside, not even into the foyer, but I will enter that hotel and its ballroom, one day. I realise that the promoter has no desire to create white noise ballrooms, in his punk-rock empire hallucinations, at least for the moment, and prefers to locate himself here—three minutes' walk away from the city's central square, or two minutes, if you are running headlong, in fear or elation—in the damp-saturated cellars and industrial ruins at the wretched periphery within this city's heart, beside the naphthalene floods of the river Aire. In my raging amphetamine silence, I would like to look down into the water of that river. 'We'll just take a quick walk by the river, and then come back,' I tell the aged proprietor, and he nods his head, looking downwards to the virulent carpet at his feet in all-engulfing sadness.

Lily glances back at the proprietor wistfully as he opens the door for us, and I know she would prefer to stay with him and the ghosts of the city of Lvóv. At the intersection, she hesitates again, as though compelled to ascend the street under the railway viaducts and wander through this city, in its dead-of-night silence, walking through walls, into those ballrooms of the Queen's Hotel and the Griffin Hotel, and piercing plywood barriers in order to enter the sealed arcades of obsolete luxuries and technologies. But we walk together onto the wide bridge over the river Aire.

I know that, ninety years ago in 1888, this bridge was the location of the first film ever made, shot from the window of an adjacent building, by the French inventor Louis Le Prince, who had travelled to this city to study machineries for refining and printing fabrics, during the era when the city specialised in such innovations for its industries, and adapted them for the construction of a film camera. His film, two seconds in duration, was projected on an immense screen in the Majestic cinema to mark that anniversary, two weeks ago, the audience of this city's film-obsessives gathering to watch the ghosts either traversing that bridge in the direct sunlight of noon, or else motionless—two figures leaning over its parapet in the lower-right corner of the frame, others walking at speed on delivery errands, a figure pivoting to acknowledge a friend, carriages, carts with precariously piled-up goods, and the newly-built tramway running over the bridge, the carriages still pulled by horses in that era, with the railway viaducts and then-thriving hotels, bars and warehouses on the riverside, among them the warehouse whose cellar we have just exited—and breathing out in awe, after those two seconds, that audience then dispersed into the city's central square after the Majestic cinema's projectionist declined in obstinacy to show the film a second time. Louis Le Prince never projected the film himself, since no projectors existed at that time or for the next seven years, and he vanished without trace, on a railway journey, two years later.

Lily and I walk into the centre of the bridge. Nobody is around, no cars, no police cars, and I am keeping silent to accede to Lily's unspoken stricture. We lean over the low parapet with its ornate ironwork of owls, bees and slaughtered sheep, which extends only to our waists. Behind our backs—beyond all of the warehouses and hotels unchanged from the era of Le Prince's film, only blackened and disintegrated across nine decades—is the tramshed, the intervening distance too far now to hear the soundtracks of science-fiction films bleeding through its locked gates. On the far side of the bridge, to the south, is the city's brewery, working through the night, its chimneys spouting hop-steam, isolated in a wasteland beyond the riverside warehouse from whose nearest window Le Prince shot his film of the bridge. Ahead of us are only the disused unloading depots alongside both banks of the river. And below us, the river Aire is coursing eastwards with its sediments and pollutants towards the North Sea. Here, it is deep black, but further along, when it mixes with the dense mud, benzene and coal-tar of its tributaries, it will turn ochre, before pouring into that sea.

I glance over to Lily wrapped in her greatcoat, leaning her arms on the bridge's parapet, her blanched face staring directly down into the river. She is utterly absorbed in her own phantom presences. She looks across into my eyes' pupils, and I know they must now be dilated to their extreme extent with the ongoing amphetamine rush, and then down at my lips, across which blood from my bitten tongue is slowly seeping. Smiling in distraction, she presses the index finger of her left hand to her lips and reaches down her right hand to unbutton my trousers, then pumps that hand into a fist in a sudden sequence of furious gestures until semen shoots across the parapet edge and scatters into the water of the river Aire, with its detrital flow towards the North Sea. Laughing with delight, Lily tracks the downward course of the semen for a moment until it is lost from sight in the river's darkness. She keeps her scarred hand entirely for herself. I turn my body around to face the opposing direction, and the pavement below the parapet quickly becomes constellated with drops of blood from the tears in my skin made by Lily's split nails, in their moments of frenzy, together with the last drops of blood trickling from my lips. I am gasping as after my Chapeltown gang-warfare chases of last winter, then I close the gaping buttons and my pupils' dilated apertures are closing too.

It's now time to return to the Futura festival, but I turn back to the river, stare down from the low ironwork parapet, and imagine how it would be to plunge into that river from the bridge—in the Victorian era, in hot summer weather, hundreds of naked apprentice boys from the surrounding factories took that plunge—and slip vertically through the surface of the black water, carried by the momentum of your body towards the riverbed, reaching stasis point twenty or thirty feet down, before starting to kick and swim upwards, breathless and lungs aching, mouth and throat closed to avoid swallowing the naphthalene-tainted water, but wanting to cry out, until you break the surface and can breathe again. Whenever torrential winter rains fall for weeks on end on the limestone plateaus of the Yorkshire Dales far to the north, where my parents were born, the river Aire gathers up those rains and flows so fast that it threatens to burst its banks, and only the strongest wintertime apprentice-boy swimmers, after their plunge from the bridge, could ever reach the bank and climb the now-rusted ladder placed there a century or more ago for such survivors... Innumerable such boys, together with those consumed in this city by the desire for suicide, or simply to fall headlong into oblivion, were carried away by the river Aire, towards the North Sea.

When I look up, I realise that Lily is gone, without a word, and I can barely see her pale hair and her greatcoat in the pre-dawn mist, at the intersection before the railway viaducts, then she vanishes from sight, for an assignation with the aged Lvóv club-proprietor or to walk the barriered arcades of this city, or some other destination. My tongue healing, I study the constellations of drops of blood on the bridge's pavement, now drying and swallowed-up into the stone, then walk back along Swinegate towards the tramshed. As I approach it, the gates still barred, it appears silent, with no trace or sign that inside, around two thousand amassed young bodies must be spreadeagled or collapsed over the slate floor or propped against the walls, in groups or in isolation, while a projector beam still transmits film images over their heads, onto the tramshed's striated far-end wall. Nobody answers my fist's pounding on the gates, and they hold no viewing-hatch for those inside to scrutinise the bodies of that hall's prospective clients, as with the door of the future F Club.

At 6am, a truck pulls up and begins to unload many hundreds of cans of beer for the second day of the festival, and at the same moment, the tramshed gates finally open up and the exhausted projectionist staggers out, his arms cradling fifteen or more film reels, some of them enclosed in battered cardboard boxes, others exposed and trailing celluloid. The delivery men work to rapidly stack the beer behind the gates, and drive away. I look around for the promoter, who is invariably present at the entrances to his punk-rock venues, scanning the bodies arriving and exiting with disinterest, but is now nowhere to be seen. It's an aberration for him to be absent. The projectionist notices my bewilderment, and says, 'He's gone off for an important meet-and-greet, or so he told me, before it all kicks off again. I'm taking the chance to make myself scarce—it's like a battlefield in there. What a fucking night.' I steady the film reels precariously balanced in his arms, but he glares as though they should not be touched by hands other than his own, then heads off on foot, back up through the dark arches towards the Majestic cinema on the far side of the city's main square.

A ferocious stench is seeping out of the tramshed—an amalgam of alcohol, urine, body fluids and emissions, amphetamine-sweat, cigarette-smoke, heat-reactivated industrial toxins, dislodged asbestos—but I slip back inside as the gates slowly swing closed after the projectionist's exit. No lights are on inside the building but I can just make out the masses of bodies sprawled on the ground and against the walls by the light of a few burning cigarette ends. Most of the festival's clientele are unconscious, and appear to intend to stay that way. The promoter abruptly appears out of the darkness, directly in front of me, limping from between the heaped and mouth-gaping bodies, and laughs, 'It's like running a fucking zoo in here.' He has Iris with him. 'Your friend has been telling me all about the new arrival up at High Royds. What a fucking tragedy. Those final demented commentaries he did last season were amazing. He couldn't recognise any players, he didn't know what sport it was anymore, where he was, who he was, but he still kept on commentating. It was so beautiful, on a par with the last words of Dutch Schultz. You need to go up and visit him—he'll need some company up at High Royds, alone with the fucking mad... And talking of Dutch Schultz,' he finishes in a whisper, putting his black-bearded lips to my ear, 'I have a special surprise guest to end it all at midnight, straight from New York, just you wait and fucking see.'

Iris looks alarmed, as though all of her professional secrets have been split-open and revealed. I have not seen her since the epileptic singer's cacophony began, over twenty-four hours ago, and she has aged a decade or more in that time. There is no way to keep track of other bodies, in that engulfing darkness, and they soon veer out of sight and touch. We walk away from the promoter, who is now seated and settling his clubbed feet on a second chair, primed for the cacophonies of the festival's second day and to dissuade any attempts at early escape. Iris takes me by the arm and whispers in my ear, 'That man has some strange friends.' I turn to look at her. Her pupils are dilated, her forehead beneath her black hair is vertically striated and abraded like the walls of this tramshed, the petrified coal-tar residues and engrained detrita of this building's surfaces are now marked deep into the skin of her fingers that grip my arm, and her body—made athletically lithe from the gestures of holding-down the convulsing figures of the enraged and the dying—exudes an exhaustion so extreme that it seems as though the last thirty hours have equated to an infinity of insane-asylum nights on the hill above this city, in the company of the raving mad. She whispers again, 'If we can just get through the rest of this alive, I can make us a Brompton cocktail tonight up at my house, if you like. And finally, we'll sleep. The last bus out leaves at ten past midnight, right outside on Swinegate, so we need to be on it.' I calculate that there are now eighteen hours of the festival remaining, and the dawn must be breaking, on the denuded, wrecked city outside, in the world beyond this one.

Iris walks away towards the toilet annex, and at that instant, the cacophony ignites again and the gantries above the amassed bodies begin to shake. The four figures on the platform at the tramshed's far wall, illuminated a moment ago by adjacent fluorescent lighting, generate an acute dissonance, so relentlessly driven in its outburst that it makes the entire tramshed-floor vibrate, and many figures who appeared comatose only a few seconds ago now slowly unpeel themselves from the ground's adhering toxic strata and stand upright, as though resuscitated. A small, gnarled figure with a gurning face, his emaciated body dressed in a wide-lapelled checked polyester jacket many sizes too big for him, joins the perpetrators of that cacophony, approaches the microphone with surly disdain, and begins to berate and insult the audience at rapid velocity. Even from the distance of the entire length of this immense tramshed, I can see that he has consumed a vaster quantity of amphetamines than anyone else now here. His abuse is drowned in feedback for several minutes, and when the malfunction ends, or intensifies, I realise that his stuttered vitriol is actually his singing, and I hear his voice virulently piercing the air of the tramshed: 'The kidneys burn, in the small of my back...'.

Many of the audience are slowly gravitating towards the platform and that crooked, wired figure, eager for subjugation to an abuse whose acidity will momentarily annul their exhaustion, but I head instead at a tangent to the tramshed-wall corridor at whose dead-end almost the entire consignment of vodka bottles remains intact, retained by the promoter for emergency situations. As I glance into the dressing-room alongside the corridor, I see an aged, skeletal man, dressed in a green fedora and an almost identical wide-lapelled suit jacket to the gnarled figure currently performing on the platform, seated before a plywood table, pouring himself a large glass of the emergency vodka with his right hand, his left hand leafing through typed and overlayered manuscript pages, in apparent paranoid trepidation either at the long day ahead or at some unknown agent of assassination. The gesture of his vodka-pouring wrist, pulling back his jacket's sleeve, reveals a switchblade attached on a steel lever to the inside of his forearm, ready to be activated and propelled into his fist at the first manifestation of trouble, and the bulge beneath one shoulder of his jacket signals a holster beneath. He darts a lizard eye at me at the door, but instantly dismisses the contents of his vision and returns his gaze to his vodka.

From one side of that corridor, an ironwork spiral staircase ascends upwards from the sodden, glacial ground-level of the tramshed, then traverses the hall's inner wall via a metal hatch to emerge onto an inspection walkway which runs at altitude along the side of the tramshed, constructed to allow tram-engineers sightings of malfunctioned pantographs extending up from the carriages for repair. From the walkway, I look down on the exhausted, spectral figures below, many of them grouped at the far end of the hall where the gnarled figure and his four associates are pursuing their cacophony, others sprawled on the floor or stacked against the blackened, moisture-streaming walls. At this altitude, any coherence in the amplified propulsions—barely there even at ground level, in the expanses of this echoing, windowless hall—is lost entirely, and all I hear are coruscating ruins of noise, together with the engrained resonances of the epileptic singer's cries of the previous day. I have taken two bottles of the Ukrainian vodka in order to concertina the second day of the festival into fragments of oblivion, and consume one and then the second in gulps. In my eroded semi-consciousness, the day goes by as with the first, in enmeshed intervals of cacophony and silence.

The Futura festival must finish exactly at midnight, after a duration of forty-eight non-stop hours, and as the final evening advances, the annulled, endured time experienced in variants by all of this hall's occupants is abruptly transformed into one, urgent time. For most of the evening, I watch the exit-gates as the promoter abuses those of his clientele who attempt to leave the tramshed, with the intention to head back up through the dark arches to take last trains of the night to the other cities of the

North. I know that the promoter is mentally scanning and archiving every young face that pleads for the gates to be opened, disbarring them without appeal from all future entry into his punk-rock clubs of this city, and once his empire expands, into every club in all cities of the North. But despite their acute exhaustion, most of the tramshed's occupants are determined to remain in that hall until the last moment. At 10pm, the legendary originating figure of punk-rock in England is due to appear on the platform at the end of this hall, for his first performance with his new associates, after a hiatus of ten months following two final performances with his previous associates, the first as a matinee for seven-year-old children and the second for adults, on Christmas Day of the previous year, 1977, at a nightclub in a frozen Pennine town to the south-west of this devil's city, as benefit concerts for the families of the Pennine town's firefighters, on strike and unpaid at that moment for nine weeks already. In the winter of discontent that is beginning tonight—Callaghan's last winter, since Thatcher is coming, awaiting her moment and her power—the entire population of the North will be on strike.

I watch through the ironwork walkway grille above the tramshed furore as my excruciating post-vodka consciousness returns, the interior spaces of my body seared and all senses accentuated, so that every passing moment jolts into greater focus, out of paralysis. With my ear pitched against the tramshed wall as I stand unsteadily upright, I feel I can hear the wretched of this city once again on the far side of that wall, in their chambers and abandoned workshops below the railway arches, screaming in denudation and agitation, but realise that it is now the crowd below wailing in exasperation, the echoes of that malcontent impacting in spasms against the wall. I can tell from the extreme agitation of the crowd that 10pm went by long ago. An armchair has been carried onto the empty platform, together with the plywood table I saw earlier in the dressing-room, a battered kettle and tea-bags now positioned on top of it, but that platform remains otherwise resolutely empty. I catch sight of the aged, skeletal figure leaning against the back wall of the tramshed, in near-darkness, his manuscripts in his hands, waiting to perform the festival's closing moment. Finally, the promoter leaves his preferred site by the tramshed's exit-gates and pushes his clubfooted, hunched body through the crowd to rage at the procrastinating figures beside the platform. His license will turn to ashes at midnight, and if this festival goes on a moment beyond that expiry, the police of this city will suspend their search for the Yorkshire Ripper, raid this hall, and confiscate his takings.

Twenty minutes before midnight, the shockheaded originating figure of England's punk-rock culture finally climbs onto the platform with evident profound reluctance, and immediately turns his back to the audience. His associates are already there, one of them reclining in the armchair, instigating an arrhythmic thud, another adding an aluminium howl, that cacophony rapidly occupying the entire volume of the tramshed so that its walls convulse for the last time, and the singer begins to howl too, in outlandish bursts of melancholy and longing, his back always to the audience, in a performance of negation and refusal, occasionally interrupting that howl to rebuke his associates and anyone else within reach. I can see that this is not what the audience expected or wanted—over half have already fled through the now-unguarded tramshed exit, and others are spitting and wailing in disabused fury at the figures on the platform. Soon, that platform's surface is covered with saliva, ejected in arcs from the raw throats of the audience, while the singer's howling continues, unchanging and relentless in its desperation.

At two minutes before midnight, I see the promoter, his head in his hands beside the platform, look over in consternation at the aged, skeletal man with his manuscripts, who now turns away in indifference, his fee evidently prepaid, and vanishes into the tramshed's darkness. The figures on the platform clearly intend to reinforce their performance's negation by abandoning it in mid-cacophony, a few moments on from now, but instead the promoter intervenes to curtail it himself, signalling with another X-crossing of his arms for the power to be cut, and the entire hall abruptly falls silent. The originating figure of punk-rock, startled in mid-howl, drops his microphone and slips away, cursing the promoter. That microphone emits a white-noise eruption as the promoter picks it up and gestures for it to be reactivated for an instant, and as the crowd floods away, he announces the Futura festival's closure: 'Let's hope you all had a wonderful time, girls and boys—now fuck off out of here!', then throws the microphone back to the ground and limps away in lamentation.

The festival's final die-hard clientele exit the now wide-open gates in silence and exhausted despondency, into the glaring midnight city. This aberrant sub-city of the hallucinatory deranged is being rendered into an annulled status, as though it and its inhabitants never existed. The siren of a police car wails outside, but the promoter has ended the festival exactly on time, and even in the abyss of their corruption, the police know they cannot confiscate his takings or revoke his future licenses to operate punk-rock clubs in the most decrepit cellars and peripheral ballrooms of this city, and they return to the nocturnal circuits of their search for the Ripper. Apart from the crush at its gates, the tramshed's floor is voided of all living forms other than the most comatose, that wasteland constellated by innumerable detrita, but the rusted tramlines and long-congealed oil-slicks traversing it are now visible once again. Bags of unsold amphetamines are spilled in neglected blue gushes and proliferations across that slate floor. The exit's crush of bodies is so dense that I know I may not reach the street outside in time for the night's final bus, but I re-enter the tramshed's now-deserted toilet annex and find a plank-barred emergency-exit door which can be shouldered open.

I land on the deserted pavement of Sovereign Street after propelling myself through the emergency-exit door, instantly immersed in the first night of this city's winter, with the seeping cold of the river Aire—separated only by the breadth of a line of derelict warehouses from this street—engulfing my body until I stand upright. In the skies to the north-west, immense black rainclouds are massing, but for the moment, the air above this city is still iced and starred. It's now nine minutes after midnight, and all memory of the Futura festival has been erased for all time. Nobody chose to film it, even with handheld super-8 cameras, and the smoke-filled, vertiginous hall clouded and set askew all attempts to photograph it, as though it resisted all images, so that festival exists only in the oblivion-shattered bodies of its population, who have now vacated the tramshed so rapidly that the crush jamming the gates only a few moments ago has dispersed, that expelled population heading at speed to the railway station for the last trains of the night out to the city's peripheries, or along Swinegate and across the bridge over the river Aire to recover their equilibrium in nightclubs and all-night cafes.

The junction of Sovereign Street and Swinegate is only a moment's walk along the still-vibrating exterior wall of the tramshed, and around the corner, the final bus of the night is preparing to leave, close to the tramshed gates, the driver already revving the engine and glancing impatiently at his conductor, who is still on the pavement taking a last inhalation of his cigarette while blithely scanning the tramshed's exiting clientele. The bus starts its route right here—the route identical to that undertaken until twenty years ago by the trams which emerged on their lines from the shed's gates, crossed the hills to the south-west and descended into the then-thriving industrial towns of the river Calder valley—and its occupants have walked reluctantly to this site from the bars around the brewery on the far side of the river Aire, where alcohol can be purchased for the lowest conceivable rate, after clinging to their drinks until the last moment. I can see none of the festival's clientele among those passengers.

As I approach the bus—the driver urgently gesturing to me to get on now that the conductor has stubbed-out his cigarette with his boot into the pavement—I pass by the wide-open gates of the tramshed, its wrecked interior now illuminated in an invasive spectral yellow glare by the streetlights outside. The concentrated stench of that interior is rapidly seeping out into the city and dispersing. Inside, the proprietor is standing with his back to me, only a few feet away, weeping in denudation, his empire shattered even before it began, his hunched back convulsing in sobs, his wails resonating around that entire space. Other figures are busily dismantling the platform at the tramshed's far wall, others moving rapidly between the few still-comatose bodies sprawled on the benzene-engrained floor, pouring the contents of previously-withheld vodka-bottles over their eyes and into their gaping mouths, and slapping their faces, to awaken them from the bliss of their stupor, as though aiding battlefield casualties. Those brutally dazed, half-blinded figures soon rise to their feet, as the walking dead, and stagger towards the exit. Only the most stupefied will need to be lifted, carried by the arms and legs, and thrown out onto Swinegate. Soon, the last bodies and the dismantled amplification stacks will be gone from that tramshed's interior, leaving behind only the dispossessed figure of the promoter, adhered in isolation to the slate floor and surrounded by his festival's detrita, weeping through the night of this city.

I jump into the bus's open entrance door as the driver begins to pull away, and climb the stairway to the upper level, most rows of seats already occupied by passengers smoking cigarettes, but the last rows are empty and then Iris is there on the back seat, watching to see if I appear. I saw her last at 6am that morning. I can tell she is now living in a zone beyond exhaustion—her all-night shifts at High Royds combined with the forty-eight just-elapsed hours of the Futura festival—but in the refrigerator of her kitchen in her minuscule house by the abandoned railway tunnel, on the hill above the river Calder valley, a large medicinal bottle taken by her delicate hand from the asylum dispensary's cupboard contains a cocktail in the variant of ingredients—morphine, ethyl alcohol, chloroform, chloral hydrate and syrup—preferred at High Royds for maximum efficacy upon the demented and terminally delirious who must be transported, across the span of one night, into death or oblivion.

Iris is leaning her head back against the razored green-vinyl seat—the city's facades pivoting in the narrow window directly alongside her face as the bus turns north at the intersection beside the F Club's future site, then west onto Boar Lane and heads towards the city's central square—and tells me, 'Everything has ended... It's over, it's all over', but I'm uncertain if she's speaking of the festival, or her life. After the elapsing of the world of the festival's past forty-eight hours, I am now pitched into another world. I sit beside her, but at a distance, and as we pass the facade of the Queen's Hotel, I see the aged, skeletal man, now wearing a smart raincoat over his jacket and carrying a vodka bottle in one hand, a briefcase spilling manuscripts in the other, entering the chandeliered hotel foyer as though heading for a convention. Iris identifies and professionally assesses him, 'That's a man who needs a large dose of methadone, right now.' She reflects for a moment, as though calculating multiple obsessions and permutations of the human body, then adds, 'They will give him Eddie Waring's suite, it's vacant now.' After leaving the city's central square, the bus turns back towards the river Aire and crosses it close to where it disappears into its subterranean channel below the railway station.

Iris tells me she will never attend such a festival again, nor will she ever visit the F Club again upon its re-opening, but I know she can only dissolve the gruelling insanity of her nights at the High Royds asylum, over the coming winter, with nights at deranged punk-rock clubs beside polluted rivers. She begins to tell me stories of her nights at High Royds and at the St. James hospital, and soon we reach the spine of hills that separates the river Aire valley from the river Calder valley—industrial chimneys and shut-down factories and the crumbling cupolas of Victorian-era magnates' granite mausolea all around, embedded among the endless rows of terrace houses that veer out in all directions over those hillsides—but, overwhelmed by nausea, I realise I cannot continue this journey towards the transparent bottle of liquid waiting in the refrigerator, in Iris's frozen house, and turn to hold her left ear for a moment in my hand, her skin finally starting to warm again and her eyes looking at me in desperation, then I walk away along the smoke-saturated aisle, down the stairway, off the edge of the bus's entrance as it slows for an intersection, and fall retching into the gutter, expelling nothing but dehydrated vodka residues. Then, gasping for breath, I simply lay on the pavement at the gutter's edge, on my back, the stars of the Northern sky high above me. At a moment towards dawn, someone heading down into the valley stops and helps me up. I start walking back into the city.

2.

THE DEVIL'S GROUND,
JANUARY 1979

This city belongs to the devil, irrevocably, for all time. If he is resting from his work, he will survey the entire city through the great plate-glass windows of the emergency rooms at the twenty-storey summit of the St. James hospital tower, or from the black-tinted windows of the bar of the Queen's Hotel where he carouses with his acolytes and looks out upon the city's central square, or from the windows of the BBC North studios high above the serial-killing and gang-warfare terrains of Chapeltown. But it's said he has a special predilection for the sloping strip of decrepit warehouses, nightclubs, abandoned buildings and unknown zones between Boar Lane and the northern bank of the river Aire: the devil's own ground. In the streets of this city, we only ever see his speed-blurred physical manifestation for an instant—the tracksuit, the white hair—since his progress is so swift, his work so pressed and arduous, the proliferation of his tasks to be accomplished so innumerable. The devil was born in this city.

For the weeks following the Futura festival, black clouds blown in from the north-west unleash relentless rainstorms on the city, and the level of the river Aire rises to the top of the vertical stone banks built in the nineteenth century to channel its course between the warehouses and factories, and under the railway station. One night, I return to the site of the festival, the tramshed gates still pitched wide open, the detrita and debris inside uncleared—dried bile and semen on the slate flooring among the petrified benzene-slicks, ripped scraps of celluloid from *The Man Who Fell To Earth*, endless emptied beer-cans, items of clothing left-behind by the expelled comatose—and all that has changed since I last saw it nine minutes after the festival's closure is that the weeping body of the promoter has finally departed. Wild animals have scavenged the unsaleable amphetamines, discarded in thousands of idly-scattered blue tablets, then bludgeoned their heads in frenzies against the blackened interior walls of the tramshed, and other animals have eaten those animals, before dying too in their own feral madness, so that the stench of their carcasses now joins the diminishing stench, exuding into Swinegate, which is that festival's legacy, along with the irreparable psychoses and cracked memories instilled in its clientele across its forty-eight hour duration. The tramshed now awaits its demolition, but that immense undertaking can only be accomplished once this winter is over.

Finally, at the beginning of January—Thatcher's first year, 1979, since everyone senses she is coming—a new bout of rain-storms above the Yorkshire Dales propels the river Aire over its banks, and the city floods in acrid, naphthalene water, extending six feet deep all the way from the brewery to the south of the bridge to the slopes of the dark arches and the railway viaducts to the north. The bridge itself is submerged to its ironwork parapet, and all the subterranean levels and cellars of the surrounding warehouses are inundated to the height of a human body. After only a few nights of operation in its new location, the F Club's venue is itself flooded, the waters forcing open the barred door and pouring down the stairway into the cellar space. The promoter has appeared on local television and given interviews to the city's newspapers, speaking in lamentations: first the Futura festival's calamitous ending and non-appearance of its star attraction, now these punk-rock club cancellations. Since the bridge is rendered impassable, the city authorities institute a network of rowing-boats to transport passengers across the flooded river, from the railway viaducts to the brewery, as though this were a medieval city only traversable by water. The passengers bitterly dispute the fee they must pay for their transit, and that city—together with all the cities of the North—is flaring with acute malcontent as Callaghan's hapless government enters its final phase of disintegration, imminent strikes of all surviving industries and public services now threatened. The dead will not be buried and will float away along the floodwater towards the North Sea, together with the uncollected refuse. The population of Chapeltown would like to riot, but desist only because they fear that they, too, will be carried away in their uproar by the floodwaters.

As I make the crossing by boat of the flooded river in the first days of the month—the rowers in their orange city-council rubberised overalls cursing at the strong flow, the sky overhead now brilliant blue, since the rains have stopped—I realise that I will now need to gather together at least three agents of cacophony for the performance which the promoter proposed to me on the first day of the Futura festival, and which I accepted in my silence. By the end of this month, I must have three bodies willing to occupy the far corner of the club under Swinegate alongside me, and execute at least twenty minutes of sonic furore, if the floods recede by then.

In mid-January, a wind rises from the far north and strikes this city, the temperature abruptly plummets and the floods freeze solid in a glacial rush, so that it's now possible to walk on a floor of ice, all the way from the railway viaducts to the brewery on the river's southern bank. The exterior warehouse walls that were streaming with water become encased in thick ice and in icicles that hold the height and dimensions of human bodies, tapering to lethal blades. All of the floodwater filling the cellars freezes too. In a thick overcoat, I walk along Swinegate towards the public call-box outside the post-office in the city's main square, look into the tramshed gates once again, and see that the uncollected debris inside is now vanished, submerged far beneath the level of the ice. The extreme cold has striated fissures into the exterior brick walls, already destabilised by the corrosive components of the toxic residues covering their inner surfaces, priming them for their demolition to come. When I reach the call-box, I dial the number of the promoter at the Yorkshire Television studios where he has his day-job. The television station is now on long-term strike—the defunct television sets of this city intermittently come to life to transmit appeals in the hunt for the Yorkshire Ripper, and otherwise transmit nothing—with only an emergency crew on hand, so it takes a while for him to be called to the telephone, his clubfooted steps audible before his voice: 'Who the fuck is it?' I ask him if the F Club cacophony performance is still fixed for the end of this month. His voice echoes as though he were speaking from Siberia, in the intimate company of muttering ghosts, rather than the other end of Kirkstall Road. 'Fuck, yes,' he says, 'I need to get the F Club up and running again. This ice will be gone in no time, then the proprietor will get together a gang of his Polish friends to pump out the cellar. Tuesday 30th, 11pm. I'll pay you £12 if I can. So don't fucking let me down.' I put the receiver down. Next I call Iris, whom I haven't seen since our journey from the Futura festival, as she arrives for her High Royds shift—she has no telephone at her house by the abandoned railway tunnel—and give her the F Club assignation. I can only hear her voice in eroded fragments. She tells me, 'There's no way I can come... I have to devote myself to the patients here now. They don't let up screaming for a moment. Bad things happen to them in this place, late at night... And I had to drink the entire bottle myself... I didn't wake up from the coma for a day and a half... So only if there's no shift that night.' It's impossible to call Lily, since I have no number for her, but the nameless club's aged proprietor from Lvóv may be able to locate her, among the vanished and the spectral bodies of this city.

As I walk back down Swinegate on the deserted ice plateau, it seems to me impossible that the frozen floodwaters will disappear in two weeks and that a clientele for the proposed cacophony can be conjured from the traumatised, oblivious population of this city, then induced to enter the just-drained abyss of that cellar beside the river

Aire. But now I need urgently to isolate the executors of that cacophony from my friends and associates, and I start mentally to visualise and reject their faces, until I have rejected everyone, then I start again, and isolate the faces I most want to reject.

At the back of the tramshed, on Sovereign Street, a rusted maintenance ladder, previously left trailing into unreachable space above the pavement, is now accessible from the raised ice plateau, and I start to climb to the tramshed roof. All of the rainwater has seeped through gaps in the thick oak beams of that roof so it holds no ice. Scattered around are old beer-glasses and tea-mugs from the tram-engineers' own climbs to this roof, decades ago. I walk to the roof's edge. It's evening, and the winter light is just about to darken. Down to the south-west, the spine of hills above the river Calder is visible but the entire plain between the Aire and the Calder, to the point of the two rivers' confluence, appears flooded and iced-over from this distance, and up to the north-west, beyond the peripheries of this city, I can see the High Royds asylum, where Iris is now just starting her all-night shift with the demented and the psychotic, infernally palatial in isolation on its hill, white with frost and icicles.

As the sky darkens totally, I descend the ladder from the tramshed roof and cross the iced-over river Aire bridge, holding the ironwork parapet in order not to lose my feet. Beyond the bridge, I take the alley which leads off into the maze of derelict Victorian warehouses and workshop buildings extending between the river and the brewery. Up to the doorway of the first building in the alley, a channel has been methodically cut through the ice, and I hammer on the door. It takes at least ten minutes before I hear my friend Jim push aside the internal bolts to open it. He immediately starts ascending the wide staircase. 'I wasn't expecting you,' he says over his shoulder. 'I'm just leaving, you can come along if you want.' He is wearing a battered European leather coat from the 1930s, belted at the waist, and a truck-driver's high-necked black jersey beneath it. When we reach the second floor, he gestures at the locked cast-iron door and murmurs, 'Le Prince', but ascends another two storeys. In his workshop below the roof, a coal-oven fire is burning and I cross the raw floor-beams to the window. Even ice-carapaced, the bridge directly below and the warehouses on the river's northern bank are recognisable from Le Prince's two-second film from ninety years ago, viewed from this warehouse storey at a higher elevation. 'I have the key,' he says. 'It was still in the lock, rusted shut, but I got it open. I haven't been inside yet. I'll take you down there sometime. It's been empty for decades, just ghosts.'

Jim's workshop walls are stacked with film-reels from floor to ceiling, and he's now gathering up four reels, handing two of them to me to carry back down the staircase. On a table in one corner of the workshop, beside the telephone, he has a synthesiser, marked 'EMS Synthi AKS', and several amplifiers and cases piled-up alongside it. I can't tell if he lives here too, or in another abandoned warehouse in this alley. Since the winter of last year, Jim has worked as the relief projectionist at the Majestic cinema in this city's main square, filling-in when the senior projectionist is too disabused or felled with alcohol addiction to pursue his duties, and taking on the all-night screenings which no other projectionist in this city will accept. I tell Jim that I saw his boss in October projecting science-fiction films at the Futura festival, and Jim exhales and rolls his eyes. On nights when he isn't working at the Majestic, he hires himself out to any cinema across the entire expanse of Yorkshire whose regular projectionist is out of action, or has vanished along with the film reels, necessitating an emergency replacement. Jim's father and grandfather did that same work before him, and on the work-benches around the room, I see splicing devices marked with manufacturers' insignia from 1930s Austria, acquired before his grandfather fled that country to become marooned in this city.

Jim pours us two shots of vodka before we head off into the frozen night, and I tell him of the promoter's proposition. Jim looks around at his synthesiser and the cases alongside it, and across the intervening Aire ice-field at the warehouse on the other side whose cellar will once again hold the F Club, if this city's hell ever unfreezes. I know that he's been a trained musician since childhood, can play any instrument, and wanted to study at the music school of the Vienna arts academy, and nowhere else, but his father refused, telling him that at least a century had to pass before anyone in that family could return to the concentration-camp lands of central Europe, and consigning him last winter to a lifetime of nights in the family business.

Jim is hesitant, and after draining his vodka, he says, 'Maybe... We could use the place downstairs to rehearse, if we need to. But it would need to be a real cacophony, a fucking hailstorm of noise, otherwise I'm not interested. And just once, never again, just once... In any case, from the 31st, I have to be at the Majestic every night for the run of the new Coppola film—it's nearly three hours long, and my boss will never get through that, so the cinema's proprietor wants me to be there for every screening, to project the final reel. Brando. I don't know how long the run will last with that title: *Apocalypse Now*.... There'll be an all-night celebration in the Majestic's basement after the first show.' He checks the time and we leave immediately, down the stairs, beyond the far edge of the ice-field, and into his van parked beside a long-emptied brick warehouse whose ornate facade appears subject to a vast outburst of fungal contamination, trees growing from the roof.

Jim drives us out to the sliproad leading to the M1 motorway. Even in the glacial darkness, figures are standing by the side of the road, hoping to catch rides to escape the North. Jim is driving at speed, playing a cassette of relentless machine-pounding which pushes him on faster—he's late, and the cinema clientele in some godforsaken town alongside the motorway will already be buying their tickets at the kiosk. No police are on the roads, all patrols assigned to the hunt for the Ripper, so he starts to drive at exhilarating velocity. We are propelled through the night, high up on the motorway's embankment. After a few moments, the towns around the Calder river valley appear to the west, in veering sequences of lights on the zigzagging hillsides.

From the flatlands to the east, the Drax power-station's seven immense cooling towers materialise in the distance, their infinite expulsions of water vapour, coal-tar residues and naphthalene blown out towards the North Sea. Further south, we start to pass the illuminated steel foundries, the open-air pouring by concentrated work-gangs of the molten steel making fire spit out into the darkness, but the vast halls and railway-yards of other foundries are darkened and disused, already voided and in the process of demolition, as that land's engulfing industrial disintegration now takes hold.

Jim tells me, 'It's the next exit. We're almost there. I still have to get the reels onto the projector and the screening starts in ten minutes.' We skid onto the exit ramp and into total darkness, no streetlights on either side of the road, but Jim doesn't reduce speed. Against the virulent ash glow transmitted vertically by the lights of a city to the south, as though that malediction-inscribed city has just been incinerated, I can see colliery pithead wheels and slag-heap tumuli. We pass through a deserted town and Jim pulls up directly outside the cinema's foyer, turning off the van's cassette-player at the same moment so that I hear a half-century of amassed film-projector components abruptly collide with one another in the back of the van. I'm still clutching the two film-reels he gave me in his workshop, and he grabs the other two from beside his seat. The cinema manager is standing outside in anxiety, beside the poster advertising the film about to be shown and under a malfunctioning neon sign: Regal Cinema. The audience are already inside, their eyes fixed on the blank screen.

While the film runs, I watch Jim's adept hands as they hover around the grating projectors, his scarred fingers easing the buckled celluloid through the gate, anticipating rips in the aged strips, performing split-second reel-changes between the two projectors so that the film runs seamlessly for the audience of ten figures in the darkness below. Jim is indifferent to the film itself but it's clear that he's obsessed with the technology of the projectors, and the more obsolete and malfunctional they are, the more he is captivated. While one projector is running, he takes the other down from its stand, unscrews it and begins to dismantle it, replacing worn steel parts from the handfuls he brings out of the pockets of his leather coat. The sweat pours down Jim's face as he works. As the anxious cinema manager hurried us through the auditorium to the over-heated projection box, he told us that his usual projectionist abruptly entered a psychotic state that afternoon and tried to throw the reels for the night's screening into the river Calder, before being captured and transported to High Royds in glossolaliac delirium. He asks Jim if he can take over all projection responsibilities at his cinema permanently, but Jim smiles and shakes his head: 'All projectionists go mad in the end: alcohol, solitude, amphetamines, the cacophony, the heat. They crack up... But I'll check my schedule, maybe for a week I can do it, then I have to get back to the Majestic.'

We're back on the M1 motorway, but driving slower now. The lights of the Calder river towns are going out, but the Drax power-station towers are still pumping. I ask Jim why he didn't project the Le Prince film of the river Aire bridge himself, at the ninetieth-anniversary screening at the Majestic last September. I didn't speak to him on that night—we were enemies, for reasons we don't remember. He says, 'I'm just the dogsbody there, nothing, the assistant. My boss has been there for ten years already, and he's biting the floor. The bastard knows it's coming down soon. I'll go in one evening and he'll be hanging from the ceiling, and I won't be sorry. I'll need to wait for that until I take over, then I can do as I like.' We reach the end of the motorway's embankment and the entire city is suddenly laid out before us in the moonlight, as a spectral apparition under its acetylene streetlight glare: the immense derelict factories with their chimneys, the wastelands on its western side where the city was aerially fire-bombed over thirty years ago and never rebuilt, the Town Hall and the hill with the BBC North studios, vast cemeteries of blackened tombs and the cupolas of Victorian industrialists' mausolea, the football stadium just below us, and the ice-glittering silver course of the river Aire winding through that city's heart, disappearing beneath the railway station and the Queen's Hotel, then re-emerging and heading east towards the Drax cooling-towers. Jim must have seen it many times before, but I hear him curse a loving malediction under his breath.

We leave the van beside the contaminated warehouse and return to Jim's workshop. He opens the windows to the night air and leans out over the frozen river, still cooling down from the overheated projection box. I can tell he's intrigued by the prospect of the F Club cacophony, and he immediately begins to pull his synthesisers out of their cases. He tells me that many of them are handbuilt experimental prototypes from 1920s Russia, where his grandfather was a pioneer of electronic music, collaborating with Arseny Avraamov and Leon Theremin, before performing for a decade or more in Vienna, supporting himself by repairing film-projectors, prior to his exile to this city on the day following Hitler's *Anschluss*. His grandfather's Russian collaborators mostly vanished into the Lubyanka cellars or the gulags, the collaborators in Vienna all disappeared into Mauthausen or Auschwitz or the I.G. Farben chemical company's slave-labour camps. After arriving in this city as a refugee, Jim's grandfather never touched the synthesisers again. 'I've had to rewire most of them,' Jim tells me. 'But they all work... My grandfather told me he once met Nikola Tesla at the New Yorker Hotel, his proudest moment—he demonstrated his experiments to Tesla in the hotel ballroom.' Jim turns on one of the ancient, obsolete synthesisers and starts to manoeuvre its settings with one hand, while manipulating the EMS Synthi AKS's dials and keyboard with the other. At first, all that emerges is the same disconnected hum that I hear each time I call Iris on the High Royds line, but then the amplifiers abruptly begin to transmit an outlandish sound that holds all of the anatomical melancholy of the bodies of this city and the disintegrating lands around it, before Jim's fingers work more frenziedly so that devastating neural beats cross the river Aire at maximum amplification, impacting against the iced warehouse facades on the far bank—I can see them vibrating—and echoing back.

Jim turns off the two synthesisers and laughs, 'We'll need some percussion too, maybe guitar. Otherwise it's just going to be all-out aural torture for the audience.' He reaches behind the stacked-up synthesisers and grabs the neck of a dust-coated guitar. Without wiping away the dust, he plugs it into one of his amplifiers and a feral wail of feedback emerges even before he touches the guitar's rusted strings. He says, 'I didn't really want it, but it came as make-weight part-exchange last winter from a cabaret artiste from south Yorkshire who planned to open a pornography cinema in Penistone and needed a couple of old projectors fitting. He was glad to get rid of it. It's a 1961 Burns guitar, a Split Sonic with special "wild dog" setting, three pick-ups, tremolo-arm. Rare stuff, since nobody wants it. It's been played in every club of the North. You can have it if you want.' He wipes the sunburst front of the guitar with a cloth and I can see the constellated incisions of fingernails, projectile-impacts, nicks, scars, cigarette-burns, scrapes. I take it from him and though I barely know how to play, I'm oblivious and it feels good. I hand it back to Jim and take a £10 note from my pocket—I still have some money left from selling my parents' house, and that will last me until the end of March—but he waves the note away with distaste. He says, 'If that hunchbacked rascal pays us, I'll take something then. I'll keep the guitar here for you.'

As we descend the staircase, passing by Le Prince's workshop on the second floor, I'm startled when Jim begins to talk of the coming of Thatcher. Everyone in this city knows we are now living the last moment before Thatcher, and in a few months at the latest, she will be here. We already have the devil and the Ripper in this city, and now we will have Thatcher, too. England is asleep—Callaghan has been swimming off the coast of Guadeloupe this week, and he doesn't think that 'other people in the world would share the view that there is mounting chaos'. Jim's voice is suddenly shaking with anger, and I know he is torn, his senses irreparably shredded by his family history of punitive humiliation, vanished bodies, and exile.

He detests the already-fallen cities of the North, but prefers them in their current collapse and awry elation than under Thatcher's coming regime. We know she is coming, but we don't yet know exactly what she will bring with her, other than totalitarian madness, the eradication of the North and its surviving industries, and the crushing into subjugation by the military and the police of all insurgent bodies. Jim can sense what is coming far more acutely than I can, and I try to divert his black mood: 'The devil will take all his Christmas holidays with Thatcher from now on—that is, if he doesn't take them up at High Royds with the Ripper, assuming that's where they'll put him, if he ever gets caught.' I'm standing in the building's ice-cleared entrance, and Jim glares at me with fury and slams the door. I hear him bolting it as I walk away.

It's 1am by the still-functioning clock-face on an abandoned warehouse's tower by the bridge. During the evening, the clear sky of the last weeks has clouded and the temperature is rising. After crossing the bridge, I enter Swinegate and reach the nameless club, hoping to speak with the aged proprietor from Lvóv about the potential whereabouts of Lily. He's nowhere to be seen but the deserted club's doorway is still torn-open from the force of the floods that traversed it, and I descend the stairway as far as I can go. The base of the stairway and the cellar are six feet deep in ice-sealed water, so that the entire lower half of the space is submerged and encased. Through the gap at the top of the club's entranceway, I can see its walls crystalline with amassed ice-particles that illuminate it as they start to melt. I think about slipping through the gap to walk over the ice to the far end of the club, but I can hear its surface already cracking with the raised temperature, the pressurised naphthalene water trapped beneath it starting to propel itself upwards. Turning back, I climb the staircase, head right at the intersection by the railway viaducts, and start walking towards the gang-warfare and serial-killing Chapeltown streets.

As I walk by the barricaded arcades, I'm momentarily haunted by Jim's fear of Thatcher and the coming transformation of this city and the Northern lands. This city is the ruin of a thriving city from the previous century, still inhabited through obstinacy, and we want to hold onto the disintegration that engulfs us and exhilarates us, for another instant. But this city is impelled by aberration, too—if we will be destroyed by Thatcher, it is because we desire it, and this city now waits for Thatcher, and desires her, to complete its fall. We know that Thatcher has taken elocution lessons, so that her vocal commands will be irresistible. We know that she loves the dictators of South America so strongly that she will surpass them. Once she eradicates the industries of the North—the coalfields and the steelworks—she must turn to the exposed bodies of its populations. The men of this city will be separated out from the women, and the children of this city will be separated out from the women and the men, and each group will be taken in turn to a place of confinement on the city's peripheries, such as the Elland Road football stadium, and made to wait for several days before their mass execution. A renegade montagnard army from the Yorkshire Dales will stream down into this city, following the course of the river Wharfe—just as the Vietnamese infiltrated Phnom Penh from Cambodia's north-eastern highlands at the beginning of this month, to end the mas-sacre regime of Pol Pot—and liberate all survivors, then head south on foot, along the tarmac course of the M1 motorway, to arrest Thatcher, execute her with all of her associates in the courtyard of her ministries and display her severed head on a pike above the fast-flowing Thames from the quayside of the Prospect of Whitby pub in Wap-ping, for all to see. Thatcher is not even here yet, we are still safe for a few months in the vertiginous ecstasy of our fall's momentum, but we already dream of her death. More likely, her fall will come at her acolytes' hands, not at our own hands. When Thatcher comes, at this winter's end, we do not know what will happen.

Once I pass the glass-faced tower of the St. James hospital, I enter the gang-warfare terrain of this city. Chapeltown itself has no gangs, only those ready to riot, but it forms the crossing-zone for the movements through it on foot of the gangs of the Seacroft housing-estates to the east, and the Meanwood housing-estates to the west. Those gangs' confrontations take place in a different site each night, ranging in size from scuffles to massed battles with several hundred participants on each side, and no participant is aged over nineteen. They are disputing territories which they despise and reject, and they hold no weapons, other than broken bottles and industrial knives intended for slicing plywood. At times, other gangs, from other areas of the city, such as Belle Isle and East End Park, intervene and attack both the Seacroft and Meanwood gangs simultaneously, so that those two gangs must form an alliance to avoid being overcome. The occupants of the police cars on Chapeltown Road disregard all gang-warfare, since they possess only one priority: to locate the Ripper, and arrest him, before he kills again.

As I enter Chapeltown, I hear the roars of the gangs coming from either direction, and realise I have to move fast, or I will fall into the path of the Seacroft gang. Each gang emits a wordless roar, incessantly, as it makes its long journey on foot towards its adversary. The main bodies of the gangs can be avoided through tracking the echoes of their roars, but the danger comes when your path crosses that of those trailing behind a gang's main body, or those whose course has been turbulently set askew by a sudden skirmish. Once I turn off Chapeltown Road onto the bomb-site-indented terrace houses of Francis Street, that gang-warfare roar is supplanted by the dub bass pulse emitted from the Roots Club, that disused synagogue's building shaking seismically in its wasteland, as though in protest at its post-abandonment resuscitation as a dub club, the cacophony ricocheting off the surrounding houses, which reverberate too. I climb the exterior marble steps and ask the dreadlocked doorman, 'Is Veronika around tonight?' and he nonchalantly gestures me inside. Through the thick smoke, at the far end of the hall, I can see Veronika's tall, lithe figure behind the bar, dressed in a black highnecked jersey, black skipants and climbing boots, handing out red cans of beer to the dwindling clientele. She seems startled to see me, as though I were a ghost—I last saw her last summer, when the promoter moved his F Club punk-rock nights away from this venue to the now-flooded club by the river Aire—but she points downwards with her index finger, as though consigning me to an infernal subterranea.

All I know of Veronika, from our encounters during last summer's F Club nights, is that she loves drumming, and she is half Jamaican and half Ukrainian, but both her parents vanished when she was a child. Her uncle operates an all-night restaurant and drinking club in the soundproofed basement of the synagogue building, and when I descend the staircase by the club's entrance and take a rickety plywood table among the insomniac old men that comprise his clientele, he recognises me and sets down a plate of fried carp and a bottle of Chernihivske beer in front of me. The basement is pulsing from the noise overhead, as though we were all lodged inside a frantic human heart, but it's quiet down here apart from a radio tuned to Radio Kharkov. 'You need to think about marrying Veronika,' her uncle tells me in a grave voice. 'We're worried about her... She's seventeen now, she's too old to be getting wild.' I say nothing, and look around at the aged figures with wounded eyes, sitting mostly in solitude, others smoking and playing cards in silence. After almost an hour, Veronika suddenly appears at the table in front of me, her long black hair pulled back from her high cheekbones and brilliant blue eyes. Her uncle immediately sets down an identical plate of fried carp for her, and she laughs, 'Fresh from the river Wharfe...'.

'You missed the Futura festival,' I tell her, 'I missed you there.' She looks at me, her eyes shot-through with mischief: 'You know I only like clubs, two nights in a freezing tramshed isn't my idea of fun.' I tell her of the F Club promoter's proposition, and ask her if she would like to play drums at that performance, just for one night. 'Maybe... But I haven't got any drums anymore, I had to sell them. But we can go and get some, just a snare-drum would be enough, that's nothing to carry. We can walk down to that music school, they probably have a ton of excess stuff in there, just get in from the roof, grab what we need. I've got the right boots on.' She points down below the table to her climbing boots. It takes me a moment or two to realise what Veronika is planning. 'The Northern School of Music?' I ask. 'That sounds a delicate operation. I've never been inside. We may need to figure out how to get in. Tomorrow night?' Veronika looks at me in exasperation. 'No! Right now, this fucking minute. *Now*. Let's go. I'm not going to wait around.'

I can see her uncle's eyes follow Veronika in lamentation from the restaurant kitchen hatch as she silently mouths *'Skoro povernus'* at him, rapidly ascends the staircase, back into the world of cacophony. The gang-warfare battle has passed close by, or has even taken place in Francis Street itself, within the last half-hour, since the gutters are scattered with casualties, bodies of my age or younger with cracked heads and fist-lacerated lips, broken and broken-bottled noses pouring blood. But the roars are already receding into the distance, the two gangs split-apart after their confrontation, heading back towards Seacroft or Meanwood, and the casualties will sooner or later pick themselves up, and follow behind, limping and trailing drips of blood, disregarded by the Ripper police. In the blackened carapaces of Francis Street's bombed-out terrace houses, no longer quivering now that the Roots Club is closing for the night and the sound-system has been turned off, children of around seven years of age are grouped together, looking out of the glass-voided windows and inhaling glue from small plastic bags. Once they fly in hallucination, they will no longer fear the Ripper, as their parents do. Nobody is sleeping tonight in Chapeltown and there is terror at work in all the dead-of-night streets of this city, but as Veronika descends the club's marble steps, gesturing for me to hurry, she is laughing at it all.

As we head down Francis Street to the intersection with Chapeltown Road, Veronika reprimands the children in the bombed-out houses' windows in rapid Jamaican patois. Already holding each other by the shoulders, those children grip one other still tighter and inhale all the harder for their castigation, as though they only have a few remaining seconds before their hallucinations burst. Veronika shakes her head, then laughs again, 'I always wanted to be a cat-burglar', and she is almost invisible as she slips through the engulfing darkness of this city with her black skin, black clothes, black hair, so fast that I have to lengthen my stride to keep up with her. Francis Street is so silent once we've left behind the zone of bombed-out houses with their hallucinating children—it's now so late in the night that even the proponents of nocturnal gang-warfare are sleeping, in the concretised housing-estates of Seacroft and Meanwood—that Veronika begins to tell me fragments of her life in the former synagogue, where she occupies the cedarwood-panelled dressing-rooms and study-rooms on the top storey previously used by the rabbi and his assistants. Her uncle lives in Francis Street with his family, sleeping all of the days, operating his restaurant all of the nights. Veronika does not sleep, and in the days last summer when she still had her drums, I would hear their relentless, intense thrashing emerge from the synagogue's upper storey windows whenever I traversed Francis Street in daylight. She prefers to work at night in the dub cacophony of the Roots Club rather than with her uncle in his restaurant. Veronika tells me she will not remain in this city, or in the North, or in England, once Thatcher is here. On her eighteenth birthday, later this year, she will obtain a passport and head either for Jamaica or for the Ukrainian Semi-Autonomous Soviet Socialist Republic.

It takes us half an hour to reach the Northern School of Music building on New Briggate, at the point at the city-centre's deserted northern perimeter where the arcades begin. Of all the Victorian-era buildings and warehouses in this city, with their pollution-blackened walls, this is the only one to have been partly restored. It was originally constructed as a music hall, and a sequence of sculpted faces stretches across the marble facade of the building's ground floor, illuminated by streetlighting, some faces convulsed in lunatic hilarity, others grimacing in agony or fury as though presciently transmitting the imminent fate of this city's entire population, with the coming of Thatcher. Veronika scans each face and replicates it for my amusement, then she tries the foyer's locked door, and pulls a disabused face. Above the still-derelict music hall, reached from the foyer by an immense oak stairway, the rehearsal rooms on the top storey must hold the students' instruments. At the side of the building's exterior, an iron-work fire-escape extends in zigzags up to the roof, and in a few moments our hands are prying the skylights until we find one, its wood cracked with age, that easily opens. We are both afraid, but it's such a thrill. We are poised on either side of the skylight and Veronika smiles at me, then reaches over the abyss and slaps me hard across the face, half-terrified, half-ecstatic, and she says, 'Now I'm the bur-glar Seck Gorgui, from Genet's *Our Lady of the Flowers*. And I'm going to piss myself with fright if I'm not careful.' She's poised on the edge of the skylight, the fabric of her skipants stretched against her thighs, and plummets into the darkness below without looking. I have to follow her. We land in a corridor, and when I recover my balance, Veronika is already shining the beam of a small bicycle-lamp at successive doors, as though she knew we would commit this act, and so came equipped, even before she descended the stairs of her uncle's restaurant to meet me. After trying several doors, she finds a negligently unlocked one, wildly swings the lamp's beam around the room and locates an old snare-drum on a stand, beside a table with two well-worn Buffet Crampon clarinets, undismantled as though their rightful owners have only just set them aside a moment ago, so that the mouthpieces still leak saliva onto the table. I take the snare-drum and one of the clarinets, Veronika takes the other. It's now impossible to exit by the roof, so we head down the stairway to the ground-level and push open an alleyway fire-escape door. The alarm bell above it immediately starts to ring in the alley, but it will be an hour or more until the police detach themselves from the urgent hunt for the Ripper to investigate.

Now we relax, and start walking back along New Brig-gate and through the ringroad underpass until we reach Chapeltown Road. I am still carrying the snare-drum by its stand and one of the clarinets, and Veronika has the other clarinet tucked into the waistband of her skipants. She takes the clarinet from my hand for an instant, scratches out the serial number with her nailfile in two or three adept strokes, hands it back to me, then erases the number from her own clarinet. From time to time, she brings the mouthpiece to her lips, and though the cane reed has split in the chaos of our getaway, she generates and repeats a shrieking blare of noise, which makes people in the houses along Chapeltown Road open their windows, to ascertain if the Ripper is murdering another victim. The Ripper police, passing at frequent intervals in their cars, are also following our course, since nobody other than the Ripper could justifiably occupy that arterial road at the dead of night, now that every glacial venue of entertainment in this entire city has shut down for the night, but the stolen instruments we carry do not engage them for an instant, and if two figures are walking together and one is not slaughtering the other, the Ripper cannot be present.

We descend the stairs of the Ukrainian restaurant, which is still almost full of insomniac aged men, and take a table in the far corner. Veronika's uncle sets down a tiny black coffee laced with *samohon* and a glass of water for each of us, assesses the snare-drum and clarinets, but says nothing. I'm not certain if Veronika is planning to invite me up to the rabbi's rooms above the dub club. She knows to swallow the coffee in one fast mouthful while it's still hot. Then she quickly recounts the death in March last year of her half-brother, Konrad, a year younger than her, in a motorcycle crash on the iced-over Sheepscar Road. One of his friends was riding with him, holding on from behind, and both boys were propelled over the roadside, a great distance, landing on their heads, one body on top of the other, after their skidding motorcycle vanished from under them. Veronica is weeping pulses of hot tears that spill rapidly over her cheekbones: 'I don't know if anyone will remember him. When I leave here, he will be forgotten... ashes...'. After drinking my own coffee, cold, I am ready to go. I tell Veronika, 'I'll call you in a week or so, from the public call-box outside the post-office in City Square, to let you know if we're going to be rehearsing before the F Club performance.' She glowers, reaches over and slaps my face again, even harder than on the roof of the Northern School of Music—but with less precision, so that her thumb collides with my nose and it will now bleed—as though I committed some reprehensible act during our encounters of last summer, now consigned to oblivion or near-oblivion through the impaired state of consciousness, blurred by alcohol abuse, in which that act took place. 'I'll be waiting', Veronika says. I take one of the clarinets and walk through the cigarette smoke to the staircase, then out onto Francis Street.

From the intersection with Chapeltown Road, I turn down towards the city's centre, its amassed lights still projecting spectrally upwards into the sky, from that city of ghosts and the sleepless accursed, even at the dead of night. My nose is now bleeding from the blow of Veronika's thumb, leaving a trail of drips behind me, and the flow grows more rapid as I walk, the clarinet gripped in one hand, the thumb and index finger of my other hand closed around the flow of blood, cursing. In this exposed state, losing blood, I cannot pass in anonymity and darkness through the night, and I now present a target for the gesture-scanning eyes of the Ripper police. I begin to wish I had stayed with Veronika in the restaurant basement of the Roots Club, and I know that she will still be sitting there at the table I left, weeping her lamentation over her half-brother's death or her own life, and she will drink shotglasses of *samohon*, set down at regular intervals by her uncle who hopes that one night she will finally sleep, until that restaurant closes at dawn and the insomniac old men from Kharkov and Donetsk will disperse to their terrace houses in Francis Street, but Veronika will ascend the stairs to the rabbi's rooms in her solitude, to pace and drum, and pace and drum.

A police car heading up Chapeltown Road from the ringroad underpass veers across the street, slows and comes up behind me. The driver winds down his window: 'Are you the Ripper then, son? What's all that blood?' He hands me a dirty handkerchief from his uniform trouser pocket, and looks across at his companion, who nods in resignation. I gesture to the clarinet gripped in my hand: 'I've been playing at the Roots Club, the last show of the night. A bad audience, I got attacked...'. He looks at the clarinet with disinterest and points to the police car's rear seats: 'Just get in the fucking back.' I know they have only picked me up because of the dearth of tenable Ripper contenders and the necessity to fulfil quotas of the detained. The officer in the passenger seat is focused on the car's radio, which emits incomprehensible words in a storm of feedback, and he mutters to the driver, 'Millgarth Road is full, we have to drop this one at the Town Hall.' Behind the driver, I watch through the windows as the blackened, voided Victorian-era buildings of the city-centre's periphery speed by, then we pass the granite facade of the City Infirmary and the great tapering cupola of the colonnaded Town Hall appears ahead.

We pull up by the side entrance. The two officers in the car say nothing, ready to begin their next circuit of Chapeltown, so I open the door and see another uniformed officer waiting at the entrance to the Town Hall's subterranean levels, and I go down. He has an aged, lined face, and tells me, 'The Millgarth cells are already packed-out with all you would-be Rippers, so you'll have to make do with us here.' The subterranean strata are immense, whitewashed corridors with dim striplighting extending in all directions. We go down further staircases, along more corridors, and it gets colder. I still hold the dirty handkerchief to my nose, but the freezing air rapidly congeals the flow of blood. The aged officer opens a wooden door in a row of seven or eight, and gestures for me to enter. I realise that these are the original detention cells built with the Town Hall in the 1850s, rendered obsolete when that building's subterranean police-station moved to its own building, many decades ago. The stone walls of the cell are painted white, and the oak floor is densely marked with scratchings, boot-marks and century-old inscriptions. All the cell contains is an oak-plank bench held in an alcove to one side, the wood dark with the absorbed innumerable fluids of bodies. Two figures are already sitting on the bench, their faces in their hands, and they don't look up as I enter and sit alongside them, the clarinet still gripped in my hand.

It takes an hour before the aged officer reappears and leads me out of the cell and down the corridor. The two figures are still sitting with their faces in their hands, and I assume that their crimes are graver still than my own. In a bare office at the corridor's end, a man in a polyester suit is hunched alone at a table with a pile of dossiers and felt-tip pens in a range of colours, smoking the last of many cigarettes whose ends surround his ashtray. As soon as I walk in, he looks intently at my face with his red-rimmed, bloodshot eyes, sighs in exasperation, and tells the aged officer, 'This one is much too young to be the Ripper. He would have needed to start killing at the age of twelve or thirteen.' All he says to me is, 'Why do you waste our fucking time?', as though I had volunteered for this sub-terranean journey. The lowly interrogator dismisses me with the same contemptuous hand-gesture deployed three months ago by the Futura festival's promoter to permit his clientele to enter the tramshed's interior. The Ripper has not killed this winter, or the previous autumn, and it is only the previous relentlessness of his killings, in this and nearby cities, over the past four years, that instils terror into the cities and the bodies of the North. But when he appears from time to time to have vanished from those cities' streets, negating them in disdain as though their occupants were no longer even worth killing, as during this winter, those cities materialise his nocturnal presence still more pervasively, and those bodies hallucinate his presence still more strongly, so that he is always with us. All of this last night, he has been seated a few streets away, alongside the devil, engaged in profound reflections on his work, in the bar of the Queen's Hotel.

The aged officer escorts me back through the corridors and up the stairways towards the Town Hall's foyer. We pass the open metal door to a vast, whitewashed vault, and I can't resist stepping inside for a moment to look at the endless shelves of spilling files, cassettes, documents, cuttings, transcripts, cards, logbooks, lists, hand-drawn maps. All of the intervening floorspace is crammed with many hundreds of precarious towers of documents, each extending above the height of a human body. That archive's day workers pass me from behind as they arrive for their work, and the night workers stream past me as they leave. For that instant, the archive is untended. I look back at the aged officer, who tells me, 'There's no space left at Millgarth, so now we have the annex here, the Ripper overspill. If we can just get a recording of his voice, we'll be able to get him. Then all this can be put on the rubbish-dump.' He points me in the direction of the final flight of stairs, but he will accompany me no further.

The immense domed foyer of the Town Hall is almost deserted, but above the marble statue of Queen Victoria on the far side, a man in black overalls is balanced at the top of a long ladder, applying gold paint to the emblem of this city—a slaughtered lamb's fleece, surmounted by three stars—positioned just below the dome. I can't tell if he has been working all through the night, or has just started his work for the day. At the summit of each of the four columns which support that dome, the name of a continent is inscribed, from the era of malcontent in the 1860s during Queen Victoria's long withdrawal from public life after her husband's death, when this city, then at the zenith of its grandeur, began to conceive of itself as the capital of the North and an autonomous city-state detached from England's capital, ready to extend its empire's power into every continent. In those curtailed ambitions, this city would be ruled by a new monarch of the North, whose summer palace would be a grand hotel constructed by the same architect as this building, on the North Sea coast at Scarborough. Alongside the painter's body, the word 'Asia' is inscribed. The painter suddenly looks down at me, my hand still holding the clarinet, and calls my name, then starts his long descent down the ladder. I recognise the face of Mr. Vala, who often took his son Farhad and I swimming in the fast-flowing river Wharfe when we were ten years of age, until other children swimming alongside us were drowned by undercurrents and swept away towards the confluence of the river Wharfe and the river Aire, then into the North Sea, their bodies never-recovered, and those excursions ceased. All I know of Mr. Vala is that he was a gilt painter in a great marble palace of the Shah of Iran, the Khak-i Marmar in Tehran, but fled with his family as a refugee to this city after an assassination attempt on the Shah in that palace and its closure.

Mr. Vala looks with admiration at the stolen clarinet, and asks if I am now a musician. I tell him that with some friends, I will give a performance in a nightclub in this city, two weeks from now. Mr. Vala's scarred, desolate face immediately lights up and he says, 'I have to tell Far-had—you know he planned to be a musician and until he was seven years of age, he trained each day in Tehran, every stringed instrument, the *tar*, the *dotar*, flutes too, the *ney*. All that was his destiny—he had already given several recitals at the Khak-i Marmar palace when we had to leave. Perhaps he can perform with you... Now he works as a trainee coal-truck driver, taking coal from the Nostell colliery to the Drax power-station, five journeys there and back every day. We're exiles now, we just survive. When his apprenticeship is over, he will become a container driver, transporting containers all over the North from the port of Hull... That is his life now. He will be arriving at the colliery, I'll call him, he will want to see you again.' He hurries to the public call-box at the back of the Town Hall foyer, while I gaze upwards in vertigo and exhaustion at the dome. He returns out of breath, gasping, 'Farhad will be here in half an hour, he can take a diversion on his way to Drax, he'll meet you on the Town Hall steps, right outside. I'm so happy you will see him again. You know, yesterday the Shah fled Tehran, and he will not be coming back, he will die in exile, as I will. For the moment, we have Bakhtiar, but he is nothing, he will be gone soon. It's Khomeini who is coming, he is still in Paris today but he is coming... Khomeini will create his own state, a theocratic state.' He smiles in helplessness and lights a small black cigarette, then inhales as deeply as he can, since he must ascend the ladder now and return to his work. He adds, 'And for you, Thatcher is coming... She will create a theocratic state too—the great theocracy of Thatcher.'

I will wait outside for Farhad for half an hour, on the steps of the Town Hall, in the last darkness of the night. I have a vision of the coal-truck drive we will imminently take out of this city, eastwards, over the flatlands into the void space between the two arterial rivers of Yorkshire, the Aire and the Wharfe, which flow east towards the North Sea. Instead of the establishing of a great city in the land between those two rivers, its construction supplanting this one and rendering it definitively ruined and obsolete, the Drax power-station and its immense cooling-towers were built on that land, five years ago, their pumped-out emissions of naphthalene steam visible from any raised point in this city. Before I go outside, I enter the toilets of the Town Hall's foyer with their Etruscan marble cisterns, and wash the congealed near-black blood from my nose and lips. I stare at my face for an instant in the mirror above the washbasin, into my own eyes, but look away in horror. I realise that Mr. Vala must have wondered why my face was covered in dried blood, and what I was doing, emerging from the depths of the Town Hall, half an hour before dawn, but he said nothing.

I sit on the steps of the Town Hall, and feel the stillness of the city's air on my wet face, still chilled but warming, the ice within it dissolving so that the frozen river-Aire floods must now crack. In the pre-dawn darkness, after this night's frenzies, all of the all-night clubs, bars and halls of this city are emptied-out. In front of me, in the streets between the Town Hall and this city's main square, the headquarters of the North's corporations are amassed together, many in Victorian-era buildings, others in glass and steel towers built over the past ten years. Every corporate deal undertaken in this city, for demolitions and constructions, for industries and shopping-centres, for bodies and their abuse, trading, denudation, prostitution and death, forms an act of corruption, struck in the bar of the Queen's Hotel, in the first-class dining-carriage of the evening express-train that runs between this city and England's capital, and in the upper-storey chandeliered salons of the Town Hall behind me, every last deal overseen and sanctioned by the devil, from his vantage-point at the emergency-room summit of the St. James hospital, and watched-over too in deep contemplation by the waiting Ripper, now biding his time in the living-room of his frozen house on this city's periphery, while his archive accumulates beneath it. To the north and south of this city, the corrupt live in their compounds and mansions. In the darkness, I can sense the corrupt North's petrifaction gathering around my body, that corruption so saturated that it is now petrified and ready to splinter. Now Thatcher is coming, and she will shatter that petrifaction, but the blind corrupt masters of the North, assigned to their work or indulged in their exercise of it by Callaghan's disintegrating government, do not see what is coming. Or if they are not blind, and the corrupt masters of the North feel shame in witnessing their subjugation of its cities, then they must actively desire their own eradication at the hands of Thatcher and her coming theocracy, since she will raze them all, with the exception of the devil, in her coming power, along with all of the industries and bodies of the North, and disperse their ashes to the winds from the seven Drax cooling-towers, towards the North Sea.

I know that on these same ice-exuding Town Hall steps which seep that corruption into my body, Winston Churchill gave an unrehearsed, badly-received speech on the 18th of May 1942, following the aerial bombing and wastelanding of manufacturing, munitions and terrace-house districts along the river Aire valley in the west of this city, in March of the preceding year, the war-planes dropping their excess bombs at random on Francis Street and other godforsaken streets of the Chapeltown district, in order to lighten their weight as they turned back towards Germany, in an era when the Second World War appeared lost for England, with the Fall of Singapore and England's humiliation only three months earlier. The thousands of spectators who stood in sardonic enmity before Churchill's figure on these steps spat and jeered the slurring, improvised performance of barked, alcohol-scrambled exhortations, transmitted from his microphone through a defective sound system, as though that clientele formed the prescient audience of a punk-rock festival three decades or so on, in the awry time of this city.

As the half hour of my occupation of the Town Hall steps elapses, the darkness fades and figures begin to emerge in the avenue at the foot of those steps. The North's corruption, ignited from the building behind me towards those in front of me and oscillating between them, is still more glaring in the dawn light, its malediction illuminated. An aged man in a tattered raincoat sees me sitting on the steps and climbs them, delighted to see the clarinet propped on a step beside me. I can tell from his spasmodic movements and exhaustion that he's wracked by alcohol abuse, or untreated dementia, and has walked all through the night. He tells me, in a broken voice of delirium, 'I'll give you a tune, son... I once saw Churchill up here, right where you're sitting now. But you're Albert, aren't you? That's right, you're Albert?—I never thought I'd see you again, I thought you were dead. 1944. Always smiling, always laughing.' I glare at him: 'No, I'm not your fucking Albert. You need to walk over to City Square and take the first bus of the morning up to High Royds.' But he appears so disheartened at my denial, his fallen face now concertinaed in deep sadness, that I add, 'Yes, you're right, I'm your Albert, but now I'm not smiling and I'm not laughing anymore. I'm dead.' I might as well be a spectre in this city as a young live body. That admission appears to give him hope, and he nods and descends the Town Hall steps, murmuring, 'Always smiling, always laughing...'.

A moment later, I hear a horn blaring in four bursts that echo against the facade of the Town Hall. I look around, and see Farhad's face and thick black hair in the window of a dust-covered coal-truck, stopped in the street at the location where I was dropped by the police car, two hours ago. The last time I saw him, we were both ten years old, wearing identical black swimming-trunks, dripping water in the summer heat and standing gaping-eyed in glacial shock on the banks of the river Wharfe as the divers' search began for the swept-away children who had been screaming with elation, alongside us but nearer to the river's fast-flowing centre, only a few minutes ago. Farhad appears overjoyed to see me and he is yelling happily at me, in the cadences of a Yorkshire accent which his father does not possess. I walk over and he reaches down to put an affectionate hand on my shoulder, then gestures for me to go round the cab of the truck and get in on the other side. He tells me, 'I can't stop, but if you have time to ride over to Drax and on to Nostell with me, let's go, then we'll have some drinks somewhere when I take my break.' I have time. I open the cab's passenger door and climb in. Farhad appears elegant, even dressed in a black industrial jacket, supermarket jeans and workboots immersed in dried ochre mud. He rams the truck into movement and heads down towards the frozen river Aire.

While we exit this city, we do not speak, and Farhad manoeuvres the rundown coal-truck into City Square, passes the foyer of the Queen's Hotel and accelerates into Wellington Street, turns onto the ring-road to avoid Le Prince's ice-carapaced bridge and crosses the river Aire on the ring-road overpass, so that I see its surface far below, now striated with dense networks of cracks, then he takes the sliproad onto the eastbound lanes of the M62 motor-way. I look in the opposite direction towards the black precipices of the Pennine mountains from which this motorway emerges through a cutting incised in the gran-ite ridges after crossing the mountains' plateau on an ele-vated embankment. The motorway is only a few years old, its tarmac still smooth below the cracked-axled wheels of Farhad's truck. The only sound in the cab is the singing of a woman's heartbroken voice from the speaker of Farhad's cassette-player, positioned between us. Farhad begins to speak quietly, so that I have to lean to hear: 'Last winter I killed two old sisters at that blackspot on Sheepscar Road, you probably know the place, the north end of Chapel-town—the road turns and there's a zebra-crossing straight after. The brakes failed on the ice and I ran them both down. I'd been driving all day, the same run as today, I'd just got my provisional license, I'd just got this job, five trips between Drax and the coalfields, then back up to Chapeltown—I keep the truck parked right outside our house. My eyes were aching and I didn't see them until a second before I hit them. I came out of the skid and I kept driving. My heart was beating so fast. I read in the newspaper afterwards that they were twin sisters, almost ninety, never spent a day apart. They'd been out to bingo. Nobody ever found out, nobody saw me, I wiped the blood off the front of the cab before I went in for my tea. I know I'll lose my job if anyone finds out, maybe I'll go to prison. I know you'll never tell anyone.' I heard the story myself, the previous winter, almost a year ago: the mystery of the aged twin sisters, found crushed on the deserted roadside, their arms around one another, their killer gone. Some said that the Ripper himself was the perpetrator, driving fast on his return to his frozen house after the murder of Helen Rytka, herself one of twin sisters, in a town of disintegrated industries among the Pennine ridges, and that incident proved that he lives at the north end of Chapeltown. The Ripper walks the streets of Chapeltown at night, while he bides his time, and sometimes he stops in Francis Street and listens to the cacophony of someone drumming wildly in the upper storey of a derelict synagogue. Farhad looks over at me, the pain and bewilderment of exile in his face, but he's also smiling in elation: 'But in that split-second, skidding on the ice, when I realised I couldn't stop, I really wanted to run them down.'

The Drax cooling-towers are straight ahead, so immense that it seems we will reach them in an instant, but they are still distant, and we will need to drive for another half-hour until we arrive there. In aberration, since it otherwise habitually blows east towards the North Sea, the vapour pumped from the cooling-towers is blowing directly towards us. The river Aire runs to the south of us, over the flatlands, clear of ice, and the river Wharfe runs to the north of us. The river Ouse has already poured into the river Wharfe, and the river Calder has already poured into the river Aire. We are running along an elevated motorway section, on concrete pillars above the unstable flatlands, and up ahead I can see beyond the Drax cooling-towers to the point where the river Wharfe pours into the river Aire, and all that remains is the river Aire, saturated with mud, silt and sediment and turned ochre, boiling with naphthalene, hydrogen sulphate, and the bodies of drowned and unrecovered children, gaining speed until it finally flows into the North Sea, and everything is lost.

We are silent again, and I've yet to say a single word to Farhad. I ask him who is singing on his cassette, and he replies: 'That's Googoosh, from Tehran. I saw her perform, in the Khak-i Marmar, the palace that is now abandoned, when I was a child. Now she lives in Los Angeles, but she'll return to Tehran soon, even with Khomeini coming. I will go back too, with the ghosts of the twin sisters, after I make my five thousand journeys to Drax.' I can see he's fascinated by the clarinet which I still hold in my hands, and I tell him about the F Club promoter's proposition. Farhad has never heard of punk-rock clubs, though he thinks he once heard about something called 'heavy-metallers', but he desperately wants to play at the F Club performance in two weeks' time—'I would give my soul, anything'—and he can play any instrument that exists, he still has the two instruments with which he arrived in this city as a child, the *tar* and the *dotar*, he has not played them for ten years, but it will take only an instant for him to be ready to perform again, and he can play at any speed: 'I will play as fast as you like.' I tell him that if plays at four times his usual speed, that will probably work. I hold out the clarinet to him and he takes it with his right hand while keeping his left hand on the steering-wheel: 'This is a gift for you, Farhad.'

We turn off the motorway onto a pitted side-road, and reach the barbed-wire fence surrounding the Drax sub-city, which powers the detrital city behind us. I look out of the cab window at the propulsions of vapour from the nearest cooling-tower. Farhad stops at the gate and tells the guard: 'I've brought my boss with me, he's keeping his eye on me.' The guard looks at Farhad with contempt and waves him on. We drive across the vast Drax terrain to the coal-unloading zone and Farhad manoeuvres his truck, pulls a lever and adds his load of coal to the infinite stacks, then we head off again. I am hallucinating with exhaustion and realise that we will need to do the journey twice, to the Nostell colliery and back to Drax, before Farhad can take his break. I close my eyes and listen to the voice of Googoosh.

After the truck has been loaded for the third time today at Nostell colliery, we drive north into Wakefield. Beyond that town is the sliproad at which Farhad will rejoin the M62 motorway, then deliver the third load of coal, and make two more journeys this afternoon, into the evening, before returning from Drax to Chapeltown. We pull up directly outside a rundown social club in the town's main street. Farhad tells me, 'I can just take an hour or so, no longer, otherwise I won't be able to get the fifth load to Drax before the gates close... I usually never stop so I don't know this place, but we can probably have some drinks here.' He jumps down from the cab onto the pavement and checks the stability of the truck's batch of coal, so overloaded that it risks spilling into the sloping street. The social club's proprietor is standing on the pavement in a threadbare polyester suit. He glares at Farhad with disdain, but can't resist telling me, 'We've got a turn from bloody Prestwich on, just about to start. Free fish and chips too. Get yourself inside, son.'

As we enter the social club, I feel its interior's stench of deep contamination spectrally pass through us at high velocity, as though it were only a hair's breadth from taking on human form, as it propels itself towards the street outside. Since the club is open to members only, we need to write our names on minuscule paper cards and are each liable to a 'life-members' fee, 10p, on top of the 40p admission charge, which Farhad insists on paying with a crumpled, coal-blackened note. He is now holding the clarinet in his arms, wary of leaving it in his cab: 'This is a town of thieves and rascals.' The proprietor escorts us beyond the foyer into the first room, one entire side of which is occupied by an elongated metal vat containing white-hot liquefied lard, into which four staff in white coats are carefully dropping slabs of fish, then pulling them out, coating them in an orange carapace of unknown origin and depositing them in heated transparent shelves above the sizzling vat, pending their consumption. Otherwise, that room is almost bare, a few formica tables with vinegar bottles and plywood chairs scattered around it. The proprietor tells us, 'Get your fish and chips inside you, boys, they're free, then you can watch the turn.' The staff are looking at us expectantly. Farhad assesses the vat with horror, and turns towards the second room, but the proprietor puts a hand on his coal-dust shimmering jacket-sleeve and whispers to us, 'It's compulsory, boys. Don't upset the fryers, they're professionals. Get that fish down you. Otherwise you'll be barred and you can get back out onto the bloody street.' At that instant, a cacophony of percussion and vocal vitriol erupts from the second room, and the proprietor adds, 'That's the matinee show starting up in the function room, just for children. No alcohol. The grown-ups' show is tonight.'

After we eat the plates of fried cod, Farhad asks if I would like us to go back out onto the street, since we are not permitted to drink here, but I head instead for the social club's second room, and he follows. I open the door, and we stand just inside it. The second room is larger than the first, oak-panelled, framed photographs on every wall from many decades of that social club's yearly excursions to the North Sea resort towns, a turning mirrorball overhead and the room's lights on at maximum illumination, an ash sprung dancefloor underfoot, an empty bar at one end sealed with a steel grille, and four figures generating an insistent cacophony from a low platform at the far end. I recognise the gnarled, toothless singer standing in front of those figures in his wide-lapelled checked jacket, from his early-morning appearance on the Futura festival's second day, still emitting abuse, this time directed towards his hapless musicians rather than the clientele of one hundred dehydrated young bodies seething in convulsions of adrenaline in front of him, overheated but with no body-fluids to sweat out, no saliva in their mouths to spit out. From perversity, the gurning singer intones an era of profligate alcohol abuse: 'I sat and drank, for three decades.' His associates are focused intently on their instruments, eyes down, fearing that the least error will bring the wrath of the singer upon them, and they generate driven pulses of raw-ended noise. Most of the clientele are younger by three or four years than Farhad and I, and I can tell they are wide-pupilled from amphetamine consumption or the precocious desire for cacophony and oblivion.

After half an hour of relentless cacophony, the four figures abruptly fall silent and the singer begins to berate the audience, his microphone's incessant bouts of feedback rendering his admonitions' content incoherent. The audience, still convulsing as though the cacophony were ongoing, surge abruptly towards the platform, then onto it, knocking the cursing singer to the ground and trampling over him. The clientele scream in their elation, push over the amplifiers, and roar the name of that town, that of the devil and that of the Ripper, into the seized microphone. The gnarled singer and his four associates extricate themselves from the uproar, abandon their performance, and push past us, out of the function room to reach the street.

The proprietor is standing alongside us and watches the still-cursing singer exit with both shoulders of his too-large checked jacket torn. Up close, the singer's thin-lipped face appears unblemished and unscarred. I look at the proprietor's own bloated face beside me, a wide scarlet stripe of broken blood-vessels below each eye, his white hair slicked back. He tells me, 'They'll be back in a minute, after they've had a cigarette and a drink and calmed down. I just put on these matinees as a bit of fun for the youngsters. It's a shame about the turn, but they were cheap to book, two shows for the price of one, the cheapest in the bloody North. You can come back for the evening show too, if you like, no extra charge.' The clientele in the function room are now turning on one another, and fights are breaking out in every corner. The proprietor ushers us back into the first room with its still-sizzling fish-vat: 'You're on the Drax run, are you? Good lads.' He raises the index and middle fingers of his left hand in the air, snaps them, and one of the white-coated staff immediately delivers two large glasses of beer on a tray. The proprietor instructs us, 'Get them down you, boys, one bloody gulp.' Farhad and I upend the glasses of tepid liquid and swallow it. Farhad pulls a face at its bitterness. The proprietor collects a well-worn wooden club from under the fish-vat, returns roaring to the function room, quells the brawl and expels that entire unruly clientele from the social club within moments, so they are left reeling and gasping, still exchanging half-hearted blows, sprawled out on the pavement.

Farhad and I slip through the expelled children and climb back into the coal-truck's cab. A stream of coal has slipped from the truck's load and is scattered down the side of the street's incline, but Farhad disregards it. He positions the clarinet carefully alongside his cassette-player. He will let me out of the cab at the sliproad of the M62 motorway, and we take the road out of this town, the course of the river Calder running to our right. I know I may not be able to reach Farhad from the public call-box outside the post-office, so I arrange to meet him at midnight, two weeks from now, Monday 29th, on the bridge over the river Aire, if it is unfrozen. If it is still frozen, we will not meet, the performance at the F Club will not take place, and we will never meet again. Farhad says nothing, his hands clenched on the steering-wheel, and I can tell that he is unsettled by the fish and beer he has been forced to consume, and the outburst of cacophony he has witnessed. At the M62 junction, I jump down from the cab. Farhad says, 'Thanks, with all my heart, my friend, for this gift.' He holds the clarinet proudly. 'Please keep my secret of the twin sisters. I know you will... I will make my five runs that day, then I will meet you on the bridge.' Farhad turns his Googoosh cassette back on, reaches over to slam the passenger-door closed, and drives away towards the Drax cooling-towers. I am high up on the south side of the river Aire valley, the wind from the east blowing strongly, and I will need to walk back into the city, once I have retched and fallen into the gutter beside the sliproad. From this elevation, I can see Le Prince's bridge in the far distance, surrounded by warehouses, and at the city's eastern periphery, the golden brick facade of the Temple Newsam palace, from the Tudor era, on its hill on the far side of the river valley. I will direct my eyes towards that palace and once I have reached it, I will turn back towards the devil's ground.

It's two weeks later, and I'm standing on the bridge over the river Aire, gripping the ironwork parapet. The clock-face on the abandoned warehouse tower beside the bridge strikes midnight, and I am waiting for Farhad and Veronika. The river below is flowing again, and the ice which carapaced this bridge has disappeared. The thaw predicted with confidence by the F Club promoter took place the day after Farhad and I visited the social club in Wakefield, and the torrent of unfrozen water was propelled down-river from the devil's ground to flood the lands to the east of this city, extending half of the way up the hill of the Temple Newsam palace, and swamping the flatland terrain of the Drax power-station so that deliveries of coal were impossible for several days, and all power in this city shut-down until the river Aire floods moved eastwards, joining with those surging from the river Wharfe valley, and finally draining in a vast detrital wave into the North Sea. Even now, the power-supply across the North is unstable, the lights of this city can only be illuminated to half their usual capacity, and more than ever, it's a city of half-seen spectres. All of the subterranean clubs and bars of the devil's ground have been pumped, and the floodwaters have seeped of their own accord from the derelict ware-houses on the river's northern bank. Only the tramshed remains flooded, the trapped waters now so congealed with engrained naphthalene and benzene residues from its walls and floor that they are unable to flow out, and that building will remain flooded until its demolition.

Now it's past midnight, and twenty-three hours from now, at 11pm, a public cacophony is scheduled to occur at the F Club, to be performed through the acts of four bod-ies, for whatever clientele chooses to attend. It will be the first night of that club's operation since its venue's pump-ing. A week ago, I tried to call the promoter to confirm the cacophony, but the strike at the Yorkshire Television station has now extended for so long that its telephone lines are disconnected, and even the station's emergency transmissions have become intermittent. This coming Wednesday, 31st January, is the first anniversary of the Ripper's killing of Helen Rytka, and once every few hours or so, the television screens of this city silently transmit a photograph taken almost a year ago, at the Ripper archive in the subterranean levels of this city's Millgarth Road police headquarters, of her identical seventeen-year-old twin-sister, Rita, dressed in a striped jersey and low-cut jeans which expose her navel, standing alongside the director of the Ripper police, pointing out the location at which she last saw her sister on the night of the killing, on a huge map of the Pennine city, fixed vertically to a wall of that archive, already heavily annotated with marker-pen arrows and vectors directed from handwritten cards affixed to the map's perimeters. A body is slipping through that map. The map is marked in large capital letters in an upper corner with Rita Rytka's name, but it appears from that photograph that it is her murdered twin-sister who stands in anger and insolence, pointing out the site of her own murder. Her eyes' spectral pupils look directly into the addled face of the director of the Ripper police with contempt, and the index finger of her left hand rests on the exact location of her death. That photograph flashes without warning on the television screens of the North for a few moments, then vanishes in a storm of static.

On my way to the bridge tonight, twenty minutes ago, I passed by the nightclub in Swinegate which will be occupied, for several hours tomorrow night, by the F Club. The aged proprietor in his suit tailored in prewar Lvóv stood by the door, ready to entice a clientele inside, since business has been bad since the river Aire floods and their freezing. He seems to recognise me and I ask him if the club has been fully pumped. He nods to reassure me, 'Yes, it was pumped three nights ago, then thoroughly cleaned and scoured, no sediment left. Go down and take a look, you won't see any trace.' His club was the very last in the devil's ground to be pumped—the pumping gangs declined to do it until every other club had been drained, and then they performed their work with extreme reluctance, in the dead of night, extending the immense rubber pipe between the cellar and the bank of the river Aire, and activating the pump generator with disdain. I ask the proprietor if he has seen the girl I visited his club with, in October, during the Futura festival further along Swinegate. His memory seems severely eroded, and I give him more details and prompts. She admired his suit, stitched with skill by the Skladanowsky brothers tailors in Lvóv, and ran her fingers along its fabric. Finally, he remembers: 'The pale one, who looks like a ghost? Yes, I have seen her—she walks by here some nights, when I'm about to close, but she never speaks to me, and she never comes inside.'

A few minutes after midnight, Farhad pulls up in his coal-truck, leans from the cab-window and tell me, 'I'm sorry I'm so late. I had to do two extra runs to Drax—the floods carried away all the coal stock, so they need urgent extra deliveries.' He leaves the truck in the centre of the bridge and jumps down from his cab, then reaches back to lift out his instruments, a battered *tar* and the stolen clarinet. We lean against the bridge's parapet and wait for Veronika. Slivers of ice are still racing in the fast current below. I called Veronika a week ago at her uncle's restaurant in the synagogue basement, from the public call-box in front of the post-office, late at night. It took her uncle several minutes to answer, and in that void time, I looked through the call-box window at the five-storey soot-blackened marble edifice of the post-office, the great hall for customers with its hundred-feet high ceiling, the clock-tower above extending to the same height as the Queen's Hotel on the adjacent side of this city's main square, beyond the Majestic cinema. My mother decided to leave the Yorkshire Dales at the age of seventeen to work on the counters of a post-office in one of the cities of the North, and was given a scrawled card by her prospective employers, inscribed with the names of three cities. She chose one city, and her request was refused, she chose a second city, and her request was refused, and finally she pointed to the name of this devil's city, and was assigned that work. On her first day on the counters, in that immense hall of ascending cigarette smoke, vocal uproar and the stench of damp clothing, three men in turn demanded to fuck her. Every night, she wept, and wished she was back in the Yorkshire Dales... Finally, Veronika's uncle picked up the telephone, the deep silence of his restaurant resounding from behind him. He recognised my voice immediately, and told me, 'You're a good influence on Veronika. She likes you, I do too. You need to think about marrying Veronika soon. We can have the reception here, in the Spring...'. But he cannot bring Veronika to the telephone to speak with me: he refuses to enter the Roots Club upstairs, if she is working a shift at the bar there, and if she is up in the rabbi's rooms, then he is barred from entering, but he will take a message, if I speak slowly, and will pass it on to Veronika, when she finally descends the staircase to his restaurant.

Now I can see Veronika in the distance, emerging from under the railway viaduct, dressed entirely in black, carrying her snare-drum by its stand in one hand. In the other hand, she holds a fistful of drumsticks, taped together. She has walked all the way down from Francis Street and tell me, 'If I met the Ripper on Chapeltown Road, I would have poked his fucking eyes out with these sticks. The devil too, I don't fear him, he won't sneak up behind me in his tracksuit and running shoes, I'll poke him in the fucking eye.' She barely looks at Farhad, but I can see her appraising the clarinet in his hand and then she glances back at me with a sly smile, as though I have forgotten something that occurred on the night we climbed the fire-escape to the roof of the Northern School of Music.

In the alley beside the bridge, I hammer on the door of the warehouse in which Jim has his workshop of film-projector components. After five minutes or so, he unbolts and opens the door and immediately begins walking back up the wide staircase. He is still dressed in his belted leather coat. Over his shoulder, he tells me, 'We'll rehearse on the second floor, in Le Prince's workshop. I've got it ready. It hadn't been opened for about eighty years. I'm just back from that cinema, the one down the M1—tonight was my last night there and from Wednesday I'll be back working at the Majestic. Brando...'. I enter the long room on the second floor. Layers of whitewash and plaster have fallen from the walls long ago, exposing raw brickwork. Jim has opened the window to let out the workshop's accumulated dust, but that space has been closed-up for so long that I can imagine the metallic smell of Le Prince's film-cameras is still intact, and among the debris on the floor, I make out the shapes of discarded bolts and levers from experimental devices and abandoned projectors. I look out of the window and see the exact perspective of the bridge over the river Aire which Le Prince filmed in direct noon sunlight in September 1888, saturated with crossing figures and overloaded carts, the surrounding buildings almost-identical ninety years on, but it is now the dead of night, the pedestrian pavements deserted, no bodies crossing, only Farhad's unloaded coal-truck positioned in the centre and the occasional transits of the Ripper police's vehicles on their way up to Chapeltown Road. Jim is still holding the workshop's rusted key and tells me that it had probably been used as an ironmonger's store up to the time when Le Prince took a hundred-year lease on it, and has been empty since he vanished without trace, leaving his family to transport his left-behind cameras and film-strips to New York, in the hope of selling them to moving-image entrepreneurs. Jim has positioned four illuminated amplifiers, together with several microphones, already spitting feedback, on the intact ironmongery display shelving which surrounds the room at waist height.

I do not introduce the four bodies in the room to one another—they will be the perpetrators of the cacophony to come, and nothing else. But for a moment, we stare at one another, and that is all the introduction that is needed. We each take up our positions against one of the room's four walls. Jim focuses upon his synthesisers and sound-mixing board, Farhad sits on the ironmongery shelving and sets a microphone above the taut strings of his *tar*, and Veronika manoeuvres a microphone directly against the skin of her snare-drum. Jim has brought down the guitar from his workshop for me, already switched to the maximum 'wild dog' setting, together with a microphone, and I realise at the last moment that he expects me to incant a vocal sound against the cacophony—I have written no words, not even a fragment, or even thought about what words must be emitted, in an instant, from my throat and vocal tract, and now I must invent them, conjured from my transits on foot through this city and the devil's ground of its streets, rooftops and ballrooms, at night. After inhaling a deep breath, Veronika suddenly begins to beat the snare-drum with rapid venom and we all begin. Twenty minutes later, we stop abruptly, at exactly the same instant, unsure whether there's been an all-engulfing power-cut in the fragile supply of this city or if we've all intended to stop at that identical moment, and we stare at one another again, astonished at what has happened.

3.

FUCK CLUB
SUBTERRANEAS,
JANUARY 1979

As I walk through the city at the fall of night, six hours before the F Club cacophony is scheduled to occur, I pass by the public call-box in front of the post-office in the central square and decide to call Iris. I have not seen her since the night I abandoned our journey towards the bottle of Brompton cocktail after the last night of the Futura festival, have feared visiting her frozen house beside the railway cutting in case her fury-propelled door would then slam in my face, and have only spoken to her by telephone once since then. She can be caught only in the margin of thirty seconds during which she traverses the High Royds administration building and signs-in for her night-shift. If she is beginning a night-shift at High Royds tonight, I can catch her as she walks through the administration building, and if she is not beginning a night-shift tonight, I will never see her again, since, on our journey after the Futura festival's catastrophic ending, she renounced all future assignations of oblivion and cacophony at the F Club.

I dial the High Royds asylum number, and ask if Iris is arriving for her night-shift. After a few moments, Iris takes the receiver, her voice bewildered and disorientated. I remind her about the F Club performance tonight and ask if she is coming, but it's a foregone conclusion that, since she is already at High Royds and about to begin her night-shift, she will be there until five in the morning. At first, Iris sounds as though she has been contacted from another planet, or by a ghost. But I stay silent, the line crackles, and I can tell that Iris is now wavering. She speaks in a whisper and first asks me if I can defer the performance until six in the morning, then she will have time to take the first bus from High Royds down into the city, after her shift. But I tell her that, according to what the club's proprietor told me, 6am is when the club closes, and the audience for the scheduled cacophony may not readily tolerate a seven-hour delay. After a few moments' hesitation, Iris tells me: 'There's a way. If you come up to High Royds yourself and collect me, and tell the head of administration, in these exact words: "I have come to collect Trainee Nurse Dunstan on account of a family emergency." Then I can abandon my night-shift.' I hear some curses and murmuring in the background and the line goes dead.

The hourly bus to High Royds leaves right here, from outside the post-office in City Square, on the far side of the road, and I can already see the driver gesturing impatiently to the conductor, who is smoking a cigarette outside the doors to the post-office's great hall for customers, which has just closed for the night. I climb over the square's low railings and cross the road, and jump into the bus's entrance door as it starts to pull away. The conductor looks at me in surprise, gesturing with his hand for me to jump off again before the bus picks up speed as it circles past the Queen's Hotel and heads towards Kirkstall Road, but I climb the stairway to the upper deck and take a seat at the front. The bus is entirely empty—all of the night-shift workers have caught the previous bus to arrive at High Royds in time, and none of the delirious, insane or demented inhabitants of this city travel to High Royds at their own volition, since nobody in the asylum's ninety-year history has ever been released once admitted. The conductor approaches me from behind along the upper deck's aisle: 'You know this is the High Royds bus? You can still get off, we'll stop for you by the Yorkshire Television studios.' I tell him I'm going to High Royds because of an emergency, and hand him the fare. Even after he manipulates the malfunctioned contraption held against his stomach so that a ticket is finally disgorged, he continues to dissuade me: 'We're going on indefinite strike tonight, along with the railway unions. It's just been announced on the radio. Our last departure from High Royds is at 10pm, then that's it—if you're not on that one, you'll be stuck with the bloody nutcases for the rest of the winter.'

It takes half an hour to reach High Royds. We follow the river Aire valley for the first part of the journey and the ruins of Kirkstall Abbey appear in the darkness, splinters of ice in the fast-flowing river visible beyond the shards of the abbey's vast halls and the void stained-glass windows of its tower. After twenty minutes, the river veers off to the west, we ascend the Menston hill, and I see the immense palace of this city's mad extending across the hill's summit, all of its windows lit-up at maximum illumination as though it were burning with the neural incineration of the mad, signalling to the not-yet-mad of the city below. The night's screaming has not yet started. The bus grates up the elevation and stops beside a stone gatehouse. The conductor tells me, 'We don't go any further—just follow the avenue. See you later, son.' As soon as I step off, the bus pulls away again, turns and heads back towards the city centre. On the far side of the gatehouse, a long tree-lined avenue leads towards the administration building, and the clock-tower above it is striking the half-hour. Whenever he visits High Royds, on his incessant rounds of this city, the devil never neglects to ascend that clock-tower, to watch over the bodies of his mad. Alongside the administration building, the separate ward buildings stretch out, fifteen on either side. A derelict railway track runs directly beside the avenue, and for many decades, the High Royds inmates were transported directly by train from the city below, in long windowless carriages pulled by freight locomotives that turned off the main line at the foot of the Menston hill and heaved the mad to the summit for their delivery. I am walking along the empty avenue to High Royds, the lines of cypress trees on either side of me shaking in the wind. I can see three other, identical avenues approaching the palace of the mad from the south, north and west, but all of those approaches are empty too. Off to the left as I reach the administration building, the cemetery field for the inmates appears, a crematorium in its centre, the graves all unmarked, the plot areas divided only by sticks of iron emerging from the grass-grown black earth.

I need to report Iris's emergency to the head of the asylum's administration, and pull open the unguarded oak door to enter the building. A long corridor extends in front of me, the worn-down floor intricately mosaiced with the white roses of Yorkshire edged with black daisies. Doors covered with official notices line either side of the corridor, seeping cigarette smoke and muted voices, but it's impossible to tell which is the door of the head of administration. At the corridor's far end, I open another oak door in the expectation that it will contain the main administration office, but beyond that door, an immense high-ceilinged ballroom stretches out, with windows running around its entire upper level. It's now too dark for those windows to light the ballroom, but hundred of bare bulbs, suspended from the wooden ceiling on long strings, illuminate the striated walls of decades-old ochre and black paint, coal-ovens and fireplaces running alongside each wall and emitting ferocious heat. It's clear that a film screening has just ended, and lines of inmates are silently dispersing through doors on both sides of the ballroom. Beside the projection screen, a technician in black overalls adeptly operates a lever to roll and retract it upwards, revealing an elevated performance space for musicians behind it. A white-coated doctor watches the technician's gestures with fascination, then abruptly switches his gaze to my body at the far end of the ballroom and walks its entire length towards me.

I begin to smell the sharp stench of engrained alcohol and urine emitted by the doctor as he reaches the half-way point on his approach. I consider exiting the ballroom, and even fleeing down the avenue towards the bus which will take me back into the city, but I stand my ground. The doc-

tor is aged, unkempt, long white hair grown over his collar, his cracked and elastoplasted glasses hooked around
his neck with string. When he reaches me, he puts them
over his eyes, and assesses my face: 'You're a visitor, are
you? We don't get many in the evenings. If I didn't know
every patient here by sight, I'd think you were already an
inmate, but by just a hair's breadth, I think you're not, for
the moment. I'm joking,' he laughs. 'My name is McDonald, the director.' He offers me his hand, and I shake it.
'How can I help you? The film show has just ended—*The
Sound of Music*, the patients love it. And we have a new projectionist, who actually projects the reels in the right order,
for once.' He gestures towards the man in overalls, who has
opened a trapdoor and is now carrying the film-reels down
into the ballroom's subterranea. 'He was the projectionist at
the Regal in Wombwell until a few weeks ago, a real professional—we're lucky to have him, since by rights he should
have been sent to the Stanley Royd asylum, not here. We
always have films on Tuesday afternoons, and a dance on
Saturday evenings. It's good for the patients, but many are
catatonic and show no response—not like when I arrived
here, thirty years ago, when we still had the epileptics and
the melancholics. Then it was fits and weeping from beginning to end of every film. We probably still have a few of
them around, in the far wards—it's not easy to keep track
of everyone. But that's the job of the administration, not
mine.' I tell him I'm here on an emergency mission, and he
leads me out of the ballroom and back along the mosaiced
corridor to the farthest door on the right, then turns away
without a word.

I knock on the door and enter. Inside, behind barriers
of cigarette smoke, four elderly women are sitting behind
typewriters, striking the keys at speed, and a man in
a polyester suit is standing by the window, looking out
towards the city below. Every wall is stacked floor to ceiling with card files. The nearest typist pauses for a moment
and looks at me with disinterest. I tell her: 'I'm here to collect Trainee Nurse Dunstan on account of a family emergency.' She sighs and looks at a list, then sighs again and
holds out a still-vibrating hand, her index finger point-

ing away to one side: 'She's working in Hawes ward in the East Division, but there's nobody here to take you. You'll have to go and collect her yourself. Now we'll have to call for someone to take over her shift. As though we didn't have enough to do. Bloody hell.' The man standing by the window looks over at me with contempt for an instant and adds: 'Go and get her tha'sen, son... We've got bigger bloody fish to fry here.' Then he turns and stares out again towards the lights of the devil's city below.

I walk across the asylum lands in the direction indicated by the typist, past one ward after another, each named after valleys or towns in the Yorkshire Dales, until I reach the farthest building, at the end of the Menston hill plateau, almost on the edge of the precipice. The exposed ward is built from slabs of limestone and granite, to withstand the erosions of iced winds and storms, blowing from the west from the Pennine mountains and east from the North Sea, and only the window frames are disintegrated, the panes cracked, several of them punched-in by spasming fists. I push open the door and feel the induced near-silence before the onset of screaming, with only the sounds of an incanting voice audible. In the low gaslight, I cannot make out Iris's figure, but I realise I am in a high-ceilinged anteroom and beyond it, through a wide doorway, I can make out the open and overheated ward of prone figures, fifty beds on either side, some of them equipped with restraints—there are no cells at High Royds, except for those so berserk that they are otherwise uncontainable, and the inmates must share their deliria and convulsions in intimacy.

As my eyes become used to the low light, I make out an aged figure sitting at the desk assigned to the duty nurse, files and cards amassed across its surface. He is dressed in the High Royds regulation-issue pyjamas, brylcreemed white hair combed back so that I see obsessed eyes, oscillating between catastrophic oblivion and perfect-recall memory, the lips of his exhausted, lined face positioned close to a rolled-up magazine which he grips in both hands. For a moment, on noticing me, he grins a toothless smile, but he has an ongoing looped commentary to deliver and he continues: 'Keep your eyes on Don Fox kicking... stiff arm tackle... the referee's having a word with the Wakefield players... a bit of a disciplinarian... nonsense or backchat... or else it's the early bath... crowd trying to put him off... simply dribbled and went on... now the thing is changed, now then... it's not a hard shot, it's always a hard shot... he's on the ground, he's in tears... he's a poor lad, there's the poor lad, they're all rubbing him... it's happened... he will never forget... what a hard life story for the boy... that's it...'. The compulsive fragments of that lost commentary gradually dissolve into glossolaliac outbursts, punctuated by abysmal silences, and the man's face suddenly appears irretrievably lost and pained, but then his commentary recoheres and the loop begins again: 'Keep your eyes on Don Fox kicking...'.

I turn to the doorway and Iris's figure appears spectrally out of the ward, her black hair merging into the darkness, above her starched blue and white uniform, then darkening again below into her black tights and flat-soled black shoes. She doesn't approach me and speaks softly, 'This is the ward for the extreme far-gone. I've just finished sedating them for the night—some of them have to go into comas, or they'd be screaming again after an hour. You don't know what it's like here at four in the morning, when everyone is awake again before dawn and the screaming starts up, from every ward.' I ask her if she's the only one in charge, since she's a trainee, and she nods her head: 'There's only me. I need to go to the administration building now to find out when my replacement will arrive. I can leave Eddie in charge for a while. He's only been here for four months and he thinks he's the boss, taking care of the mad in his retirement. He hasn't totally gone yet, he's the sanest man in this entire place, that's including the doctors.' She smiles at the aged man and he momentarily grins in return, but he has his work to do. I expected Iris and I to leave immediately for the bus at the end of the avenue and head down to the F Club, but I know that Jim and Farhad will transport the amplifiers and instruments across the river Aire bridge, and placate the promoter if need be, and that Veronika will arrive only at the last instant, after curtailing her shift at the Roots Club, so I convince myself that I can wait for Iris.

Iris puts on a black serge sailor's coat over her uniform and we walk back to the administration building. I sense she is still furious with me for leaving her on the journey back to her frozen house after the end of the Futura festival. I wait on the black daisy mosaic in the corridor while she goes into the administration office and consults with the typists. She is shaking her head when she emerges: 'My replacement can't get here until 9pm—she's coming all the way from Ilkley, from the far side of the Wharfe. Are you sure you told them it was really an emergency?' From the clock-tower's chimes, I realise we will have two hours at High Royds before Iris's replacement arrives. She points to the door at the far end of the corridor: 'Let's take a walk through the ballroom. Don't worry about the mad in Hawes ward—they've just had their main dose for the night and will be out for hours, and even if they awaken, Eddie's commentary will soothe them back to their dreams.' Iris opens the door to the ballroom and switches on the hundreds of bare bulbs which hang from its ceiling. The immense ballroom resuscitates itself, even in its emptiness. The coal-ovens are kept on permanently, and as with the rest of the asylum, the space is overheated. The sprung ash floor is marked with the stilettos and scrapes from the dancing bodies over many decades of the delirious, demented, epileptic and melancholic, and the far corners of the ballroom's ceiling, above the ochre-painted walls and the upper-level windows, hold the engrained cries of the mad, in the ecstasy and convulsions of their dancing. Now that we are out of earshot of the administration staff, Iris tells me: 'The head of administration is going to stare out of that window all night. He says he's just watching over the entire city to follow the gangs crossing it for their battles, and keeping an eye out for suspicious cars down on Chapeltown Road, so he can alert the Ripper police. But there's always the chance that the devil will arrive here without notice for his usual visit, so the head of administration needs to watch out for that too.

But the devil won't deign to come here until the dead of night, long after we've gone, if at all.'

I'm concerned that Iris is spending too long at High Royds, and is growing delirious herself. I ask her if she's thinking of requesting a transfer back to the St. James hospital, near the city centre, especially now that the bus and train strikes announced today will make it impossible for her to travel from her frozen house in the Calder river valley up to the asylum every night. Even with the buses running, that's a journey of two hours each way. Iris shakes her head: 'I'll be sleeping here—there's a building for resident nurses. I'm giving up my room in that house. I'm still thinking it over, but I'm sure I'll never go back to St. James. It's better for my career to be here. I have a professional commitment now to the insane, to the inmates here. I'm thinking of the future too... Thatcher is coming, by the Spring, maybe earlier, and she'll be here for decades unless one of her minions upends her, and this punk-rock era of the last two years will soon seem like some kind of paradise.' She gestures in the direction of the city below, beyond the cracked walls of the ballroom: 'That city could even be destroyed—civil war could break out once Thatcher is in full swing and decimates everything in the North. At least I feel safe here, up here with the mad. You may not know it, but High Royds is under powerful patronage—Dr. McDonald has been talking to some very influential people about expanding the hospital and opening an annex in the city centre. We could even take over the Queen's Hotel now that nobody stays there anymore, and use Eddie's old suite as the administration office.'

Iris's eyes are fired, and she turns to face me, tears streaming down her cheeks. We've reached the far end of the ballroom, alongside the performance space for musicians. The projectionist appears up the steps from his office in the subterranean levels, still wearing his black overalls, alarmed at the ballroom's sudden illumination. I motion for him to go back down again, that there's no need for him to fear. He asks me: 'Do you want another projection now? It's no problem if you do. I love it here. I've got two 1930s Gaumont-Kalee projectors at my disposal, in perfect working order. I can do the reel changes with my eyes closed. And there are over two thousand reels of film down there. Do you want *The Passion of Joan of Arc*?' He waits open-mouthed and wild-eyed for his instructions, eager to collect the film reels, take them to the projection booth at the other end of the ballroom, and dim the lights in readiness. I tell him firmly, 'No, we don't want to watch anything just now. Maybe later. Go and check the films.' He reluctantly retreats back into the space below the ballroom.

Iris needs some air, and she knows the way to the roof of the ballroom, so we climb onto the musicians' space and Iris points to the staircase against the back wall which goes part of the way, then a ladder leads to a trapdoor in the ballroom's ceiling. I stop for a moment on the floorboards of the musicians' platform, and Iris tells me: 'You'll need to come back on a Saturday night for the dance. We usually have one every week, but the inmates' band has broken up—they started fighting with one another mid-performance, their hands around each other's throats, and they were always pestering Dr. McDonald for bigger fees. So he's looking for stand-ins until the inmates calm down. I think he's got something arranged for all of the February Saturdays, some lads coming all the way from Prestwich, but I can ask him to book you for the first Saturday in March.' I say nothing, but I can see Iris has already taken a notebook used to record fits and mishaps from her uniform pocket, and is inscribing the date with a tiny pencil. When we reach the top of the ladder, I look down on the ghost-saturated ballroom from ceiling level, then Iris opens the trapdoor and we are out on the roof, protected from the fierce wind by the clock-tower directly alongside us. To keep warm, we huddle together, and the illuminated city is spread far below us with the three northern arterial approaches—Kirkstall Road, Chapeltown Road, Sheepscar Road—all converging on the city's central square, and below that, I can see the strip of the devil's ground, the derelict tramshed and the warehouses around the river Aire.

Iris is still scarred by the last night of the Futura festival, but she appears not to blame me for abandoning her. She is disabused with her punk-rock heritage of the last two years, between the ages of fifteen and seventeen, and though she is desperate for new cacophonies, she will countenance no further affiliation with punk-rock clubs—tonight, 30th January 1979, will be her last visit to the F Club—since with the final performance at the closing moment of the Futura festival, punk-rock irreparably failed Iris, and it's now over, it's the end, if it ever existed in the first place, or it has mutated into its own vanishing detritus, animated by phantom punk-rock bodies and the epileptic gestures of singers who cannot hold on. Iris points out the vast cemetery of the nameless mad directly below us, the iron markers just visible in the moonlight. For the first twenty years of this asylum's existence, after it opened in 1888, untold thousands of bodies were buried there, unrecorded, body upon body, ten deep, until almost the entire space had been filled, and a crematorium was constructed, so for the last seventy years, the inmates' ashes were interred just below the surface or else cast to the winds.

Iris is still weeping, and she shows me the key she covertly cut last October to the High Royds central dispensary. She throws it over the side of the ballroom so it lands in the cemetery ground below. Iris says, 'I don't need that any-more. I'm trusted here, and I can take whatever I need. If you want, we can share Eddie's dose for tonight—he doesn't need it, he can keep commentating all night. It's premium grade stuff. I'll go and syringe it into a Van Slyke pipette, then bring it back and we can drip it into each oth-er's mouths until it's all gone.' But I shake my head—I need to be lucid for the F Club cacophony, which is scheduled to occur two hours from now. Iris stares into my face again, and I stare back into her eyes. I can see that her life is now torn-apart by urgent dilemmas that can only be solved by doses of oblivion, and she grips my arm tightly and whis-pers: 'The devil is in league with both Thatcher and the Ripper. How can that be? How can that be? The North is fucked, England is fucked. You and I, we're fucked.'

As the clock-tower strikes 9pm, Iris and I descend from the ballroom roof and leave the administration building. As we exit the door, I look at the windows of the main office and see the head of administration, still gazing out at the city below, so intently that he either doesn't notice me at all or disregards the sight of me. We approach Hawes ward. Iris has left the door locked, but nobody ever attempts to escape High Royds: every inhabitant of the Northern cities knows with absolute certainty and from early childhood that, if you are consigned to High Royds, Stanley Royd or any other asylum of the North, you will never escape or leave in any other way, and you will die there. The replacement has not yet arrived, and when Iris unlocks the door, we hear the commentator's looped voice, stuck now on one repeated fragment: 'It's not a hard shot, it's always a hard shot...'. Iris wordlessly gestures for the commentator to abandon his work for the night, and he grins in acquiescence, sets down the rolled-up magazine and vanishes into the ward. Iris checks her patients and returns: the mad are all calm or in comas. She keeps her coat on and murmurs: 'I need to wait for my replacement, my double... Go and wait for me by the crematorium, otherwise she'll see you and she'll never believe I'm excused for a family emergency.' I cross the cemetery, the overgrown grass impeding my way. On the door of the crematorium, a note is sellotaped listing the seven names of the mad whose bodies will be incinerated tomorrow.

It's almost 10pm when I see an elderly, stooped figure slowly crossing the asylum lands from the administration building, occasionally halting as though convulsed by a vertebral seizure. In just over one hour, an irrevocable cacophony must occur far below this hill in a subterranean nightclub beside the fast-running river of ice slivers and naphthalene in the devil's city. The replacement enters Hawes ward and I hear raised voices of reprimand, but I can tell it's the replacement who is reprimanding Iris and not Iris castigating the replacement for her sloth. The altercation awakens those of the mad who are in the shallowest comas and screams begin, then are transmitted to the occupants of the adjacent Askrigg and Burtersett wards. Finally, I see Iris in her serge sailor's coat slam the door of Hawes ward behind her in a fury and walk across the terrain of the mad dead towards me: 'Let's go!', she hisses, but to have any chance of catching the final bus of the night down from High Royds into the city centre, we must run now, and we go headlong, hand in hand, along the course of the derelict asylum railway, between the lines of cypress trees, in exhilaration, Iris's mood abruptly transformed from rage and desperation to elation, her legs in her uniform's tights pumping against the gravel and the sleepers. When we reach the half-way point, a black Rolls-Royce Corniche heading in the opposite direction passes us at speed on the avenue, as though its arrival has been precipitated by the outburst of the mad at the altercation marking Iris's departure. The High Royds clock-tower is striking ten as we reach the gatehouse at the avenue's end and the bus is revving to leave, the conductor taking the last inhalation from his cigarette, the driver urgently gesturing for him to get on board. Iris jumps on first and the conductor throws away his cigarette end, then follows me as I hand him the coins for two fares, asking: 'Are you taking one of the nutcases with you then, son?', but Iris looks back at him with eyes flashing with anger as she ascends the stairway to the upper deck, and he immediately lowers his head in contrition: 'I didn't recognise you, Nurse Dunstan. I'm sorry.'

Even before Iris reaches the ripped green-vinyl seats at the back of the bus, I can tell she is regretting leaving High Royds. I sit alongside her and tell her: 'We'll be there in time, we'll just need to run through the dark arches down to the F Club', but she isn't looking at me and doesn't hear me. She turns and stares back up at High Royds with its blazing lights as we reach the foot of the Menston hill and the river Aire starts to run alongside us. Now we are approaching the city and soon we will pass by the ruins of Kirkstall Abbey and enter the razed terrain once occupied by ordnance factories whose buildings stretched alongside the river Aire, still wastelanded over thirty years after their war-era firebombing. We will pass by the Yorkshire Television studios, still on indefinite strike and reduced to their emergency split-second ghost transmissions of images of the face of Rita Rytka, staring with contempt into the alcohol-addled vermilion face of the director of the Ripper police as they examine the map of her twin's murder, which took place a year ago tomorrow. Finally, we will turn into this city's central square, entering it between the Queen's Hotel and the Majestic cinema, and come to a halt outside the main post-office, then Iris and I will run at elated speed, glancing at one another and speechless with laughter, trying to trip each other's heels, through the dark arches, past the Futura tramshed and down to the entrance of the F Club at the heart of the devil's ground.

When I look over at Iris, she has her face in her hands, but tears are streaming over her wrists, dripping down to the linoleum flooring scattered with cigarette ends and dried semen. As we pass Kirkstall Abbey, Iris reaches a hand to the bell which alerts the driver to stop the bus, and pushes it twice. I hear the ring down below, in the driver's cabin, and he immediately applies his brakes, even though it's an unscheduled stop. I realise that Iris is abandoning her journey, and she will not endure even her final punk-rock club night. She stands and looks down at me, so her tears fall into my lap: 'I'm going back to High Royds, I'm never leaving again. I'll walk back up the hill. Don't forget, I'll see you on the first Saturday night of March, 7pm.' Iris walks rapidly along the aisle to the stairway and disappears from sight without looking back, but as the bus starts up and accelerates, I see her again from the back window as she crosses the road beside the entrance to the abbey's ruins. Her dark figure is now so indistinct that I'm uncertain if she's entering the ruins or else turning to begin her long ascent of the hill towards High Royds. Beyond those unlit ruins, the river Aire is flowing in its own darkness into this city.

The conductor comes up the stairway and stands in front of me, wordless alarm in his face. He looks down at the tears scattered on the floor, then he hands me several coins: the refunded difference between the accomplished transportation of Iris's body from High Royds to Kirkstall Abbey and her abandoned fare from High Royds to City Square. I ask him if he and the driver can make one more run tonight, even though I know they will be officially on strike, back from outside the main post-office to High Royds, to pick up Iris as she walks by the side of the road, and take her all the way to the asylum clock-tower. The Ripper must be out tonight, relentlessly cruising the northern arterial roads—Kirkstall Road, Chapeltown Road, Sheepscar Road—unless tonight he is himself part of the clientele of this city's F Club, or Wakefield's Hellfire Club, or Bradford's Royal Standard Club. And the devil is up at High Royds tonight. The conductor looks relieved: 'Yes, we'll do that, son, don't worry, we'll look after her and deliver her back to her nutcases. One more trip up to High Royds and back won't hurt. In any case, we're on strike now until the Spring so we can do just as we bloody well like.'

The bus picks up more passengers after it reaches the darkened building of the Yorkshire Television studios. The F Club promoter works there, but by now, he will already be positioned at the foot of the subterranean staircase of the F Club, greeting his clientele with disdain and taking his fee, ready to castigate me for my arrival at the last instant. I leave the bus and walk slowly past the Queen's Hotel, down through the dark arches, slower still, almost immobile, alongside the tramshed and across the intersection beside the river Aire bridge, and stop at the F Club entrance.

Outside the club, the aged proprietor is pacing the pavement of Swinegate, wearing his immaculate suit and bowtie. Although he has rented his venue for the night to the F Club promoter and will receive no further payment himself, he appears compelled still to do his best to attract a maximal clientele. As I approach, he recognises me instantly, and tells me, 'Business is good tonight!—And best of all, nobody is complaining about the chemicals used to scour the walls after the flood. There must be at least one hundred clients inside, but we could still get ten or twenty more in. You must be an eminent musician... And your beautiful friend is here, the one you are always looking for. She's wearing a magnificent black overcoat, finest alpaca and silk, expertly tailored—pre-war, perhaps from Chisinau, perhaps from Odessa, I couldn't tell. But she looks paler than ever, and her hair is almost white under this light.' He points to the crackling fluorescent tubing above the club's doorway: 'I just hope the electricity holds out tonight—there have been severe powercuts all through the evening because of the shortage of coal at the Drax power-station. And from Thursday, the electricity workers right across the North will be on indefinite strike. Would you like to buy this club?—before Thatcher comes...'. He turns away, looking along Swinegate for prospective additions to the club's clientele.

I enter the doorway and immediately hear a raw grating of noise from the subterranean level. I have not been inside this building since my visit here while the interior was still packed tight with frozen floodwater, before the subterraneas were pumped and scoured. There are two flights of stairs to descend, then I will meet the promoter, and he will berate me. The noise grows louder with every step, and I can smell a deep stench of naphthalene and caustic chemicals rising from the walls of the club. At the foot of the stairs, the promoter is sitting alone, across two plywood chairs dislodged from the bar area, his hunchback resting on the first chair, his clubbed feet on the second chair, his squat body suspended in the intervening space, alongside a plywood desk. I approach him, but he is absorbed in his work on a long list of his club's excluded patrons, divided into sub-sections of the lifetime-barred and those barred only for the duration of this winter. Membership-cards bearing the same faceless figure who appeared on the Futura festival's entrance-card are scattered across the table, alongside the promoter's battered tin cashbox and a torn sheet of paper marked in biro with the words: 'Members free, Non-Members 50p'. Finally, he looks up and curses: 'Look what the fucking cat dragged in... Don't you know anything about professionalism? You're supposed to be here two hours or more in advance, to do a soundcheck. At least your friends were here on time. Anyway, you're on in five fucking minutes.' He gestures into the club's interior. Although he is angry now, I know that an all-consuming cacophony will rapidly placate him. 'I've just been up at High Royds, John, in the Hawes ward, listening to Eddie Waring's all-night commentating,' I tell him. The promoter swings his thick-soled boots off the second chair, looks down at the ground and nods approvingly. 'I should have guessed what you were up to,' he says, and adds: 'If I could just get him back down here for a performance of that demented delirium, maybe a double-bill with those epileptic Macclesfield Nazis, then I could close-down this club and retire in fucking glory.' I am tempted to tell him about Iris's proposition for a performance in the High Royds ballroom, but keep silent and turn away.

I enter the bar area, which is near-darkened, lit only by a few bare bulbs hanging from the low ceiling, and filled to capacity with figures in worn-out leather coats, ripped shirts and stockings, and the charity-shop suits and dresses of the recently dead. Almost nobody here is over eighteen years of age, but many look far older, their eye-sockets pitted and their bodies emaciated, as though a punitive incarceration or forced-labour sentence was inflicted upon them, long ago. The extremity of their punk-rock experience over the past two years has excoriated those bodies, and now wrenches them still more intensively in its vanishing. Since the club has nowhere to leave winter coats, every throat is wet with streams of hot sweat from the proximity of so many obsessed and overheated bodies. At the bar, an elderly woman is dispensing bottles of beer and shots of vodka. It's the first night of the F Club's re-opening after its flooding, and I know that none of this clientele are here for the particular cacophony that is about to erupt. Any aberrant cacophony could take its place, as long as it propelled them into vertiginous sensory disarray. Although the club's proprietor assured me that its walls have been comprehensively scoured following the flood, it's clear that they are still seeping an ineradicable river-Aire detritus of desiccated ammonia and naphthalene, along with residues of the chemicals deployed for those walls' scouring. But the clientele appear oblivious to the stench which the club emits, as though its toxicity has been designed to their own specifications. Although small groups and cliques are laughing together in apparent celebration of the F Club's re-opening, many of that clientele stand resolutely alone, indifferent to all human communication, leaning in isolation against the contaminated walls and waiting for void time to pass. I look out for Lily, but she is nowhere to be seen.

I slip through the crowd and enter the club's second zone, angled so that the platform at its rear cannot be seen from the first zone. I feel a hand on my shoulder, and turn to see Jim and Farhad standing together by the bar, which also extends at a right-angle from the first zone. Jim is serious and focused, and he points to the platform on which all the instruments and amplifiers he and Farhad have transported over the river-Aire bridge from Le Prince's workshop are arranged in a tight semi-circle, the illuminated amplifiers carefully positioned on plywood chairs, between the sound-system stacks. 'You've left it late,' Jim says. 'But everything is ready. I've set the mixing-desk sound levels myself. Just so you know—I'm only doing this once, never again. One terminal cacophony, and that's it for me. From tomorrow I'll be busy anyway with the start of the *Apocalypse Now* run at the Majestic, then there's a celebration afterwards.' I tell Jim that we've already been offered a second booking, for the High Royds ballroom, a month or so from now, but he shakes his head firmly: 'Only once, only once.'

I look over to Farhad, who has an undrunk bottle of beer in his hand. He is dressed in a black cashmere lounge suit, his shirt buttoned to the collar, and his thick black hair smells of rosewater. He smiles at me, but his smile immediately splinters into bewilderment and fear. I can tell that he's exhilarated at the imminent performance, but that elation is layered-over with trauma. I whisper into his ear: 'Don't worry, Farhad, whatever happens, it'll all be over in twenty minutes.' He smiles again, and I know he does not want to speak, but the words still pour out: 'It's happened again, I think I've killed someone again, on Sheepscar Road... At the end of my Drax runs, coming back down here from Chapeltown, in a hurry, to help Jim with the instruments... I saw a figure in a black overcoat by the side of the road, hardly there, then suddenly right in the centre of the road, as though time had jumped, and I couldn't stop, I couldn't brake, it was too late, I had to keep going. I barely saw anything, but I think I heard a scream.'

I turn away from Farhad's desperate face to look at the crowd, who saturate the club's space, engulfed in their rituals and gestures, all of them now doubled for me by the convulsive rituals and gestures of the High Royds inmates I witnessed tonight. All of the bodies gathered here in this club exist for a moment and simultaneously disappear. But Veronika has still not appeared. Now the promoter abruptly extinguishes the club's lighting, and the crowd turn to face the platform at the far end of the club's second zone and start to hiss in expectation. Without Veronika's drumming, we cannot perform, but now the instant has arrived to perform. I'm torn between standing at the microphone and announcing the abandonment of our performance even before it's begun, or else performing a silence whose negation will run so deep that the crowd will attack us, smash our instruments and chase us out onto Swinegate. But as I move towards the stiletto-scraped platform behind Jim and Farhad, I feel Veronika's body embrace mine from behind, transmitting intense heat, and she laughs: 'How can they call this place a club? It's the pit of hell. And it stinks in here.' I turn and Veronika's face is there in front of mine, her lips painted blue, her eyes intoxicated, her hair wild, four drumsticks held vertically in her fist and prison-barring the space between our faces. A cacophony will now be exacted.

Veronika does not hesitate, pushing Jim and Farhad aside so that she can reach her stolen snare-drum in the shortest interval, and she is already drumming at ferocious velocity before Jim activates his prototype 1920s USSR synthesiser and Farhad begins adeptly to thrash the strings of his amplified *tar*. I see Veronika pause for a split-second to move the microphone closer to the snare-drum's skin, and Jim simultaneously initiates a relentless bass drone from the EMS Synthi AKS synthesiser positioned behind him. I step onto the platform from the crowd as they surge to its edge, almost overwhelming me with their insurgent corporeal heat and violence. Even before I turn to face that crowd, I can tell that the cacophony generated by Veronika, Jim and Farhad is already opening up deep sensory fissures in the one hundred bodies facing us. I pick up the Burns Split Sonic guitar and see that Jim has fixed the dial to the wild-dog setting and sellotaped one or two words of essential advice to the guitar's body, but I need no guidance as I enter the cacophony's propulsion and I follow Farhad's adroit fingers with my own inept fingers, so that the cacophony intensifies, then I stand against the microphone to incant my journeys through this devil's city at night.

Once the cacophony is ongoing, it appears unstoppable and irreparable. I soon realise that Jim has set the sound-levels to such a volume that we are creating an infinitely proliferating entity of noise. From time to time, I look obliquely at Veronika, whose hair is streaming over her face as her arms pump at the snare-drum, and at Jim and Farhad, focused with such acute concentration on their instruments that they will not look back at me. As the cacophony accumulates, I know we are exacting a brutal sonic assault on the bodies in front of us, impelling them further into their punk-rock obsessions with madness or addiction or despair, and then onwards. By accelerating that cacophony into an unprecedented terrain, we could transform those bodies beyond all fixed categories of existence. Those bodies will be shattered and detrital, and will need to reassemble themselves from fragments into new configurations. Otherwise, we could perform in silence, as I envisaged in Veronika's absence. But we are on a fragile knife-edge precipice of noise, and when I look down on the entranced eyes of the crowd, it's impossible to tell if they are absorbing that entity of noise, or else are ready imminently to stream onto the platform, kick aside the microphones in disabused contempt and call an end to the cacophony.

In the heart of that cacophony, I experience the hallucination that I am back in the High Royds palace of the mad, around 4am, four hours in the future from now, at the moment when the effects of the inmates' narcotic cocktails erode and the screaming begins. All that holds together those voices' outbursts of screaming is the loop of the commentator's voice, in its oscillation between memory and oblivion, but that voice too is attuned in intimacy to delirium, cut by abysses of silence into which the inmates' screams will fall, until High Royds returns to its restless calm at dawn. And at any moment, the devil can end or revivify the screaming with one flick of his gold-ringed fingers. In the darkness between the naphthalene-engrained nightclub walls, I feel that my body and voice are flickering in volatile space, from the ward of screams to the nightclub of cacophony and back again. Now, my fingers are bleeding and my voice is raw.

Abruptly, I sense that the cacophony is undergoing some kind of disintegration, and I glance back at Jim, who gestures with the flat of his hand to indicate that the F Club's power supply is malfunctioning, along with that of the entire city. In response to that malfunction, I can see him making intricate shifts to the programming of the prototype synthesiser, while Veronika is drumming in convulsive percussive bursts, so that the cacophony fragments into sequences of momentary implosions, and I watch the walls of the club shaking so severely that the desiccated chemical residues are being repeatedly propelled inwards as ash and dust, while the meshing over the sound-system stack's speakers emits smoke and flames, and the bodies in front of my eyes appear close to collapse. Beyond those bodies, at the angle between the two zones of the club illuminated by the bare bulbs over the bar area, I catch sight of the promoter and the proprietor standing side by side, both gesturing wildly towards us.

The interval of disintegration lapses as the current returns, and Jim adjusts the cacophony so that it is now driving at far-excess velocity, the packed bodies in front of us pitched somewhere between convulsion and dancing, so overheated and sensorially disorientated that they emit a dense steam of sex and negation that rises to the low ceiling of the subterranea and gathers there, ready to fall. I look over to Farhad and see the exhaustion of exile in his face, but his left hand is still moving over the *tar* strings at blurred speed. Veronika nods and smiles at me in exultation between the thrashing transits of her hair. And Jim is still absorbed in bleeding intensities of noise between his two synthesisers. We can go on indefinitely, until the club's 6am closure or further still, and then, as though slipping between our fingers, the cacophony suddenly ends. Simultaneously, the crowd is roaring, and the cacophony's final echoes are reverberating from the club's walls, gradually dispersing until nothing at all of the performance remains. Nobody will remember this night. The promoter has already raised the lights, and I can see the one hundred bodies in front of us in harsh illumination, many of them now so drained and dehydrated that they sink to their knees on the ground. Released by the immediate cooling of the air, the amassed steam of sex and negation pinioned at ceiling level is now raining down onto those bodies, their skins already soaked with sweat, heads held back and gasping for air, so that rain of lust and terror falls directly into their mouths. The still-upright clientele around them are shouting ecstatically and calling for more, as though another cacophony could somehow be generated from zero, but that acclaim alienates Veronika, and she throws her drumsticks to the ground in disdain and kicks them away with her climbing boots, curses at me and shouts: 'Fuck you all... This was for Helen Rytka—not for you...' into the still-live microphone as she jumps down from the platform, pushes her way through the audience, and leaves the club.

I set aside the blood-streaked guitar, still spitting feedback, and step down from the platform to lean against the bar. Immediately, the promoter is at my side, holds my shoulder and hands me a crumpled envelope. I glance inside at the ten notes. 'I've had to hold £2 back for the damage you did to the club's sound-system and walls,' he tells me. 'Now all that dust and ash will need to be swept up, and I'll need to compensate the fire-control services.' I look over and see the elderly woman who usually dispenses bottles of beer now pouring a washing-up bowl of dirty water over the still-vibrating speakers at this side of the platform to put out the final flames, but those at the far side are only emitting smoke. I glare at the promoter: 'You fucking bastard, let's have it all, now.' He reluctantly reaches into his pocket, adds two crumpled notes to the envelope's contents and says: 'Only because that was a fucking miraculous cacophony. I don't know how you did that. My clientele loved it.' He gestures at the audience, most of whom are still kneeling open-mouthed on the ground, eyes staring straight ahead in oblivion as though just subjected to one of the electro-convulsive therapies that, from what Iris told me, Dr. McDonald administers at 6am each morning in a room behind the High Royds ballroom, to those of the inmates who will not stop screaming. The club's lights are glaring down on those bodies, and they appear as the corporeal remnants of a catastrophe which has struck the devil's city tonight. I can see thin trails of blood leaking from eardrums, and the dancefloor closest to the platform is crisscrossed with arrows of urine. Those bodies are exposed to an acute skinned-alive exhaustion, and I know it will be an hour or more before they stand to dance again or disperse onto Swinegate. Jim and Farhad are already passing repeatedly between those petrified figures, avoiding body-fluids, carrying the instruments and amplifiers to the club's entrance.

The promoter gestures with his right hand and the club's lights go down again, the habitual raw grating of noise occupying the volume of the club. Now that it's dark, he feels he can make a proposition, and he rests his hunched back against the bar and puts his lips to my ear: 'I'm going to hire the ballroom of the Griffin Hotel, for four weekend evenings in March. You know the place—it's four times the size of this club, a prestige venue. So I want another cacophony from you, Saturday the 3rd, midnight, £15. I'll give you a written contract. And that's just the fucking start. By the end of March, I'll be ready to take over the ballroom in the Queen's Hotel basement, five nights a week. It'll be the premium venue of the North. I'll leave this place with its chemical stench behind—it's time to move on. And if Yorkshire Television ever starts to broadcast again, I'll get you on to do a live transmission.' I've spent many evenings in the always-deserted ground-floor bar of the Griffin Hotel, just off City Square on the street which forms the northern boundary of the devil's ground, and sometimes taken the stairs to the fifth-floor ballroom, which is ruined and abandoned, never refurbished since that now-decrepit hotel was built in the 1870s, at the same time as the original Queen's Hotel, gargoyles, animals and demons emerging at every storey from the stone cladding over its blackened brickwork. An illuminated clock-face, the twelve letters of the hotel's name replacing the usual numbered hours, burns all night and marks the relentless maledictions of this city's time. The hotel is still open but almost nobody visits this devil's city anymore and, alongside its long-term residents, any guests are there by disorientation, stranding, or mishap. I've heard that the hotel's desperate proprietor has been trying to rent out nights at the ballroom all of this last winter, occasionally luring potential promoters by holding high-volume drunken receptions whose invitees finally spill out of the ballroom into the adjacent corridors at the dead of night, break open the locked doors of the fifth-floor guest-rooms and upend the guests from their beds.

'No way,' I tell the promoter. 'We already have a confirmed booking on March 3rd. Up at High Royds, in the inmates' ballroom there. So you can stick your contract and your £15 up your arse and set fire to it.' Even in the darkness, I can tell that the promoter is taken aback, and hear him inhale: 'Fuck, you're moving fast. £20 then, the next night, March 4th.' He takes a crumpled sheet of lined paper from the same pocket as the two pound notes, amends the pre-inscribed fee in scrawled biro, and sets it down on the bar. I will still need to convince Jim that two further cacophonies are viable, but I sign the contract and walk away.

I know that Jim and Farhad will already have the instruments and amplifiers amassed in the doorway of the club, and will be waiting for me so that we can transport them together across the river Aire bridge to Le Prince's workshop. I take a last look at the F Club's clientele in the semi-darkness, most of them still immobilised and dazed, though one or two of them are now rising from their knees, shaking their heads in vertigo and moving towards the toilets to retch or rehydrate. I reach the bar area and find Veronika's uncle waiting for me. He shakes my hand gravely and whispers: 'Veronika didn't see me here. I followed her, to make sure she was safe from the Ripper on her walk down from Francis Street. She's left to finish her shift at the Roots Club. I need to leave in an instant and follow her back to Chapeltown—she threw away her drumsticks, so she won't be able to poke the Ripper in the eye if he comes for her. You know that Veronika says she will leave Francis Street as soon as Thatcher arrives. I'm worried that if she goes to the Ukrainian region of the USSR, where her mother is from, the MPLA guerrillas training there will recruit her, take her back to Angola and make her fight with a machine-gun in their civil war. And if she goes to Jamaica, where her father is from, it's still more dangerous there. I'll never see her again, she'll disappear or be killed. I've already lost her mother and her brother...'. Veronika's uncle is weeping in distress now, the smell of fried carp rising from his checked polyester jacket as he embraces me. 'So come to my restaurant tomorrow evening at 10pm, and speak to her. She only listens to you, nobody else. You've done so much for Veronika already—I could never believe she would be performing in a top establishment like this.' He waves a hand at the club's striated, naphthalene-exuding walls, then embraces me again. 'Please convince Veronika to stay in Francis Street... I have to go now, before I lose sight of her.' Veronika's uncle rapidly ascends the F Club's stairway.

As I reach the stairway myself, the aged proprietor is coming down to assess the damage inflicted upon his nightclub. It's 1am, but he still appears immaculate, and the club will not close for another five hours, so he still has most of his work for the night to accomplish. 'Your associates are waiting for you outside. That was a most remarkable entertainment,' he tells me. 'But on the loud side. It will take the rest of the night to expel the clientele, but I have some buckets of cold water ready. Now I fear the subterranea has been destabilised, and I'll need to commission an assessment of the entire structure. We were fortunate that the building above didn't collapse on our heads. There are at least three more bricked-up cellar areas under the warehouse, each the size of this club or more. The best solution now will be to brick-up this club and open up the other cellars.' I ask him if he saw the white-haired girl in the black overcoat leave. At first, he seems confused, or to be contemplating an underhand subterfuge. I try to activate his memory: 'The magnificent black overcoat—you said it yourself. From Chisinau, or maybe Odessa.' The proprietor looks me in the eyes: 'No,' he says. 'It is by no means unusual for the clientele of this club to enter by the doorway but to leave by other means.'

Jim and Farhad are waiting outside, shivering in the cold as it starts to snow. I hand them each three one-pound notes. Farhad takes his fee and, to my astonishment, kisses the middle finger of my left hand. Jim looks at the notes with disdain, scrunches them into a ball in his fist, and flicks the paper into the Swinegate gutter. 'The promoter kept me talking,' I apologise to them. 'He thinks he's going to be the king of the fucking North, opening up his clubs in the ballrooms of the Griffin Hotel and the Queen's Hotel.' Farhad looks at me in incomprehension: 'The king of the North?—but we already have two kings, at least in this city, the Ripper and the devil. We cannot have a third king, that's sure. And when Thatcher comes, she will arbitrate and make a choice. I believe she will choose the devil over the Ripper, and invite him into her home, since he will not go where he is not invited. And the Ripper will finally be captured, and sent to High Royds. But the promoter is only a lowly man, discontented in his body, so he wants to be a king.' Jim nods in agreement, holding his arms around his ancient leather coat to prevent the wind-whipped snowfall infiltrating it. He asks me: 'You mean the ballroom on the top floor of the Griffin, along-side the clock-face? That place hasn't been touched since the 1870s. And the ceiling is about thirty feet high. With all that dirt, dust and nicotine on the walls, the acoustics must be fucking incredible.' We start to walk over the river

Aire bridge, Farhad moving ahead in his eagerness, while Jim carries a synthesiser case in each arm, and I'm holding Veronika's snare-drum.

I can tell Jim is intrigued by the promoter's plans, so I pass on the proposition: 'As well as a performance at High Royds on March the 3rd, we've now been offered another show, in the Griffin ballroom, on the next night. But if the power strike is still on, we won't be able to do either.' Jim stops and shakes his head. 'What we did tonight has to be a one-off. Nobody recorded it, nobody filmed it, so it's only held in the audience's bodies. And once they've got their ears working again and had some sleep, they'll soon forget it too. So no more, no fucking way. Anyway, from tomorrow night I'm working on the *Apocalypse Now* projections at the Majestic. If the film's run goes on for more than a month, there's no chance I can do more cacophonies.' I can tell that Jim's desire at this moment is to lock up all of the instruments in Le Prince's workshop, bolt the reinforced cast-iron door and throw the key into the river Aire, so that those instruments won't be found for another forty or fifty years, when the door to the workshop will finally be blown open with explosives by film-obsessives and the mysterious detrita of tonight's performance will be discovered.

I try to persuade Jim: 'What would your grandfather have done if he'd been offered the chance to perform his experiments in the ballrooms of an insane asylum and a near-abandoned hotel?—he would have seized the chance to test out the capacities of his synthesisers in those kinds of environments. And you told me yourself that his greatest moment was when he demonstrated his synthesisers to Tesla in the ballroom of the New Yorker Hotel.' Jim is now stopped dead in the centre of Le Prince's bridge, thinking the matter over. Five minutes pass, and Farhad eventually comes back and stands off to one side, puzzled. I gesture to him to keep silent. The snow is accumulating in a layer on the shoulders of Jim's leather coat. Finally, he nods his head: 'You're right. My grandfather would want me to do it. But I'll only use his prototype synthesisers—I won't contaminate everything by mixing-in 1970s technology as I did tonight... Just don't give me any more of that promoter's dirty fucking money, or there'll be hell to pay. And two more cacophonies, no more. If necessary, we can rehearse again in Le Prince's workshop, even if the strike goes on—I have an emergency generator.' He puts out his hand and I shake it.

Farhad is overjoyed at the prospect of the two further performances, and while Jim strides ahead with the two synthesiser cases, he stands in front of me, takes my shoulders and grins into my face. His cashmere suit is now sodden with snow and reeking of chemicals from the F Club walls, but he doesn't care. He tells me, 'It was such a fortuitous morning, when my father met you in the Town Hall foyer. I'm happier now than I've been since I was seven years old, playing the *tar* in the marble palace in Tehran. I'm going to practice twenty hours a day, every day, from now until the High Royds performance. By then I'll be able to play the *tar* at seven times the usual speed, if that's what you want. With the power strike starting on Thursday, I don't need to make any more coal deliveries. No more Drax power-station truck-journeys. And when I don't need to drive my truck, I won't be killing anyone else on Sheepscar Road.' Farhad's face falls, and I see the desperation of exile in his brilliant blue eyes. 'But if I'm arrested, I'll be imprisoned or deported back to Iran. And on Thursday, Khomeini will fly back to Teheran from Paris, to seize supreme power. I've heard that a crowd of many millions will be waiting for him. If I'm deported to Iran, the revolutionary guards will torture and execute me instantly. *Hichi*... Nothing will remain of me at all. My ashes will be buried in an unknown place. The horror of the era of new theocracies is beginning, Khomeini's on Thursday, Thatcher's too, in a month or two.' Jim impatiently gestures for Farhad and I to catch up, and Farhad's face is transformed again from terror to pleasure as he leaves me behind. I stand and watch them as the snow thickens and their figures blur, only their voices now clearly discernible as they animatedly begin to discuss *tar*-string tensions, and by the time they reach the far side of the river Aire bridge, they've vanished from sight.

I cannot see either end of Le Prince's bridge in the gathering snowstorm, and when I lean over the parapet to look down towards the river Aire, gripping the century-old ornate ironwork with my hands still raw and blood-streaked from their guitar-string collisions, I can barely see the black water in its propulsion eastwards, the snow melting as soon as it touches the surface of the fast-flowing river. It's silent, and the sudden snowfall has deterred even the Ripper police patrols from crossing the bridge on their way to Chapeltown Road. After tonight's furore at the F Club, I want to absorb the solitude for an instant, and I take off my overcoat and cover Veronika's snare-drum with it to prevent the skin from being damaged. I can feel the cold, but I will survive it. I could be exhausted, or simultaneously exhilarated. I touch the parapet again with both hands, and feel a reactivating presence, as though Le Prince's two-second film of this bridge, the first film ever made, inhabits it and can, at any moment, revivify all of the bodies who were crossing the bridge in that interval when the film was shot, from the window of Le Prince's workshop, ninety years ago. I can't see the clock-face on the derelict warehouse tower at the riverside, but I hear it striking 2am. I feel that I will now be living entirely within the medium of film for the next twenty-two hours, between the ecstatic sensation I experienced only an instant ago that my body was being spectrally traversed by Le Prince's film of this bridge and the figures crossing it in the September noon sunlight of 1888, and the moment when the film I will see projected at the Majestic cinema begins, at midnight.

In the peripheral vision of my left eye, I see a figure in a dark overcoat approaching soundlessly from the F Club side of the bridge. A voice I've never heard before, or which is speaking for the first time, tells me: 'You're cold, you're cold...' and a small hand reaches down to the buttons of my trousers, rapidly pulls them open, and executes a sequence of such finely-timed, adept gestures that the transits of semen are propelled downwards into the river after a ferociously short interval and I watch them fall, as they did on the night of the Futura festival, immediately carried away in an amalgam with naphthalene and transported out of this city, towards the North Sea. As I gasp, lost for breath, attempting to remain conscious, I pull my left hand from its spasming grip on the parapet's ironwork and reach out until I can seize the thick cloth of the overcoat. That fabric feels still warm, as though its wearer only exited an overheated place of sanctuary a few instants ago, to accomplish her work, and I feel the blood scraped from my already-raw hand by its convulsive grip on the parapet now begin to infuse that luxurious cloth.

The same hand that expelled the fall of semen now ascends into my hair, and I feel lips against my left ear, whispering into it: 'I've been killed tonight in a hit-and-run incident on Sheepscar Road. I saw you talking to my killer a moment ago. He should not have killed me, nor the twin sisters. But he will die too, soon... And I will still watch over you and take care of you, between the High Royds screaming inferno and the infernal cinemas, ballrooms and nightclubs of this city... I don't fear the Ripper, I don't fear the devil, I don't even fear Thatcher... But I'm leaving this city, you'll never see me again after tonight... I'm taking a journey east now, back through time, the reverse direction to the journey my parents took—so young, ghosts already—thirty years ago, through Europe's ruins and ashes, to arrive at this city. I will travel backwards, via Wroclaw, Lvóv, Chisinau, Odessa You won't see me again, you won't feel my touch again.' I close my eyes, and the hand holding my hair twists my face around so that icy lips touch the very surface of my cracked lips, then that hand rotates my head firmly back to face towards the river. I feel myself close to losing consciousness, oscillating between blackouts and instants of lucid clarity, and abruptly release my hand's grip on the overcoat. After a few minutes, I turn around, open my eyes and look to the right and to the left, but see nobody at all in the diminishing snowfall, only the abandoned buildings, nightclubs and factories at either side of Le Prince's bridge.

4.

ZONES OF EYES,
JANUARY-FEBRUARY
1979

I'm crossing City Square towards the Majestic cinema, between the Queen's Hotel and the main post-office. It's 9pm on the first anniversary of the murder of Helen Rytka, and when I passed the bar of the Queen's Hotel, a moment ago, I saw the flickering television set inside tuned to the on-strike Yorkshire Television channel as it transmitted the black-and-white photograph of her twin, Rita Rytka, eye to eye with the director of the Ripper police, before reverting to void static. Tonight, at midnight, as this winter of discontent intensifies, the entirety of the public-service workers of this city will join those already on strike: the bus and train drivers and conductors, the television-station technicians, the dustbin-emptiers and the buriers of the dead. Callaghan is flailing in extremis, his government ready to fall, but Thatcher is calm, waiting for her moment. I'm carrying Veronika's four drumsticks, which Farhad salvaged from the F Club dancefloor after Veronika kicked them aside, then handed to me last night when I finally caught up with him after the hiatus in my river Aire bridge crossing. An ambulance is now heading at speed from the square, its siren at maximum volume, but the driver brakes to a sudden halt at the junction with Wellington Street, as though unsure which way to go. The doors of the Majestic cinema are still locked, immense hoardings to either side announcing tonight's film premiere, but I enter the building by the back stairway and climb ten flights to the projection booth.

I knock on the door and Jim is poised over twelve containers of celluloid reels. Behind him, I see the two vast projectors, and beyond the glass partition, the auditorium below is poised in near-darkness. Jim looks at me for an instant but waves me away: 'I'll see you later. I have to assemble the entire film myself, it lasts for almost three hours and the reels have arrived in the wrong order. I'm in charge now... The senior projectionist is gone—some kind of delirious alcoholic meltdown. It's been building for years, and the tension before tonight's screening sent him over the edge. The ambulance crew didn't know whether to take him to High Royds or St. James... St. James is on strike from midnight and the patients already there are being expelled into the streets. High Royds can't go on strike because of the mad, but they have a resident projectionist already there. While the crew were arguing, the projectionist ran screaming down the stairs into the square and they chased after him. I just hope he didn't take a reel of the film with him.' I know that the ambulance crew will begin their own strike at midnight, so they will need to decide fast on the senior projectionist's transportation to High Royds or St. James. 'I'll leave you to it,' I tell Jim. 'I'm going up to Chapeltown, to give Veronika her fee and her drumsticks.' Jim is so concentrated on his work that he doesn't hear.

As I pass the public call-box outside the post-office, I decide to call Iris at High Royds, to make sure the final bus picked her up as promised from the side of the road last night and deposited her at the asylum clock-tower. I call the number and ask to speak to Nurse Dunstan, but realise that she will not be arriving for her night-shift, passing through the administration building, after making the long journey from her frozen house by the railway cutting alongside the river Calder. Now, Iris will indefinitely inhabit the asylum itself, moving only between the nurses' home and the Hawes ward, transiting the asylum grounds. A voice tells me: 'She can't come to the telephone. She's already at work.' I put down the receiver and begin the walk up to Francis Street for the assignation Veronika's uncle gave me after the F Club cacophony. Last night's vanished snowstorm has left only iced residues in the deep cracks of this city, and the night sky overhead is streaked with stars. I pass by the arcades, the godforsaken nightclubs and sex-clubs of the Merrion Centre, through the ringroad underpass and onto Chapeltown Road, the Ripper police patrols heading in either direction, figures on both pavements walking back from work towards the city's northern peripheries.

At exactly 10pm, I descend the stairway of the restaurant, and look over the tables of solitary men, immersed in their memories of famines and internment camps, or smoking and listening to the quiet voices of Radio Kharkov from the transistor radio taped to the wall. It's still early, the restaurant only opened a few hours ago, and I take a table in the far corner. Veronika's uncle crosses the restaurant floor with a bottle of Chernihivske beer, shakes my hand gravely as he did last night, and tells me: 'Veronika will be down in a moment.' He points up at the ceiling, which is shaking with the Roots Club dub furore. 'She's not working in that place tonight, and I told her you'll be here. I'm depending on you to have a serious talk with her tonight. Yes, a very serious talk. You'll see what I mean when she appears.' I say nothing, and pour the beer into the glass which Veronika's uncle sets down beside the bottle. I know I will have to leave within an hour in order to reach the Majestic cinema in time for the *Apocalypse Now* film projection.

After ten minutes or so, Veronika descends the restaurant staircase. She appears to hesitate when she sees me in the far corner, glances over at her uncle in the kitchen, then slowly approaches. I see she's carrying her stolen clarinet in her left hand, and she's wearing a black boxing-outfit, lettered in pristine yellow on the front with the words 'Everlast—Bronx USA', the shorts extending halfway down her thighs, her climbing boots below laced tight. Her wild hair is tied back with a thick elastic-band,

and her throat is streaming with sweat, as though she's been pummelling a punch-bag for the past two or three hours. I can see she's still hesitating to sit down, but she finally hooks the chair aside with one of her boots and slides down onto it, places the clarinet on the table, and looks me in the eyes under the harsh illumination of the restaurant's bare lightbulbs. Immediately, I see that her face is bruised and beaten, from her forehead, across her nose and down to her mouth, her lower lip split. I take her right hand, the skin also bruised and lacerated, a bandage wrapped around it, every knuckle skinned: 'Veronika, what happened?'

Veronika's uncle sets down a beer in front of her and she lifts it to her lips, drains the entire contents and puts it back down on the table. But, apart from the gulp of her throat, she is silent. 'You left so fast last night,' I tell her. 'You didn't meet the Ripper on Chapeltown Road?' Veronika smiles wryly, but it's clearly painful for her lips. 'No, not the Ripper—I would have put his fucking eyes out with my fingernails, even without my drumsticks.' I look over to the kitchen, where Veronika's uncle is busily preparing two plates of fried carp. 'It wasn't your uncle?—I know he was in a desperate state at the F Club last night. I talked to him, and he was ready to follow you.' Veronika shakes her head dismissively: 'No, my uncle won't ever hurt me. I soon out-distanced him, once I'd passed under the railway viaduct and reached the arcades.' I listen for a moment to the noise of the gang-warfare cries in the streets outside, audible even down here as the Seacroft gang and the Meanwood gang start to manoeuvre into position for tonight's battle. 'Did you get caught in those gangs' cross-fire? I know that when the stragglers get detached, they go haywire.' Veronika slips her hand from my own, reaches behind her neck with both arms and detaches the elastic-band that held back her hair, so that it cascades down over her shoulders. 'I've lived in Chapeltown all my life,' she says. 'I know how to keep a distance from those gangs.'

I've now reached the end of my list of candidates for Veronika's assailants, and I wait for her to speak again. I can only assume that Veronika gratuitously provoked a passer-by, but I'm wrong. 'I just had a confrontation, that's all,' she says. 'It's nothing. When I was walking past the Merrion Centre, three big guys came out drunk from one of the clubs in there. It's always the same with their shouts—you black whore, you're the Ripper's supper, you deserve it, you black whore—and I went berserk. Two of them I could manage easily, but three was hard work. So I got hurt a bit, but I made it back to Francis Street. And now I'm working out, getting myself ready for the next time. I need to be able to punch with both fists, fast. I don't have time for any more cacophonies, so here's the clarinet back—give it to the Iranian kid. I know he has one already, but maybe he can grow another mouth.' Veronika laughs, but I can see it hurts.

I take the clarinet in one hand and give Veronika her drumsticks back with the other hand, as though we were exchanging gifts. Then I reach into my pocket, take out the promoter's envelope with Veronika's cut inside, and hand it to her. She smiles without looking inside the envelope, and sets it aside. I tell her, 'If you change your mind, we have two more performances at the beginning of March... The High Royds ballroom, then the Griffin Hotel ballroom. Your snare-drum is safe—we took it back to the workshop by the river last night. We won't perform without you.'

At that moment, Veronika's uncle arrives with the plates of fried carp and more beers, but he retreats quickly, eager to leave us to talk. Even though Veronika has just renounced all further cacophonies, I can see that she is tempted by the ballroom performances. 'High Royds? I've never been there, but I'll be going soon, if I stay in this city... Performing for the nutcases? That would be fun, and you can be sure they won't applaud—I can't stand that. I'll think it over.' She has to use her left hand to fork the fried carp into her bruised and split mouth, and I can see that the bandage on her right hand is now seeping blood. 'But I'll do it for you, if you want me to.' I ask her if she still plans to leave this city, and leave England, on her eighteenth birthday, in the Spring, for the Ukrainian region of the USSR or for Jamaica. We both know that Thatcher will be here, by then, and the real hell will begin. 'Not the Ukraine,' she tells me. 'I've changed my mind after last night—I'd get it a thousand times worse there than in this fucking city. But maybe I'll go to Jamaica, visit some clubs, swim in the sea, just relax...'. I look into Veronika's face, so tense and strained that the pulsing tendons in her neck are vibrating in time to the dub thuds from the club upstairs. She closes her eyes: 'You can come too.'

It's time for me to go back down to City Square. I'm still holding Veronika's clarinet, but now I place it on the table, and leave it there. I ask her, 'Are you coming to see the film? Jim will project it at midnight. I'll walk back here with you afterwards.' Veronika shakes her head: 'If I had my drums here, I'd be playing all night, in the rabbi's rooms, never stopping, in memory of Helen Rytka. I'm not leaving Francis Street with my face like this. So I'll just keep working with my fists, and go out to check on those children who sniff glue in the burnt-out houses. I don't want them to die.' I stand up, and Veronika abruptly stands too at the same instant, kicking her chair aside, and takes my face in her hands. She's laughing and weeping: 'You know my uncle thinks we should get married, like in a film... But you're so much younger than me, six months or so, you should still be sniffing glue in the bombed-out houses down the street, wide-eyed and hallucinating... I'll see you in a month's time, at the insane asylum.' I want to kiss Veronika's lips, but they're too bruised. So I hold her shaking body for a moment as it transmits extreme heat to mine, her wild black hair in my face, the yellow lettering 'Everlast—Bronx USA' of her boxing vest pressed against my chest. Then I cross the restaurant floor, between the tables of solitary, aged men, look back for a moment as I reach the staircase, and see Veronika sitting at the table again, already downing the first spirit-glass shot of *samohon* brought to her by her uncle, her back to me.

As soon as I've descended the synagogue's seven marble steps and started to walk along Francis Street towards Chapeltown Road—the dub thud of the club that convulsively shakes the pavements now gradually receding—I curse myself for not convincing Veronika to come down into the city's centre with me for the *Apocalypse Now* projection and the all-night dance furore. I can envision with certainty that she's still sitting at the restaurant table in her boxing outfit, taking a shot of *samohon* every ten minutes, and it's still early in the evening. At some point, two hours or so from now, when the other restaurant tables are all occupied by exiled, solitary men, Veronika's uncle will whisper to her that it's better if she ascends to the rabbi's rooms, and she will put on her gloves there, pummel the punch-bag with drunken fury for hours until the old leather splits and the sawdust spills out, then she will lay on the floor, face up, exhausted but wide-awake, her face beaten and sweat still streaming from her body, her bruised lips murmuring maledictions. I would turn back, but I am now walking so fast, to avoid the attention of the Ripper police patrols and the gangs traversing the northern avenues for their imminent battle, that I've already reached the edge of the city centre. When I pass St. James hospital, I have to cross the road to evade the amassed, panic-eyed patients expelled from their wards in anticipation of the strike, milling on the pavements as though they were refugees in their own city, unsure where to go, their operation wounds still trailing transparent pipes leading to drainage bottles, the staff already leaving, the hospital's lights turned off and the doors locked. The unburied bodies of the dead, habitually housed in the subterranean mortuary of the hospital, have now been transported to the great freezer chambers of this city's slaughterhouse, on its eastern periphery, alongside the river Aire, to be held in suspension until the buriers of the dead finally consent to work again, or the ghosts of the dead dig their own graves.

Everyone in this devil's city knows that, at the far side in time of the strikes that will begin at midnight, we will have Thatcher. Callaghan's government, already crumbling, will not withstand the turmoil of the coming weeks, and his ministers are paralysed. Ennals announced yesterday that the hospital strikes can only worsen. Even in England's southern regions, widespread strikes of public-service workers are beginning too. The masters of the North, along with their corrupt corporate allies, appear set on self-ruination, along with the all-engulfing disintegration of this city and the industries of the Northern lands. Last night, after travelling to meet with Callaghan, they stepped out onto platform 5 of this city's railway station, from the first-class dining carriage of the final train from England's capital before the transport strike began, red-faced with alcohol, and headed reeling through the station's halls to the Queen's Hotel bar, to celebrate the imminence of their own eradication and the denudation of this city. Thatcher's eyes are wary, and she will not act until she is certain of success, but when those watchful eyes see the moment to seize power, in the coming weeks, she will take it.

When I enter City Square, the clock-face on the post-office has just struck eleven-thirty, and I cross the plaza to the Majestic cinema. That cinema's curved sandstone facade is now illuminated from below with spotlights, and up on the roof's pediments, I can see three sculpted figures of angels, all of them pulling shrouds away from their naked bodies with their left hands, as their eyes watch over this city and its inhabitants. The Majestic cinema was the most luxurious in the entire city when it was constructed in the 1920s, its prominent site between the original Queen's Hotel and the main post-office drawing seething crowds every evening, arriving at the tram-stop directly outside the cinema so that the spectators' bodies were disgorged directly into the foyer. But at the end of the 1950s, those film-captivated spectators vanished, and the Majestic's auditorium was used as a bingo hall for twenty years or so until last September, when the screening of Le Prince's film induced the proprietor to experiment with showing films again. The cinema's outside doors are now wide open but the auditorium is closed, so the high-ceilinged foyer, lit from above by chandeliers, is crowded to overspilling with hundreds of figures, eager for the proprietor to signal for them to be allowed inside the auditorium. Through the cigarette smoke, I can see that almost the entire audience from last night's F Club cacophony are also here, risen from their knees and rehydrated, but still wearing the same clothes, and for the first time, I can feel eyes upon me, so that my anonymity in this city is broken. I pass through the crowd towards the ticket kiosk and sense that bodies are edging away from me, to create a channel for my passage, as though I were at the origins of viral contamination. At the auditorium's doors, the proprietor is issuing orders to his ushers. He wears a shining black suit, cut so ineptly that it hangs from his emaciated body. Although I've never met him before, he seems to recognise me, approaches and hands me a ticket. 'From the projectionist,' he tells me.

At that moment, I see Jim approaching to consult with the proprietor. He nods to me but waves me aside, and I stand at a distance and listen to their discussion. Jim reports that, after five hours' work, he's assembled the reels of the entire film and it's now ready to be shown, but he is concerned that, at exactly midnight, the electricity in the cinema will fail and the projection will need to be abandoned. The proprietor replies: 'Don't worry, son. It won't be until seven tomorrow morning that the grid controllers arrive at the generating-station on Kirkstall Road and pull the lever to switch off the current for their strike. Until then, we're still in business. So you'll have your projection tonight at least, and I'll let you do whatever you like in the basement until 7am. I'm just grateful you took over from that bloody nutcase. For tomorrow, we'll have to see.'

Jim heads back to the projection box, but he takes my shoulder in passing and whispers that he has a surprise film, to show instead of the trailers and advertisements, and that I should come up to the projection box, when the night's films are over. Once he's gone, I look up at the hand-painted mosaic extending around the foyer's four walls, below the chandeliers. It holds deep cracks, and many segments have fallen over the years, but I can still see the panorama of this city in the 1920s, with its splendid hotels, thriving industries and department-stores, the pristine river Aire running alongside them. From the corner of my eye, I catch the proprietor approaching, and he tells me, 'I'll need to get that fixed, one day, when this place is making money again. We have the biggest screen in the North here, son. We used to get over a thousand for our Saturday bingo nights, then the audiences declined in fear of the Ripper and stopped altogether a year ago, with his killing of Helen Rytka. You probably won't appreciate bingo at your age, but it's an art form—especially the moment when someone has a full house but is frozen, too terrified to open their mouth to shout out. If this film's run isn't a success, I'll start the bingo nights again. In fact, it's not too late even for tonight.' He looks with distaste at his dishevelled, film-obsessed clientele. I tell him: 'Just for tonight, it's better to show the film', and he turns in resignation to his ushers to signal for them to open the auditorium doors.

The patrons stream into the auditorium to take the best seats in front of the immense, curved screen. From the stalls, I look up at the three tiers of balconies which ascend to the domed, ornate ceiling. Marble friezes around the sides of the auditorium walls and along the balconies' edges show Greek sun-god chariots pulled by teams of frenzied horses, moving at such speed that they appear ready to pitch their drivers down among the worn velvet seats. And, beneath my feet, I can sense the presence below this auditorium of the subterranean space in which Jim will hold some kind of celebration furore after the projection is over. The stalls are now already filled with elated bodies, and I have to climb to the highest balcony, so close to the damp-stained ceiling's plaster that I can almost touch the striations that embed it.

It's still twenty minutes or so before midnight, but the lights abruptly go down in the cinema and I feel the audience's voices fall silent, as another noise emerges into that darkened space, with the end of vocal language. Hundreds of eyes are experiencing the ecstasy of film's exit aperture—releasing and propelling their bodies from this infernal devil's city, transforming those bodies and their vision in that propulsion—as it materialises spectrally in this space, rendering our bodies and this city filmic, just as I experienced film's ecstatic aperture on Le Prince's bridge last night, exactly twenty-two hours ago, in the instant before Lily's apparition. That noise is a low hum emitted involuntarily by the throats of this cinema's spectators, the electric static of the contact between the cinema's air and the spectators' exposed skin at the first instant when film's images are transmitted across space from the projector to the screen, the sound of heartbeats and intakes of breath, and the audible sensation emitted by the audience that film is a vital malfunction in our lives.

That elated expectation of the audience is overturned in a split-second as their eyes begin to register the film Jim has chosen to project to them, instead of the trailers and advertisements that usually occupy the timespan between the extinguishing of the cinema's lights and the main film. Those trailers habitually indicate a future pleasure for the spectators' eyes and bodies, but Jim is instead showing them the past, or the past's erasure and disintegration. The opening shot shows a barbed-wire fence and the name of a place in cyrillic characters, sub-titled into Polish: *Oswiecim*. I realise that Jim, from all of the hundreds of reels stacked floor to ceiling in his workshop, is projecting the film footage shot by the Soviet army as it liberated the Auschwitz concentration camp, thirty-four years and four days ago. In the first sequence, aerial film from a reconnaissance aircraft flying at low altitude demonstrates the massive dimensions of the main camps and sub-camps, together with the adjacent factory complexes, frozen-over with January snow, as though that aircraft were traversing a petrified city of the dead. In the second sequence, the Ukrainian battle-units and tanks are fighting their way westwards towards the camp, but when they reach it, its operators have fled, taking most of the surviving inmates with them on westbound and northbound death-marches, the bodies of the many thousands of prisoners shot immediately before that evacuation scattered in the deep snow of the ground between the wooden barracks and the now shut-down electrified fences, or accumulated into mounds of the naked, skeletal dead. But other prisoners have been left behind, alive—out of chaos, or through their age or incapacitation, and the Soviet cinematographers film their faces close-up, focusing upon their eyes, as they give their names and those of the cities from which they were deported, and to which they will return, if those cities still exist. The crematoria have been detonated or relocated to the still-functioning concentration camps to the north of Berlin. In the final sequence, the children discarded in the camp by its operators now stand together and demonstrate to the cinematographers the numbers tattooed upon their left forearms. Four days have now passed since the Soviet units arrived, the snow has thawed and the camp's terrain is waterlogged. Those children's eyes show that, in their liberation, their hell now begins.

The twenty-minute document ends with a flurry of hand-inscribed numbers as the film-reel spools out of Jim's projector. Although the cinema remains darkened, I can see many of the audience leaving their seats and making their way to the foyer. I know that this city is inhabited by many survivors of Auschwitz and other camps, their refugee journeys from the first months of 1945, from Poland or other razed lands of the East, ending in the terrace streets of Chapeltown and other districts of this city. I descend from the balcony to the foyer and watch as the proprietor is berated with fury or else congratulated by his livid, sobbing clientele, and he glares upwards towards the projection box but will not intervene in Jim's work. Other escapees from the cinema's space have left it entirely and are now outside in the deserted City Square plaza, smoking cigarettes or gasping for breath.

I re-enter the cinema and take a seat this time in the first row of the stalls. Now, Jim projects a four-second black-and-white film which I have not seen before, evidently shot two years or so ago with a handheld 8mm camera, showing the Rytka twins together in a train carriage during a journey. Behind the two sisters, the cloth-covered headrests of the train's seats are visible, along with fragments of other passengers' bodies. I can tell that the film has not been shot in England—it could be in Italy, where the Rytka twins' father was from, but nothing is visible beyond the train's shadowed window. The eyes of the twins are looking directly at the film-camera, or at the person holding it, and their faces are smiling with deep joy and excitement in their journey. Rita Rytka is closer to the film lens, one bare arm outstretched to keep her balance against the train's jolts, looking younger, her hair straighter, than in the photographs of her standing alongside the director of the Ripper police, and she wears an open-necked shirt with pearls around her throat. Helen Rytka's face is angled obliquely as she leans on a seat-rest alongside her twin, one of her arms folded back to support her head, her left forearm exposed as it extends from her short-sleeved jersey. From her eyes' gaze, she appears to be dreaming, and she is alive and revivified, in the four-second interval of that film's projection. Two seats to the left of me, a woman begins to cry in infinite terror and will continue to cry for the next three hours. The film of the Rytka twins vanishes. It's midnight, and the anniversary of Helen Rytka's death is over.

Even before the first image, the audience hear the noise of fan-blades or helicopter blades, then the screen in front of our eyes holds an elongated stretch of jungle, a helicopter veers immediately ahead of us, surrounded by rising yellow smoke, then the jungle erupts in napalm flame and a voice is singing of the end of everything. I realise that Jim has the cinema's sound-system far in excess of its usual levels to pinion the spectators in their seats, and the film's axis of noise oscillates vertiginously from side to side of the auditorium. When I glance around, I see many spectators with their hands pressed to their ears, but all are wide-eyed, entranced. We watch the desperate figure of the assassin Willard stagger across his hotel room, shatter the glass of the mirror with his hand, and collapse bleeding onto the bed, before he is awakened and taken by helicopter to be assigned his covert mission, given his boat and his hallucinating sailors, and his journey up the river towards the compound of Colonel Kurtz begins.

By the time Willard and his sailors reach the river's Do Long Bridge, immersed in screaming guitar feedback and amplified curses from the Viet Cong fighters on the bridge's eastern side, the body temperature of the cinema's audience is sinking. Although the cinema has its respite of seven hours from the strike's first moment until the electricity supply will be terminated, the building's heating has already been deactivated, and only the conflagrations on the screen maintain residual body-heat for that audience. As Willard interrogates the abandoned soldiers around the bridge about their chain of command, the image abruptly jolts, overheats to distortion and combusts, through a mishap in the Majestic's aged projector gates or else an undone suture in Jim's assembling of the reels. The auditorium's lights are suddenly back on again and the faces of the spectators look at one another in acute disorientation. After a moment, the emaciated proprietor appears before the screen with a microphone in his hand, and tells the audience, 'Ladies and gentlemen: The film will be back on in just a moment, we've had a small technical problem, easily rectified. And we're very sorry the heating has gone down, but you're such a wonderful audience...—in fact, you're strangers in the night.' And the proprietor begins to sing, unaccompanied, the microphone channelled through the speakers at either side of the screen so that his voice mutates beyond his control, bleeding out from the film's soundtrack, the words of Sinatra's song resonating with the virulent curses and feedback we heard an instant ago. The audience are themselves now cursing, and begin to hurl projectiles at the proprietor's body so that he hunches to avoid them, many of the missiles badly aimed and impacting instead against the screen, leaving stains and incisions. But nobody is leaving the auditorium.

After fifty seconds, Jim has sutured the rip in the celluloid, the lights go down again, and the proprietor retreats towards his foyer with his hand over his head to protect it. Willard's journey along the river continues, but his sailors are diminishing and by the time he crosses into Cambodia and reaches Kurtz's compound, he has only two companions left, one deranged, one fearful. The cold in the auditorium intensifies, as though coldness itself has become an integral entity of the cinema and is itself watching the film, with its own capacities of vision, but the audience's captivation now feels relentless in all of the bodies surrounding me. Kurtz appears between movements of shadows in his temple ruins, their grounds strewn with the executed dead, and his voice taunts Willard in contempt for his masters, and invites his own assassination, performed by Willard as he interrupts Kurtz in his recording of radio transmissions and wields a machete into his body, against the sound of the same voice we heard at the film's opening, itself now out of control and convulsing. Then we see the isolated head of the assassinated Kurtz, face up and dying but still speaking his last words: 'The horror... The horror...'—and the screen finally erupts into napalm conflagration again as Kurtz's compound is destroyed by aerial bombing. The auditorium is now silent for an instant, apart from the sound of unremitting crying, sustained for almost three hours, two seats to my left, from the now-raw throat which bound this film to the film of the Rytka twins, and that film in turn to the Auschwitz liberation film, and all of those films to the disintegrating city of terror and elation outside the walls of this auditorium. Jim has chosen not to illuminate the cinema at the film's end, and the audience disperse through the frozen darkness, stumbling along the rows and against other bodies, towards the foyer. Those who intend to stay on for the dance furore, including last night's F Club audience, separate themselves out from that departing clientele and mass together at the bar behind the stalls area. The only means they possess to re-heat now is through alcoholic and dance frenzies.

I climb to the projection box and find Jim sitting exhausted on a plywood chair, directly behind the still white-hot projectors. He's already placed the reels in their containers, ready for tomorrow night's screenings, if they will take place. While everyone else in this entire cinema is frozen, he is overheated. We do not need to say anything to one another about the film we have just witnessed for the first time: its images will immerse our future lives and acts. But Jim whispers only one word: 'Brando...', and closes his eyes. I tell him that the clientele for the all-night celebration are already gathering. He nods, but he has another preoccupation: 'We need a new regime now that I'm in charge of this cinema's projections. The proprietor,

Mr. Sokol, will have to go along with what I want. No more advertising, no more trailer films that make audiences think there's still another moment to come.' I ask him where he found the four-second film of the Rytka twins, gazing at the camera in joy on their train journey, and he tells me, 'It was left outside my warehouse door, on a plastic spool in a paper bag—I found it this afternoon, on my way here to assemble the reels. Maybe Rita Rytka left it... Nobody has seen her since the Ripper press conference with the maps and that drunken idiot Oldfield, nearly a year ago. For all I know, she was in the audience tonight. But whether she intended me to archive that film or project it, I don't know.'

Jim points to three sets of film reels stacked on the projection box floor, evidently transported from his workshop, and tells me: 'There's a projector down in the basement too, and a screen, so I've brought a few films along.' I read the titles scrawled in marker pen on the sides of the containers: *Scorpio Rising, Un Chant d'Amour, The Man with the Movie Camera*. Jim tells me, 'That one was edited in 1928 by the same woman who went on to edit the Auschwitz liberation film I showed tonight: Jelisaweta Swilova. My grandfather worked with the director Dziga Vertov on synthesiser cacophonies for the soundtrack, the year before he left the USSR... But Vertov and Swilowa stayed behind. And I showed the Auschwitz film in memory of my grandfather's 1930s Vienna collaborators, who ended up in that camp, or Mauthausen, or were worked to death in the I.G. Farben chemical factories. If my grandfather hadn't left Vienna for this city when he did, I would never have been born. I wanted to remember him tonight—if you can call it memory... Oblivion, more like it, in this fucking city, in England.'

Despite his anger, Jim is finally cooling and puts on his ancient leather coat, picks up half of the reels while I carry the others, and we head down the ten flights of stairs towards the cinema's foyer. Halfway down, Jim turns to me and tells me: 'Farhad is already in the basement, watching over my synthesisers—he wasn't interested to see tonight's screening. I'll need to operate the projector and the synthesisers simultaneously. There's a lot of free alcohol down there, supplied by the film-company. They sent it to celebrate the film's premiere, but for me it now feels like it's also there to celebrate my taking over as the senior projectionist.' By the time we reach the foyer, it's after 3am and most of the audience have dispersed into City Square, but the hardcore anticipating the dance furore are still gathered at the bar behind the auditorium's stalls. Mr. Sokol's face abruptly lights up when he sees Jim approach, and he congratulates him on his work, the issue of the advertising films' replacement now forgotten. Jim starts to apologise for the film's Do Long Bridge interruption, but the proprietor reassures him: 'One rip is nothing. And it gave me the opportunity to do a bit of my singing—the first time since the bingo nights.' He smiles at me and pats Jim on the shoulder: 'There's a good lad, my best employee ever... That's a good lad. I need to keep you here for years, so don't ever go mad on me.' He opens the door at the far end of the foyer which leads into the subterranea.

A long stairway twists down from the foyer, a guide-rail running along its centre, the edge of each step marked by a lightbulb embedded into the adjacent wall. It's cold and almost dark down here, but Jim turns on the overhead lights and we see Farhad, who's been sitting for the last three hours, his hands on Jim's synthesisers to protect them. Farhad is evidently relieved at our arrival and comes towards us: 'I couldn't find the lights.' Jim shakes his head and gestures at the basement space, from which all of the seats have long been removed: 'This place was built as an overspill area for when the cinema first opened in 1928—they expected such huge crowds that they would never fit into the auditorium above. So films were shown simultaneously down here, for a cut-price ticket. Nothing has changed—you can still see the system of mirrors that projected the image from the big screen above, down onto this screen.' He points to the screen at the far end of the room. It no longer has a curtain and looks close to collapse, ripped at the edges and tainted by damp and age. But the room still has its own grandeur, with ornate mouldings at ceiling level, many of them cracked-apart as though a seismic event has fissured this subterranea at some point in the past decades. The walls on one side of the room, coated in ancient crimson paint, appear buckled and awry, and the supporting columns look precarious too, as though the auditorium above could fall into the basement at any moment. Jim sees me looking at the damage. 'A high-explosive incendiary bomb fell right outside on Wellington Street in 1941 and caused that,' he tells me as he starts to set up his synthesisers. 'The crater was deep enough to swallow a double-decker bus. You can still see the shrapnel scars on the cinema's outside wall on that side. If the bomb had landed a few paces to the right, it would have burnt-up this cinema like the jungle in *Apocalypse Now*. Or a few paces to the left and the Queen's Hotel would have been a furnace.'

Jim activates the two experimental prototypes he's brought with him from his collection of his grandfather's synthesisers, and each propels a repetitive dissonant beat, as though in conflict with one another, at extreme volume through the speakers at either side of the screen. Once Jim has spooled the first reel of *The Man with the Movie Camera* through the decrepit projector's gate and the film's first sequence begins, he turns off the basement's overhead lights again, so the room is illuminated only by the film's sequences and the lines of bulbs at either side of the stairway. We are transported back over fifty years in time, engulfed in the unchanged space of the subterranea, the film's images and the synthesisers' cacophony, all of them from 1928. And at the same instant, we are right here, caught in the contemporary moment, 3.30am on the 1st of February, 1979. So far, none of the celebration's clientele have descended the stairway, but the alcohol dispatched for the premiere is amassed on the basement floor at the foot of that stairway, its expanse signalled by the two lines of lights: two hundred or more bottles of Polish vodka and many cans of high-alcohol content beer. I cross the basement and take three bottles, but both Farhad and Jim decline theirs: Jim is focused on his projection, and Farhad is standing by the synthesisers as though he expects them to be assaulted at any moment. From time to time, Jim leaves the projector to finetune the synthesisers' cacophony so that the entire subterranea is shaking.

Around 4am, the first of the clientele descend into the subterranea, clearly frozen and holding their coats around their bodies. They hesitate at the foot of the stairs, as though they're being lured into some kind of experimental environment or arena in which they must now perform. But they cannot resist once they see the amassed alcohol at the foot of the stairs. They overcome their fear and take vodka bottles to upend the contents into their throats, gulping at the transparent fluid as their temperature starts to rise. And then they begin to dance, in wild convulsions, their bodies impeding the projector's beam so that the images of Jim's films inhabit those bodies as their fast-moving, contorted screens. More bodies are now flooding down the stairs, so that the room is rapidly at maximum capacity, holding two hundred or more figures. The clientele are so packed that they can barely move, and the heat rises from them in the intensity of their dance. The subterranea has no ventilation, and I can see bodies struggling to breathe in the depths of their ecstasy. Many of them have taken off their coats and shirts, and let them fall directly from their hands or thrown them towards the walls of the room. When one film ends, the room is cast into near-total darkness until Jim projects another, and the cell-confined prisoners of Genet's film and the leather-clad motorcycle gangs of Anger's film veer at speed across the bodies of the clientele.

Once I've finished the first bottle of vodka, and drunk half of Farhad's bottle, I start to dance too. It feels to me that we are exacting a final celebration for this devil's city—which none of us here love, with its serial-killings and gang-warfare, in its corruption and sensory malfunction, but cannot escape—before its punitive denudation and voiding under Thatcher's imminent regime. It's impossible for anyone to speak in the cacophony, but I can hear elated cries and screams emitted from the mouths of the dancing figures, so exhilarated and soaked with sweat now—many of them almost naked in the near-darkness, pressed against one another as they convulse—that they are indistinguishable. Although the air around us is freezing, we are generating far in excess of the heat needed to sustain ourselves, and I can see corporeal steam rising up the stairway, so that if the proprietor re-opens the cinema's doors, it will be pumped out into City Square and beyond, as the ghost trace of these bodies. The films seize the eyes of the dancers, and the cacophony impels their bodies: bodies, eyes, dance, noise, film. Jim's synthesiser beats will repeat themselves infinitely, in oscillation, and he will keep projecting his films in permutations, inserting a reel of one film into the projection of the reels of another film, so that this frenzy can now extend indefinitely, forever.

Abruptly, at the heart of that dance furore, the electricity cuts out—Jim's film images immediately fade away and the final frame projected, unable to transit the hot projector gate, melts and combusts. Jim needs to extinguish that toxic celluloid fire before it runs out of control and the smoke suffocates the entire clientele in this basement, but he is equipped with a torch and illuminates the flaming projector gate as he douses it with beer. The synthesisers' repetitive beat has been arrested too, and as Jim moves to deactivate those instruments, his torch's flailing beam reveals the bodies left in suspension on their dancefloor, bare-skinned and gripping one another in wide-eyed fear as though they will now be collectively exterminated. In the darkness, they disentangle themselves from one another, put on their clothes as best as they can, leaving a tangle of abandoned coats, shirts and dresses heaped at the dancefloor's periphery, and start to disperse up the stairway.

Jim takes my arm, and directs his torch-beam into my eyes for an instant to calibrate my drunken incapacitation: 'It's over. Go and stand in the cold outside for a while to clear your head. Farhad's still here somewhere—we'll be able to dismantle everything.' I climb the stairway into the foyer. The emaciated figure of the proprietor is standing by the opened doors of his cinema, as he watches his clientele scatter across the darkened plaza of City Square, many of them staggering and close to collapse. I join him by the doors, inhaling the zero-degree air, laced with flurries of snow. The proprietor disappears into his office for a moment and returns with a plastic cup of black nescafe for me. He tells me: 'The dawn will come soon.' I pour the scalding liquid down my throat and turn to nod at the proprietor, who still looks immaculate at 7am in his bowtie and oversized polyester suit.

The last bodies are disappearing into the corners of the plaza, and the proprietor points towards them: 'There they go, the rascals... It looks like they had a smashing time downstairs. Are you a Sinatra fan too?' I look at him but say nothing. I can see his face darken as he appraises the near-moribund punk-rock detrita of this city vanishing into its abysses. He asks me: 'Why is everyone in this city already resigned to Thatcher? Just tell me that. There won't be any more bloody strikes allowed once she's arrived. The unions will be crushed, even the miners... Everyone in this city needs to get organised instead, into militant units, form cells for resistance activities, appoint soviets... And then set up an autonomous republic of Yorkshire, with a nihilist faction if necessary, to placate those bloody punk-rock rascals... Any opposition, and labour-camps can be set up on the wastelands around Armley and Wakefield jails. It's essential above all to institute pre-emptive measures, and a hit-squad assassin like the one in that film can be dispatched down South to terminate Thatcher, with extreme prejudice, right now, before she even takes power. Her minions can just get show-trials in due course, to condemn them for what they would have done, given half a chance, if we'd been bloody stupid enough to let Thatcher take over.' I look across in disquiet at the proprietor's manic face, and to placate me, he slips his right hand between his lips, pulls out his false teeth, and then gurns his face towards me into a monstrous, inhuman mask. Then he continues in his toothless delirium, in his broad Yorkshire accent: 'I'm from bloody Tirana, you know, me.' He suddenly pulls up the sleeve of his polyester jacket and shows me the still-livid tattoo of digits, inscribed in plum-coloured ink on his left forearm. 'Here's my tattoo, like those kids had in that film. Not at Auschwitz, me—I was at Bergen-Belsen, fourteen years old, after having to walk up the whole of bloody Europe, from a labour-camp in Albania by the Adriatic nearly all the way to the Baltic. Then we were liberated by the British army, not the USSR's army… So that's how I ended up in England, in this city.'

I turn back to look out over City Square. The snowclouds are clearing and the first signs of dawn are arriving as the sky shades from black to metallic blue over the Griffin Hotel's clock-tower, but there will be no sunrise. I glance at the proprietor's face and he appears now to have calmed and returned to his professional priorities. He replaces his teeth and tells me: 'There'll be no more film projections for the foreseeable future, while this strike is on. Bingo instead—you don't need electricity for that, just a bloody loud voice to call the numbers. And intermissions for sing-ing.' Behind him, I can see Jim approaching from the sub-terranea's stairway, carrying a synthesiser-case under one arm and a set of film-reels under the other, and from his dismayed face, I can tell he's overheard the proprietor's decision to suspend the *Apocalypse Now* projections. The proprietor follows my gaze, and sees Jim standing there. 'But you'll need to come in anyway at the usual times, son,' he tells Jim. 'I'll still be paying you. All you have to do is sit in the projection box. And as soon as this strike ends, we'll be back in business with films, don't you worry. I certainly don't want to lose you.' Jim puts down the synthesiser-case and film-reels, and holds out his hand, but the proprietor takes it only momentarily, his eyes fixed on the ground, before slipping away towards his office.

Jim shakes his head wryly as he watches the proprietor's office door close behind him. 'He's a rogue, that one,' he tells me. 'Did he show you his forearm tattoo? He made that himself, with his right hand—it's an amateur job. He has a lot more tattoos besides that one. He arrived in Eng-land with the rest of the Albanian mafia in the early 1960s to take over the Soho clubs, but some kind of gang feud blew up after a year or two and he was ousted, minus his little toes, and ended up here. I hear the devil slapped him down too, when he tried to take over the Yorkshire dancehalls. He's just a third-rate former gangster now, running a run-down old cinema in a city that's fallen apart. But I like him anyway… He indulges me because he knows I hold his secrets.' Jim picks up the synthesiser-case and film-reels, positions them under his arms, and starts to walk away, down towards the river Aire bridge: 'I've had enough of this place for one night. Tell Farhad to follow me when he appears… And if you want to rehearse this month, before High Royds, you know I have an emergency generator.'

The cinema foyer falls silent. No vehicles are moving around City Square. The traffic lights are off and most of the delivery lorries that would be at work in this dawn light are now on strike. I cross the road, jump the railings and stand in the centre of City Square. The city feels depopulated, as though every inhabitant has been led out to a killing zone by the Aire, compelled to kneel in lines and face the river, before being shot in the back of the neck and pushed into the eastbound current, or else transported to Yeadon airport to be rendered unconscious and dropped out of helicopters hovering high above the Yorkshire Dales. Or it could be that everyone is still asleep, attempting to dream or hallucinate about any obsession other than this city, but returning always to its blackened and abandoned buildings, its abused and crazed bodies, and its maledictions. I turn a complete circle in the dawn light: the Majestic cinema, the main post-office, the ruins of the air-raid shelters, the Royal Exchange Chambers, and finally the marble edifice of the Queen's Hotel.

My eyes track down from the hotel's facade to its revolving doors, and I see the figure of Lily emerge, carrying a battered leather suitcase, still dressed in her alpaca and silk overcoat, her near-white hair streaming down over the black cloth. She is heading in the same direction as Jim, towards the railway arches and the tramshed beyond them, down to the river Aire bridge, but she glances over into the centre of the City Square plaza, recognises me and waves. I cross back over the railings, unsure if it's really her. But when I reach the hotel's doorway, it's Lily, and she's vibrant and alive, her lips deep red, laughing at the sight of my astonished face. I tell her that I wasn't expecting to see her again, and ask if she's been involved in a recent traffic accident, on Sheepscar Road, not expecting a reply. But Lily replies immediately, still laughing, as though I were deranged: 'No way... I've been in that crazy party in the Majestic basement all night, but you ignored me. Then I came to pick up my suitcase from the reception desk here—I knew I couldn't take it into the Majestic, so I asked them politely and they looked after it for me.' I ask her if she's now beginning her journey to Odessa. Lily gazes at me as though I were insane, and pushes strands of hair away from her face, the pallid skin of her hands encased in leather pilot's gloves: 'Odessa—no! Why would I want to go there? I'm just leaving for Berlin. I'm going to East Berlin for a while... I heard so many times there's an interesting punk scene going on there now, and this city is voided, finished. I've been wanting to go ever since the Futura festival, so I thought I'd take a look... I'm all set—I've got a visa, from the East German consulate in St. Paul's House.' She takes it out of a coat pocket and hands it to me, momentarily grave, as though I were a border-guard. The paper is shoddily printed with a hammer and compass insignia, stamped four or five times in different coloured inks, but the handwritten details appear so askew and blurred that all I can make out is Lily's date of birth, 3rd October 1961, the same as my own, then I turn the visa over and find on the reverse two maps drawn in pencil, one of the eastward course of the river Aire in the direction of the North Sea, and the other of Berlin, divided jaggedly into two cities.

I still can't believe that Lily is directly in front of me, now laughing again in delight at my consternation, tears forming in the corners of her eyes. I ask her: 'How will you get to the port? There are no trains running, no buses.' I know that the ferry for mainland Europe leaves from the port of Hull, crossing the North Sea overnight to the Hook of Holland port, and from there, a Trans Europe Express train departs for Berlin. As with all the children of Yorkshire of my age, I learned German at school—'a wise step, in case the Germans come at us a third time, before the end of this century', as the teacher told us—and was taken there on an outing, crossing by that same ferry, at the age of ten. Lily tells me, 'I'll walk if I have to. Along the left bank of the Aire, all the way. I have my map, you just saw it. I go due east. Finally the river joins up with other rivers and widens into an estuary, and the port is on the northern bank. It's only about fifty miles, so it can't take me more than five days. Do you think there are hotels like this one, on the banks of the Aire?' I tell Lily that she will freeze if she travels that way, but she appears supremely oblivious, as though her body were already operating far below a zero-degree status. 'I don't care about that, I'm way beyond all that now,' she murmurs in exasperation, as though she were suddenly angry with me.

Behind Lily's face, I see Farhad emerge from the Majestic foyer, the other synthesiser-case and the remaining film-reels gripped under his arms. 'Farhad will take you there in his truck, if you want,' I tell Lily. 'He's on strike now so he has nothing else to do, and he knows the Drax route by heart... After Drax, it's not much further to the port.' Lily frowns, her white eyebrows furrowed, but I call Farhad over and I know he will agree to take Lily to the port. I think I hear Lily hiss at Farhad as he approaches: 'You killed me, you killed me'—but when Farhad and I look at Lily in alarm, she's already laughing again and appears resigned to the journey. Farhad says: 'Yes, of course I'll take you, if you don't mind listening to my Googoosh cassettes on the way. We'll be there in an hour.' He points to his truck, parked directly alongside the Majestic on Wellington Street. I can sense that Farhad is troubled, either because of the journey I've assigned him, or because he will have to drive past the Drax power-station without stopping. But when I ask him if he wants to delay the journey for a few hours, so that he can sleep first, while I sit with Lily on the steps of the Majestic cinema, he shakes his head: 'No, thank you—I need to keep busy. At this moment, Khomeini is leaving the Paris Orly airport for Tehran Mehrabad airport, on an Air France flight, to begin his regime of revolutionary theocracy, and if I ever now return to Iran, I will be executed.'

We walk over to Farhad's truck and he sets down Jim's synthesiser-case and film-reels at the foot of the Majestic's shrapnel-incised wall. I will now carry them down to Le Prince's workshop myself. When Farhad opens the cab door, Lily lifts her suitcase to place it on the seat, her left arm extended, and I try to help, but only reach as far as her outstretched wrist, just below her pilot's glove, and grip the grid of unhealed razor-scars on that wrist's underside. I pull back my hand as though all of the electricity withdrawn from this city an hour ago is now being transmitted from Lily's charged skin, simultaneously ice-cold and molten. She laughs again as she climbs into the truck, whispering: 'Berlin! Berlin!' But she does not touch me again, or say goodbye, as though she were an apparition manifested only momentarily through some aberration of vision in the dawn light, the illusion of that spectral projection sustained by the immediate proximity of this cinema, or as if I were myself a negligible ghost inhabitant of this city. Farhad also climbs into the cab, activates his cassette-player, then winds down the window and looks down at me in terror, as though his execution were imminent. The truck roars away in the direction of the M62 sliproad, and I can still hear the voice of Googoosh in the distance for a few moments, until it disappears into the silence. Lily is alive, but she is gone. I turn and trace with my fingertips the shrapnel scars on the cinema's sandstone wall, some of them so jagged and deep that I can slip my entire hand into them.

5.

WHITE NOISE
BALLROOMS,
MARCH 1979

I'm standing in the centre of City Square again, but over a month has now passed and the depopulated silence of that plaza in the dawn light after the Majestic cinema dance-furore has been erased. Bodies are streaming past me on every side, the revolving doors of the Queen's Hotel are spinning fast, buses are circling the square before turning into the adjacent streets, and the two entrances into the railway station are dense with time-pressed figures. To one side of the hotel's facade, I can see posters pasted by the F Club promoter to the walls of the derelict Royal Exchange Chambers, announcing tomorrow night's performance at the Griffin Hotel ballroom, and on the other side of the Queen's Hotel, the Majestic cinema's doors are being unlocked and Mr. Sokol is ushering in a waiting young figure, putting an arm over his shoulder as that figure slips inside the foyer. City Square is reactivated after its month of shutdown stasis, but that activity appears outlandish to me, as though these Saturday late-afternoon crowds have only just been released from arenas of incarceration or massacre, and are now generating an excess of gestures to distract their own attention from the precariousness of their reprieve. I walk down through the dark arches and past the tramshed, still intact but now surrounded by demolition crews who stand in groups as they await their orders. In the warehouse alleyway on the far side of the river Aire bridge, Jim and Farhad have already loaded the backseat and boot of Jim's car with all of the instruments and amplifiers we are taking to High Royds. In one hour, tonight, the 3rd of March 1979, we will perform at the hospital's ballroom for an audience of the demented and the insane, at their Saturday evening dance. Jim is at the car's wheel, signalling for me to hurry, and I take the passenger seat, while Farhad is already outstretched on the floor behind the front seats, as though ready to cross an illicit border.

For the entire month of February, during the all-engulfing strikes of public services, utilities and industries which paralysed the cities of the North, brilliant blue skies illuminated the piled-up detrita of the streets. Whatever could be deposited in the river Aire was carried away in the eastbound current, no longer seething with naphthalene and ammonia since the chemical-industrial complexes to the west of this city could no longer operate, but a vast immovable residue still accumulated: the uncollected, the unburied, the untransmitted, the unprojected. Even the emergency transmissions of the face of Helen Rytka disappeared from the blanked-out television screens. As the first weeks went by, this city's population grew habituated to their lives without power, and began to wander the daytime streets in joy, as though the strikes had generated a liberation from all constriction and enslavement. The usually pervasive presence of the Ripper and the devil dissipated. But by the middle of February, the city had begun to emit an all-enveloping stench of decay, as though exhaling the profound malediction at its core. And at night, when the temperatures fell and constellations of brilliant stars appeared in the unpolluted skies, the city appeared petrified. From the fragments of news we gathered of the cities of the South, they had been incapacitated too.

During that month, I visited Jim each night for an hour in Le Prince's workshop, after he had finished his evening-long shift of inactivity in the Majestic's projection box, listening to the bingo shouts and the proprietor's unamplified caterwauling in the candle-lit auditorium below. The workshop's lights, powered by Jim's emergency generator, appeared to be burning in ferocious isolation against the surrounding city's darkness whenever I approached it from the far side of the river. Since the telephone network was also on strike, it was impossible to call Veronika's uncle at his restaurant below the Roots Club, and ask him to pass on to Veronika assignations for the rehearsals of cacophony. Whenever I walked through Chapeltown and passed by the Roots Club, it appeared deserted, a grille of vertical steel bars sealing the entrance at the top of the synagogue's marble stairs, the restaurant closed too, and all I could hear from the building's upper rooms was the distant noise of erratic thuds. Even the gang-warfare factions suspended their confrontations, and the glue-sniffing children of Francis Street pursued their addiction half-heartedly. But Farhad appeared most nights during my visits to Le Prince's workshop. Since Veronika never showed up, we could not rehearse, but Farhad would take his clarinet or *tar* and play, while Jim and I looked out over the river, the windows wide-open. Jim appeared disconsolate at his projections' suspension and the annulled rehearsals, but from time to time he would ask me questions about the High Royds ballroom: 'What kind of sound-system does it have? How high is the ceiling? What's the inmates' exact body-capacity?' I could tell he was formulating sensory equations of cacophonies against spatial dimensions, and even when I had no answers to his questions, he nodded as though I were giving him significant information for his calculations.

The strikes ended simultaneously, in deadlock and with every issue of contention unresolved, two days ago, at one minute past midnight on the 1st of March. The television and radio stations immediately returned to their transmissions. Callaghan is now derided as England's worst leader for centuries, as though his self-effacement and inaction were a means to subjugate himself in preparation for Thatcher's arrival. And the strikes' curtailment signals an aura of mass capitulation, in anticipation of Thatcher's regime. It's forecast in every opinion poll that Thatcher will gain a victory if a general election is to take place this Spring, but first she must provoke a vote of no-confidence in Callaghan in order to upend his government and compel him to call an election. Adept, she will wait a moment longer, before she makes her final move. This city is fissured with disquiet: everyone knows that the imminent moment of Thatcher's arrival will be a momentous one. England will be transformed beyond recognition, and the North will fall.

Now Jim reaches the ring-road underpass and accelerates onto Chapeltown Road. We have to be at High Royds for 7pm. I can tell Jim is unhappy to have been compelled to arrange for a relief projectionist at the Majestic for tonight and tomorrow—one of Jim's cousins, only fourteen years old but already renowned for the speed of his reel changes and his ability to defuse any catastrophes that arise during the act of projection. The reels of *Apocalypse Now* have been collected after only one projection and avid audiences will watch the next film on the Majestic's programme: *The Texas Chainsaw Massacre*. Jim murmurs to me: 'That little bastard will undercut me, or Mr. Sokol will replace me... I was right that we should have performed only one cacophony, no more.' I reassure him that he will be back on duty at the Majestic from Monday evening, but that feels a long way into the future.

We turn into Francis Street and I'm relieved to see Veronika already sitting on the synagogue steps in her black highnecked jersey and skipants, holding her drumsticks and ready to go. She approaches the car, looks at Farhad hidden behind the front seats and laughs: 'I'm not getting on top of him.' She opens the passenger-door and squeezes over me to occupy the seat-edge space between Jim and I. As she moves, I can see beneath the jersey that her muscles are now tautened, as though she's spent the entire month of the strike ceaselessly fist-pounding the punch-bag in fury in her rooms above the club. Although Jim has never been to High Royds before, he knows the way. We take the west-east route towards Meanwood used nightly by the Seacroft gang-warfare faction, via Savile Mount, over the Sheepscar river and then onto Kirkstall Road, turning north at the junction alongside the abbey ruins where I last saw Iris at the moment of the abandonment of her F Club bus-journey. Now High Royds appears directly ahead of us, on its hill above the city. I can hear Jim still cursing under his breath.

We pass through the High Royds gatehouse, ride along the avenue of cypress trees, and approach the main building's clock-tower as the sky darkens. Every light of the asylum is already on. Veronika slips over me and is out of the car first, gazing up at the tower and across the ward-buildings which extend out in either direction. I can tell she's trying to be nonchalant, but she's awed by the palatial magnitude of High Royds and its emanation of proliferating psychosis: 'So this is where the nutcases end up,' she whispers. 'But nobody is screaming yet.' I expected Iris to be here to meet us, but she's nowhere to be seen. 'Are you sure this is the right evening?' Jim asks, as he notes my confusion. 'If not, I've still got time to kick my nephew out of the Majestic and do tonight's shift myself.' I enter the foyer of the administration building, followed hesitantly by Veronika, Jim and Farhad, and at the far end of the corridor, beyond the floor-mosaic of black daisies and white roses, we see two hundred or so asylum inmates lined up in densely concertinaed queues next to each of the ballroom's side doors, the men on one side, the women on the other side, dressed in the decrepitude of their best clothes. They are waiting in spectral silence for the dance to begin, and their eyes turn towards us in desperation.

I knock on the door of the administration office and we enter. Only a few of the staff are still on duty, and the man in the polyester suit who meticulously surveyed the city below on my last visit, awaiting the devil's arrival, is now absent. An elderly woman hammers the keys of a typewriter, and we stand by her desk and wait. After a minute, she stops, glares at us and asks: 'Well?' 'We're tonight's turn, for the dance,' Farhad tells her. 'Are you now?' she replies in contempt, but finally picks up a schedule of some kind, runs a finger down the typewritten lines, and nods in resignation. She takes four photocopied forms out of her desk drawer and hands them to us, and at first I assume we are about to be paid in advance for our cacophony, but when I look at the form, I realise it's a disclaimer, exonerating the asylum authorities if any of the four of us is injured, maimed or incapacitated for life by the inmates. Jim asks: 'What kind of maiming, exactly?', but the typist simply waves for him to sign: 'We have to have these, after what happened with those poor lads from Prestwich.' As soon as we've all signed, she walks to the door and yells down the corridors for Dr. McDonald.

We're no longer allowed in the administration office, and stand in a tight group on the black-daisy mosaic, all of the eyes of the silent inmates still fixed upon us. After five minutes or so, Dr. McDonald appears from the ballroom's main entrance. He seems to recognise me from our last encounter, and he's evidently relieved that we've arrived: 'So you made it up here? That's good! The patients can't dance in silence.' But he appears still more dishevelled and exhausted than when I last saw him. Veronika is assessing the multiple stains and discolorations on his coat and trousers. 'It's been non-stop,' he tells me. 'No strike here!—If we had a strike, the patients would only plead for us to return to work and redouble their treatments.' I ask him if Nurse Dunstan will be at this evening's dance, but he shakes his head: 'She must be on duty, in Hawes ward. She's the senior nurse there now, totally devoted to her patients. Since she came to live up here at the end of January, she's been an essential part of our long-term staff.'

I notice that his hands are bloodstained and dripping, and ask him if there's been an emergency incident. He points towards the ballroom: 'It's the warring projectionists. You'll remember the one we had before, from the Regal cinema? He did a wonderful job, projecting *The Sound of Music* every Tuesday afternoon. But another arrived soon after, from the Majestic cinema, with exactly the same symptoms, but this one a trouble-maker. As soon as he arrived, he wanted to put on a season of Fassbinder films for the patients. So that pair have been at each other's throats for the past month, fighting over their rights to the projector. This afternoon, it all came to a head, and now they're both in the infirmary with splicer wounds.' Jim is listening intently, and he tells the asylum director that he was present himself when the second projectionist went berserk and ran out of the Majestic cinema into City Square. 'Are you a projectionist too?' Dr. McDonald asks, alarmed. 'All I ask is: don't go insane while you're up here. Two projectionists, that's bad enough.'

He disregards the lines of expectant inmates and takes us towards the ballroom's main doors. The overheated air inside is propelled against our bodies as the doors open, and I can hear Veronika catch her breath at the decrepit splendour of the immense ballroom, lit from far above by many hundreds of bare bulbs suspended from the ceiling, and she reaches down to touch the abrasures and incisions of the ash dancefloor with her fingers. At the far end of the ballroom, two parallel lines of blood and body-fluids extend towards one of the side doors from the hatch that leads down a flight of stairs into the projectionists' basement office, as though two wounded, incapacitated bodies have just been dragged away by attendants from the site of a confrontation. Veronika is now gazing up in elation into the ghost-saturated high-altitude space of the ballroom, gradually revolving her body. Jim is excited too—he grips my arm and points to the sound-system, seven large, mesh-faced cabinets stacked on either side of the empty platform in front of the film screen: 'That's a vintage system from the end of the 1920s, probably 1928—the same era as my grandfather's prototype synthesisers. He must have used an almost identical system for his performances in the Soviet Union during that era. I never thought I'd have the chance to play his synthesisers through a system like that.' Now Jim's desire to return to the Majestic and oust his cousin is annulled.

Dr. McDonald corrects Jim: 'I can see you have a close professional interest, but our system is actually from 1930, not 1928, and it certainly wasn't manufactured in the Soviet Union. The Donisthorpe company in Huddersfield made it to our exact specifications and delivered it for our first amplified dance party in March 1931. Since then, it's worked perfectly and nothing has had to be repaired or replaced. We have a long tradition here of entertaining our patients, twice each week. They're the only occasions when the male and female patients meet—otherwise, we operate a rigorous segregation. When you're dealing with the mad and demented, you have to work to schedules and rules. We've never missed a single Saturday evening in forty-eight years. Even when all of the munitions factories along the river Aire valley down below were burning during the 1941 incendiary bombings, we didn't cancel our Saturday evening dance. Afterwards, so I was told, the patients were taken up on the roof to watch the cities on fire, but several sadly jumped.' He looks at his watch: 'But we need to get down to business. It's time for you to start, otherwise the patients will grow restless. If you can set up your instruments promptly now, I'll admit them in ten minutes. You'll be playing for around three hours, with a short intermission. You can choose yourselves when to have the intermission, just don't over-extend it. We need to get the patients into their beds at 10pm.'

Dr. McDonald turns and leaves at speed by the ballroom's main entrance. Jim looks at me, aghast: 'Three hours! But we've never played for more than twenty minutes.' Farhad is already heading back towards Jim's car to collect the instruments and amplifiers. He says over his shoulder: 'Don't be concerned, I'll perform a solo recital for the first part of the evening, lively and pleasurable works of the *tar* and the clarinet, for about two hours and thirty minutes… That's nothing to me—when I was seven years old and performed recitals in the Khak-i Marmar palace in Tehran, I had to play for five hours straight… Then we can have a curtailed white-noise cacophony after the intermission.' I look back at Veronika from the ballroom's doors as Jim and I follow Farhad towards the car, but she's lost in visions or hallucinations, her eyes closed, already starting to dance, alone in the ballroom, her body tensed, on a precipice between the movements of relentless assault that have consumed her during her punch-bag boxing sessions of the past month, and a fragile dance of exposed gestures, as though she's ready to receive a blow which will make her fall.

Jim works fast once we have all of the instruments and amplifiers arranged on the platform, accessed by stairs on either side. I can see that channelling everything through the archaic mixing-board, which appears to work with an intricate system of detachable mahogany pins, is testing Jim's capacities, but after a moment or two, he has it all worked out. A melancholic trustee with a bucket and mop is wiping away the parallel lines of blood and body-fluids, and a second trustee with a cloth then dries the dancefloor with spasmodic zigzagging movements to ensure that the inmates will not slip and fall once they begin to dance. I can hear them groaning with disquiet and exclaiming restlessly from behind both side doors, their entertainment already delayed by fifteen minutes, as Jim finishes his work and Farhad sits on a plywood chair with his amplified *tar* ready. Then Dr. McDonald admits the inmates, the women before the men, and they stream inside.

As soon as the women enter, they appear to undergo disorientation, unsure which way to face, and their bodies resonate for me with those of the Futura festival's patrons once they'd been admitted into the abyss of the darkened tramshed by the hunchbacked promoter. But the ballroom is illuminated, the inmates locate themselves, and once they've lit their first cigarettes, they appear less agitated. No seating is provided, but a trestle-table with plastic beakers of orangeade has been set up on one side of the ballroom. The female inmates range in age from sixteen or seventeen to stooped, toothless figures who must have attended this ballroom's first amplified dances in 1931, and I realise that I recognise several of the youngest faces, now lost and oblivious, from last summer's F Club audiences, when the promoter was still using the Roots Club as his preferred venue. Once all of the men are admitted too, they gaze in raw obsession at the women, but remain poised around the ballroom's peripheries. Even with four hundred or more bodies inside, the space appears less than half-full, and I imagine that during the golden era of this city's insanities, from the 1890s to the 1930s, when High Royds held several times its current population and formed a thriving, autonomous city in its own right, the ballroom was habitually saturated to a suffocating crush.

Veronika is still immersed in her dance of intercut assault and exposure, and she is soon lost among the bodies of the mad and demented. It will be difficult to extricate her, when the intermission comes, but her snare-drum is now ready for her on the platform. I look at Farhad, a microphone beside his lips and one beside his *tar*, his fingers a split-second from striking his instrument's strings for the first time, and he seems to be panicking as he looks out over his audience—the delirious, the glossolaliac, the demented, the catatonic, the paranoid—who are generating their own cacophony, in incessant murmurings, in dual deliria with themselves, in hissed monologues, in exclamations of multiple voices and languages, in repeated loops, or in silent internal dialogues during which the inmates' mouths work convulsively, but no words are expelled. I'm relieved when Farhad introduces himself, hits his strings for the first time, and the audience abruptly fall silent. The music Farhad makes is astonishing in its beauty, sung with the heartbroken intensity of his Googoosh cassettes, his voice soaring through the ballroom's altitudes and echoing against the windows below its ceiling. His *tar* playing must now be as adept as when he was seven years of age in the Khak-i Marmar palace, vastly decelerated from the aberrant speed Jim and I have imposed upon him for our cacophonies, but still impelled by pulses of repetition and sudden shifts, and I can see the insane start to dance to it, the men now moving from the ballroom's peripheries to stand between the bodies of the women, all of them moving in the infinite variants of their dance.

I move to the back of the hall and find Dr. McDonald by the main doors, accompanied by seven orderlies in white t-shirts. He barely sees me, and I realise he's either captivated by Farhad's performance too, or else is professionally alert, scanning his patients' bodies for signs of fits and emergency incidents. I know that Farhad has been trained never to pause in his recitals even for a moment, so that his playing can always entrance its audience. Jim has now moved away from the mixing-desk, satisfied with the sound-levels, and is standing with his left ear pressed against the meshed face of a speaker, holding the side of that varnished teak cabinet to steady himself, assessing the aged system's fissures of noise that are audible only in such extreme intimacy. I can see him calculating the malfunctions generated by the passage through the speakers' cones of over forty years' sonic transmissions.

I slip through the ballroom's doors, along the black-daisy mosaic hallway and out of the main building, then cross the terrain between the asylum's cemetery and the wards, until I reach the door of Hawes ward. Inside, Iris is seated at her desk on one side of the ward's anteroom, wearing her pristine blue and white uniform. At a second desk, facing her, the aged commentator is still sitting with his rolled-up magazine, but I can tell immediately that his dementia has accelerated in the month or so since I was last here, and instead of the tightrope vocal oscillation between total-recall and oblivion in his looped commentaries of that era, his commentary is now reduced to utter disintegration, fragments of players' names and their acts fired-out at random between sobs and coughs.

Iris looks up and smiles at me, as though she's been expecting my arrival in the ward: 'Are you not performing? Are you the manager now?' I sit down beside her. The sound of Farhad's recital is just audible, infiltrating the commentator's delirium. I tell Iris, 'This is just the first part, then we'll have a cacophony after the intermission.' Iris nods to herself: 'One last cacophony, for me.' She tells me that when her trainee arrives, we can return to the ballroom. A tear falling from the corner of her eye, she points across the anteroom at the commentator: 'Eddie will come too. He's the only one in this entire ward who still attends the dances. I have the far-gone cases to look after here, or to dispatch... And there's always the danger that the devil will be around at the dead of night, looking to come in and embrace the catatonic or those in Brompton cocktail comas, so I need to be alert, on guard.' I'm alarmed at Iris's words, and ask her, 'The devil really comes into Hawes ward?' Iris nods: 'Yes, he's here right now... Somewhere at High Royds, in the director's office or up in the clock-tower—I saw his car arrive. He has a standing invitation and consults with Dr. McDonald on the future of the hospital.'

I can tell that Iris intends never to leave High Royds again. She evidently no longer raids the drugs cupboard, or incites the suspicions of the administrators by receiving telephone calls as she arrives for work, and she prioritises her professional duties to her patients. She tells me: 'I don't have my room anymore in that freezing-cold house, by the Calder. You'll remember it better than I do, now. It's much better living here, in the resident staff quarters, behind the treatment wing. I'll stay here throughout the Thatcher era, however long it lasts—there will be madness. I'll be needed here. Nobody needs me, in the punk-rock clubs of the North, and they'll disappear soon anyway—I'm nothing there, just another consumer of someone's useless rage and arrogance. It's over, all of that.' She says nothing more, and we sit together and listen to the commentator's exhausted but unendable delirium. The trainee enters the door of Hawes ward nervously. She's no older than sixteen, her young face constellated with eczema, the skin flushed from hearing Farhad's recital through the ballroom walls on her walk here, and it's clear she's excited and wants to ask Iris if she can be allowed a moment to enter the ballroom, and even to dance there, just for an instant, but Iris reprimands her trainee with severity, though she's only a moment late: the High Royds clock-tower has just struck half past nine.

Iris takes the commentator's arm and tells him in a quiet voice that it's time for the Saturday evening dance. He sets down his rolled-up newspaper, his lined face radiating happiness. Once he's up on his feet, combing his brylcreemed white hair, I see that he's still strong and agile, from decades of climbing ladders into commentary boxes high on the roofs of the North's stadia, and requires no support from Iris's arms. We enter the main doors of the ballroom as Farhad is coming to the end of his recital. The audience are still dancing as before, from near-imperceptible spasms to convulsions that shake the entire body. After over two hours' singing accompanied by his *tar*, Farhad switches instruments, picks up the clarinet and executes four piercing, diminishing exhalations, then stands, announces a short intermission, and bows deeply, as though anticipating applause, aware that his performance has been an extraordinary act. But nobody applauds, apart from Dr. McDonald's thick-set orderlies at the back of the ballroom, and the mad and demented instantaneously revert to their cries and murmurings.

I scan the spectators to locate Veronika, but she appears now to have become inextricably meshed with their bodies. I look back at the orderlies as I start to panic, wondering if I need to appeal for them to intervene and pull Veronika out from the mad. But then I see her, and she's already striding up the steps at the far end of the ballroom, her drumsticks in her hand, and I realise she is going to start beating her snare-drum immediately. The intermission has lasted less than twenty seconds. Farhad is caught off-guard too, standing by the trestle-table and drinking from a beaker of orangeade. I start to run around the periphery of the ballroom and join Jim as he reaches the mixing-board to re-set it. He points at the sound-system and warns me: 'We can only play for five minutes, no longer—the system is too fragile.' Veronika has already initiated the cacophony in ferocious beats powered by her boxing-enhanced arm-muscles, her face focused as though in supreme fury, and now we have to catch up, but Jim has already activated his synthesisers. An acute velocity of noise abruptly erupts and is propelled from the sound-system cabinets into the bodies of the audience, echoing in the high-altitudes and against the main doors, where I can see Dr. McDonald with his hands over his ears, looking aghast. Farhad's fingers are now moving over his *tar* strings at five or six times their speed during his recital, and I follow him with the Burns guitar. For this performance, with only five minutes of cacophony to deliver, I decide not to incant the city at night, and instead stand back from the microphone to watch over the insane.

I see the commentator has detached himself from Iris and is threading his way through the bodies of the audience, who are no longer dancing. They appear immobilised, staring in horror, but attentive. And behind us, traversing the back wall of the ballroom, I can hear bouts of screaming originating from the treatment wing, gradually enveloping the cacophony and directing it with still greater precision into the torn sensory capacities of the audience. Cries are accumulating too from the distant wards on either side of the ballroom, accentuating the cacophony so it feels that we've instigated a volatile corporeal entity that is rapidly running out of our control. Jim and I glance at one other in unease, unsure what is going to happen in the next seconds. Veronika's hair is flying around her face as it did at the F Club, and her concentration on her drumming now appears total, excluding the space of the ballroom. Farhad is evidently exhausted from the shift in the speed of his *tar* playing, the jacket of his cashmere lounge-suit drenched in sweat, but he nods to me to indicate that he is not going to falter. All we can do is intensify our cacophony to precipitate the moment at which we will abandon it.

The commentator is now at the front of the crowd, staring at the live, unused microphone. I can tell that it's irresistible to him after his nights in Hawes ward with the rolled-up magazine, and without even climbing the steps, he arduously pulls himself up onto the platform, so that his back faces the audience. He's still wearing his regulation-issue High Royds pyjamas, in contrast to the best outfits of his spectators, and he makes a professional assessment of the activity of Jim, Veronika, Farhad and I, as though we were his on-location sound crew, before finally smoothing his brylcreemed hair back with one hand, turning to grin at his audience and putting his lips to the microphone. His amplified voice is still strong and it instantly occupies the entire space of the ballroom in the way that the epileptic singer's voice inhabited and transformed the Futura tramshed. But at first he emits only repetitive fragments: 'Hard shot! Hard shot!... Rubbing him! Rubbing him!...', so that his spectators scowl in disabused incomprehension, as though they are affronted to be entertained by the demented. Iris appears beside him in her uniform, ready to lead him away back to Hawes ward. The commentator's voice is gradually falling apart into gasps and sobs, and I expect him to surrender the microphone to Iris at the next instant, but then his face suddenly clears and I'm certain he is spitting out a lucid incitation to the four hundred bodies of the mad amassed before him, and to the entire population of the Thatcher-resigned city below the High Royds hill: 'Rise up! Rise up!... The North! The North!...'.

The audience are no longer petrified and horror-stricken, and they turn around to glare at Dr. McDonald and his orderlies. Alongside them, by the ballroom's main doors, I glimpse the devil in his track-suit, standing with his arm around the shoulder of Dr. McDonald, but he adeptly slips away and vanishes, as the riot of the High Royds mad begins to cohere. His face illuminated, the commentator is still repeating his phrases, delighted at their evident activation of his audience, and I can see that Iris is torn between participating in the cacophony-impelled riot or working to dispel it. The trestle-table of orangeade has already been overturned. Some groups of the mad are at each other's throats, wrestling one another to the ground, but others are pointing in the direction of the treatment wing beyond the ballroom with urgent gestures, as though they plan imminently to stream through the side doors to release the strapped-down patients' clamps as the technicians prepare to administer high-voltage shocks. And a hardcore of the audience will not take their mesmerised eyes from the commentator's pyjamaed figure for an instant as he repeats his cacophony-driven provocation.

As Jim warned, the vintage 1930 sound-system cannot withstand the assault it is enduring, and the addition of the commentator's voice to the cacophony appears to send that groaning system over the edge. It ignites and spits fire, instantly rendering the cacophony null and void, but its catastrophe is far more engulfing than the F Club speakers' malfunction of a month or so ago. A great conflagration rapidly consumes the fourteen teak cabinets in their two stacks, so that they splinter and collapse into the crowd, and the orderlies prioritise putting out the fire with handheld extinguishers and a waterhose, over quelling the inmates' riot. In our cacophony's dissolution, I can hear the High Royds clock-tower above us striking 10pm.

Even though the synthesisers, *tar* and guitar are no longer amplified, and we can set them aside with relief, Veronika is still frenziedly hitting her snare-drum as though she perceives no reason to curtail its beating, and against that beat and the clock-tower's ten chimes, the commentator projects his final incitations into the dead microphone: 'Rise up! Rise up!... The North! The North...'.

The commentator realises the microphone is no longer transmitting his voice and his dismay jars him back into vocal disintegration, shifting without transition from his provocation to the sobs and cries that preceded it. Veronika too is no longer beating her snare-drum with the feral precision of a moment ago, and she abruptly halts, then throws the drumsticks from her bloodied hands into the crowd, jumps from the platform into their bodies but, on landing, immediately passes straight through the turbulent figures and leaves the ballroom via its main doors. Iris is now leading the semi-collapsed commentator away and she glances back at me, narrowing her eyes, but I can't determine if it's a look of reproach or approval. Only Farhad, Jim and I are now left on the platform, and a glass bottle of orangeade skims past my left ear, the projectile shattering against the ballroom's back wall. Farhad takes my hand and whispers: 'Are the nutcases turning on us now? Will they maim us?' But I can tell that the fury of the riot is already leaking away, especially now that the commentator has left the ballroom. The crowd's desire to rescue the treatment-wing's patients—then strap-down the technicians on the vacated tables and fire maximum-voltage shocks into their heads—is vanishing as their eyes look in fear at the orderlies, who have now finished their prioritised task of extinguishing the sound-system and are turning towards them. Even with only seven orderlies against four hundred rioting spectators, I can see that the pacification operation has a foregone conclusion, and I watch as each orderly transits the dancefloor in an intricate sequence of movements that initially appear erratic and random. After twenty seconds, the orderlies have corralled the insurgent mad and demented into tight groups and silenced them in readiness for their dispatch back to their wards.

The inmates' exhilarated riot has evanesced so completely that I now wonder if I somehow hallucinated the commentator's phrases of provocation, within our cacophony's uproar. More likely, he was simply extracting from his eroded memory a few fragments incanted long ago in commentary boxes poised among gantries above the stadia of the Northern cities, and the cacophony distorted those banal fragments into revolutionary incitations. The orderlies corner the final hardcore rioters in one of the ballroom's far corners with their firehose, the water directed at such pressure that the inmates hug their drenched best clothes to prevent them being torn from their bodies. Finally, that hardcore relinquish their riot and flee by a side door, pursued by the orderlies. Now, the ballroom is silent, and Jim and I descend the steps to look at the collapsed wreckage of the sound-system. On one side, the conflagration has been so fierce, the cabinets trampled in their extinguishment, that only a detrital mass of waterlogged ashes remains. On the other side, the resilient teak cabinets are almost intact, toppled across the dancefloor in a vertical line, but their interiors are so gutted by the conflagration that they are irreparable. Jim looks distraught. Dr. McDonald joins us by the line of voided cabinets—he clearly sought refuge in his office during the riot and only returned to the ballroom after its quelling. I look at his face, which appears resigned, as though he fully expected the furore. 'I suppose this rules out the chance of our being offered a weekly residency?' I ask him. 'Tonight was the last dance,' he murmurs, shaking his head. 'From tonight, the Saturday socials are cancelled for the foreseeable future. But I think that little incident did the patients a lot of therapeutic good... Even the catatonic were dancing and rioting.' To my surprise, he doesn't attempt to withhold our fee, and reaches into his pocket for the envelope: 'Here's your remuneration, in any case.' I take it, and he walks away.

Farhad has already moved the instruments and amplifiers onto the dancefloor, in readiness for them to be carried back to Jim's car. He smiles at me, clearly expecting some praise for his extended recital, but I say nothing, and Jim rebukes him: 'You need to play faster.' I can see that Farhad is hurt, and he looks down at the dancefloor, but whispers: 'I'll try harder, tomorrow.' I pick up Veronika's snare-drum in one hand and the Burns guitar in the other, but when I reach the ballroom's main doors, I stop and turn back. Farhad and Jim have already passed through the doors, and I'm now alone in the ballroom. The stench of the intense conflagration and the elated inmates' body-fluids is heavy in the air, and in the high-altitude corners between the domed windows and the ceiling panels, our cacophony's ineradicable sonic traces are now clinging to the innumerable ghosts amassed there. That cacophony's residue is still destabilising the ballroom's linear existence in time, and in its current cracked-walled decrepitude, I can see that space simultaneously overlayered with its appearance of exactly seventy years ago, a moment before the thousand or more inmates' admission into the weekly dance, when an immense crystal chandelier still hung from the ceiling, and the sunlight-illuminated windows shone down on the polished dancefloor, its periphery marked by many hundreds of wooden chairs prepared for the inmates, palm trees and great swathes of orchids arranged in each of the ballroom's four corners. An instant from now, the side doors will be opened, and the High Royds spectral patients in their 1909 formal suits and elegant linen dresses will flood into the ballroom before me.

Outside the administration building, Veronika, Jim and Farhad are waiting for me, and I distribute the fee into four parts, but I will not join them on their drive back down into the devil's city. Veronika is sitting on the bonnet of Jim's car in the darkness, and she smiles at me, puts out her hands and shows me the deep abrasions burned into the palms by the intensity of her drumming: 'I'll need to get these bandaged for tomorrow night... That was a wild evening. I'll be able to tell my uncle that I've entertained the nutcases, and even danced with them too. He often says that when he was an accordionist as a young man, he faced some really tough audiences in the dancehalls of the

Donbas coal-fields, especially the girls conscripted into the mines for the most dangerous work. But tonight's audience must be the best ever... They never applauded, even for an instant.' I tell Jim that I need to check on Iris, so they can leave without me. It's clear he's still distraught from witnessing the destruction of the 1930 sound-system, but he has a plan for tomorrow: 'We'll all meet in the Griffin Hotel bar at 10pm, two hours before we perform—then we can soundcheck. It's time we started being professionals.' Farhad is lodged in the space behind the car's front seats. Veronika laughs at my obstinacy in not joining them, then opens the passenger-door and slips inside. They roar away along the avenue of cypress trees and I'm left alone in silence beside the High Royds clock-tower. I realise that Dr. McDonald may be right in concluding that the riot formed an effective therapy for his patients—nobody in the entire asylum is screaming tonight.

I walk over the cemetery grounds to Hawes ward. Even from a distance, I can see Iris's face looking through the window by the ward's locked door, the black hair over her forehead pressed against the pane, but rather than anticipating my arrival, she's instead gazing into the far distance, her eyes following the eastbound naphthalene flow of the river Aire in the valley below and tracking the streetlight-illuminated northern arterial roads as they all converge towards the devil's ground in the heart of the city, which Iris has now definitively renounced. I know that her attendance at tonight's ballroom cacophony formed her last punk-rock commitment. I look through the window and behind Iris, I see the figure of her trainee, combing the commentator's hair, rendered disordered by his performance, as his crumpled face weeps in the distress of his dementia's terminal onset. Then she leads him away from his abandoned commentary desk with its rolled-up magazine, into the abyss of the ward of the extreme far-gone. Even though it's evidently too late to discover if the commentator intentionally provoked his riot, I gesture for Iris to unlock the ward's door for me, but she shakes her head in adamant refusal, even as she compresses her face as close as she can to my own, against the window, so that her features distort. I turn around and head for the avenue to walk down from High Royds into the city below. I know I will not see Iris again. We are now each stranded in two separate zones that eliminate one another.

Lodged into a marble triangle above the entrance to the Griffin Hotel, a great carving of the mutant beast—part-lion, part-eagle, its mouth convulsed in a scream, its wings vertically pinioned, its tail curled into an immense 'S' shape—appears as a malediction definitively forbidding entrance to the hotel, so that even to step inside forms an aberrant initiatory act that will unleash turmoil. Although the strikes that paralysed the cities of the North have now been over for four days, that entrance is still part-blocked by month-long accumulated rubbish. I look upwards at the hotel's facade, profoundly black in multiple layers of soot, chemicals and industrial residues, never cleaned in the century or so since it was built as a refuge of pre-eminent luxury for travellers who arrived in this city by train at the nearby station. Three levels of blown-out neon signage are attached to precarious scaffolding overhead: 'Residential/Griffin Hotel/Restaurant'. At each of the facade's five levels, the heads of gargoyles and monstrous entities gaze out into the street, as though their bodies are still embedded inside the hotel's rooms. At the fifth-storey level, the illuminated clock marked with the twelve letters of the hotel's name shows 10pm, and alongside that clock-face, the decrepit ballroom, usually darkened, has its chandeliers lit-up too. Above that top storey, I can see the hotel's elongated chimney-stacks, extending in rows a further fifty feet beyond the roof-level, and sculpted human, animal or demonic figures over the windows of the attic rooms. I have been here many times before, to the bar on the ground floor, depopulated by living bodies but still inhabited by the ghosts of those once planning powerful acts of corruption for this city. Now, such acts are always formulated in the bar of the Queen's Hotel, and the North's current masters would never deign to enter the Griffin Hotel's disintegrated hallways. The devil is never sighted here. But for many decades after this hotel's construction, its bar and ballroom formed the originating zones of conspiracy for all of this city's projects of subjugation, enslavement and fraud, designed to enhance the glory of the North's empires.

I pass through the foyer in which the ancient clerks are already sleeping at their desks and enter the voided palace of the hotel's bar, which stretches across the entire ground level of the building. The handwoven Afghan carpet covering the bar's floor cracks under my feet, inundated so many times by urine, alcohol, semen and river-Aire floodwater that its accumulated residues have hardened it to a brittle crust. The hotel's management can no longer afford to light the bar's roof-level chandeliers, and the faded hoardings along the walls for the ballroom's magic shows, performing-animal spectacles and bioskop-projections of the 1890s, barely legible in frames that were last cleaned a half-century ago, form windows into annulled pasts. The four bartenders are all decades past retirement-age but are kept on unpaid through their refusal to leave after sixty or seventy years of employment here, along with the impossibility that new staff would ever dream of replacing them. They appear shocked to see me as I approach the bar, and though I have been here so often that I can differentiate each incised and collapsed face, they show no sign of recognition, as though they entered a terrain of terminal oblivion many years ago. But one of them gestures a shrunken hand towards the far table where Farhad and Jim are sitting.

Farhad leaps to his feet when I approach and again, to my astonishment, he leans to kiss the middle finger of my left hand. But he looks exhausted, and slumps back to his seat. I ask him, 'Have you started your Drax runs again?' Farhad is wearing his crumpled cashmere lounge-suit underneath his industrial jacket, and his rose-pomaded black hair and workboots are covered in coal-dust. 'I started this morning. I only had two hours to rest after we drove back down from High Royds and unloaded everything at the workshop. I couldn't sleep after that moment when I feared the mad would maim us in their rioting. Today, I've done ten non-stop runs, Nostell to Drax and back—the coal-supplies are still low and Drax is working full-tilt.'

One of the bar-staff sets down a large glass of beer in front of me, alongside the untouched glasses of Farhad and Jim. Jim is silent and I can tell he's still distraught from witnessing the destruction of the vintage sound-system in the High Royds ballroom last night. He tells me: 'If we'd only let Farhad do the entire performance, and not got lured into a five-minute cacophony, those cabinets would still be intact. I could have struck a deal with the asylum director to go up there each morning, while those two raving-mad projectionists are still incapacitated, to test all of my grandfather's prototypes thoroughly. There's no sound-system of that era remaining in any city of the North—all of them have been discarded, abandoned, worked to death or abused, even the top-grade one they once had upstairs in the ballroom here. And it's urgent for me now. I've going to have to hire a van, put all the prototype synthesisers in the back, and drive around cities on the edge of the USSR—Riga, Chisinau, Magadan, Vladivostok—until I find a ballroom so lost in time that they still have a functioning 1928 sound-system. But how is that going to happen? From tomorrow night, I have to oust my nephew at the Majestic and start projecting *The Texas Chainsaw Massacre* four times a night. It looks like it's going to run for fucking months.'

The bar begins to shake, the chandeliers overhead splintering, and the noise of century-old walls being pummelled and torn apart reaches us through the Griffin's own disintegrated walls. The demolition crews around the tramshed, on the far side of the dark arches from this hotel, are finally being activated tonight. I've spent the afternoon and evening hours watching the crews, gathered from all of the cities of the North, assemble at the site. The tramshed cannot be detonated, since its location is so close to that of this city's railway station, and the reverberations of such an explosion would destabilise the innumerable strata of catacombs, cellars, subterraneas, mine-workings and tunnels that underpin this city from the centuries of its industrial exploitation, so that a co-ordinated detonation of the tramshed risks precipitating an all-consuming collapse that could see the entire city and its build-ings—from the devil's ground to the hotels around City Square, and further out to the St. James hospital and even High Royds—disappear into a sinkhole, into which the river Aire would then pour, disrupting its eastward course. As a precaution to avert the possibility of such an event, the tramshed is to be pounded with many hundreds of crane-directed wrecking balls, as well as dismantled by hand. Over the evening, I've stood to one side of the operation in Swinegate and heard the supervisors discuss the chal-lenges that face them: in particular, the entire tramshed floor-level remains flooded by a part-frozen coating of riv-er-water, naphthalene and other detrita. I know the crews will also hit an unforeseen obstacle when they attempt to demolish the tramshed's roof-gantries and discover the ineradicable sonic trace of the epileptic singer's voice there, from the first night of the Futura festival. But the tramshed walls are striated and unstable, in part through the severity of their erosion by this last winter's ice, and they will fall rapidly, with concerted action. So far, only preparatory demolition is underway, and the main work will begin at midnight. It must be undertaken in the span of one night, by 5am, since it requires the participation of so many crews, and needs to be finished—the tramshed's site transformed into a flattened, toxic wasteland—by the moment when the first trains of the morning run.

As the noise of the preparations for the tramshed's demo-lition intensifies, Veronika appears in a full-length black vinyl coat that opens to reveal her long legs in bright orange low-cut flared trousers, her wild hair haphazardly tied back with an elastic-band. She appears ill at ease, but I can tell she's made an effort to dress-up for the occasion, in the rabbi's rooms above the Roots Club. Beneath the coat, I can see she's still wearing her Everlast boxing-outfit. She sits down, her gaze taking in the Griffin bar with revul-sion, and snaps a command at the bar-staff, who bring her a large glass of vodka. When she reaches out a hand to take it and swallow it in one gulp, I see the thick crepe bandages safety-pinned around both of her hands, seeping blood. 'My uncle tied them,' she tells me. 'He says the drumstick wounds are nearly an inch deep, and I shouldn't be performing tonight. When I tried to hit the punch-bag this morning, they started to bleed, and they won't stop. And I only have two drumsticks left—I must have thrown the others into the audience last night. But I came down from Francis Street anyway. I'm not going to let you down.'

The four of us fall silent, against the senile deliria of the bar-staff's banter and the sounds of the demolition engines being manoeuvred into position beyond the dark arches. Each of us knows that this will be our last performance. Farhad's Drax-run duties preclude all further time-commitment on his part, and Jim's projection schedule and fear of being usurped in his senior projectionist role will not allow him another night's respite from the projection box. And I can tell that Veronika is fragile, and needs to leave this city by the end of the month, before Thatcher makes her move. When I telephoned Veronika's uncle this evening, to check that she'd arrived back safely from the High Royds riot, he confided in me that he is about to lose the lease for his basement restaurant along with the top-storey area, intended for alcohol storage, which Veronika currently inhabits in the synagogue building. The Ripper police fear the Roots Club, with its unruly clientele, is distracting them from their Chapeltown-focused search, and have summarily withdrawn all licensees' permissions for entertainment and consumption from the entire building. The Roots Club nightly dub cacophony will also be erased, and a three-storey Chinese restaurant is due to occupy the entire synagogue's space from the beginning of next month. Veronika's uncle has so far said nothing to her, but they must vacate the building by the 31st, and he asked me to make one final visit to his restaurant, tomorrow evening, so I will be there when he breaks the news of their expulsion to Veronika.

Jim finally begins to expound his ideas on the increased professionalism he wants us to display in our cacophony tonight: 'We need to take a break of a few seconds every five minutes or so, then it'll appear that we're performing separate pieces—songs… And we can breathe for a moment, too.' Veronika rolls her eyes: 'But you know—you've said it

yourself—this is the final performance.' Jim nods in resignation, and at that moment, we're joined at the table by the
hunchbacked promoter, who sits alongside me, pulling up
a second chair for his clubbed feet. He whispers: 'My spies
tell me you whipped up a bit of unrest last night. And blew
up the fucking PA too—I've had to hire an indestructible
one for tonight. I'll go and check it in a moment, then you
can do your soundcheck. And I hear you only managed
five minutes at High Royds. You'll need to play for longer
tonight, twenty minutes at least. It's in the contract. And
where's your special guest vocalist tonight? I suppose he
must be arriving in an ambulance direct from High Royds
with his nurse, just before midnight. Is that right? Or have
you got someone else lined-up for your encore tonight?
The Ripper—singing *Louie Louie*?' I tell him: 'You'll have
to wait and see.' He slaps my arm: 'You're a fucking wily
one.' His voice drops to a murmur: 'But you're still not
nearly as sharp as me, son. I've got a special last-minute
show on tomorrow night, in the Queen's Hotel ballroom. I
seized on a cancellation. It's secret—don't breathe a fucking word. Here, I'll give you two tickets.' He presses the
shoddy slips of grey paper into my hand, kicks over the
second chair with his metal-soled boots as he stands, then
limps towards the service elevator to ascend to the ballroom. I look at the tickets, which are printed with one
word: 'low'.

Jim and Farhad used the service elevator on their arrival
at the Griffin Hotel to transport our instruments and
amplifiers up to the fifth-storey ballroom, but now we
take the stairs. The first floor of the hotel looks almost
habitable, and a few stranded businessmen and travelling-
salesmen, too impoverished to stay at the Queen's Hotel,
are milling around the lava-lamp lit lounge on that level,
or are burning holes in the chocolate-brown polyvinyl-
chloride covered sofas with their cigarettes while watching the malfunctioning television set. But as we ascend to
the third and fourth floors, the hotel appears increasingly
decrepit, and we are moving backwards in time as we
ascend vertically. It's impossible to gauge whether anyone
still occupies the rooms on those floors. By the time we

reach the fifth level, it's clear that the corridors and fixtures have not been renovated since the hotel's construction one hundred and seven years ago, or cleaned for at least three decades. At the top of the staircase, a wooden sign with a pointing hand directs us towards the entrance to the ballroom.

A small plywood table with two chairs has been set up by the entrance and the promoter already has his tin cashbox positioned alongside a torn sheet of paper scrawled in biro: 'Members 50p, Non-Members £1'. Our cacophony is being promoted as part of the F Club empire. Hundreds of golden cans of beer are piled under the table, ready for sale. Although I've climbed the Griffin's stairs before to peer into the ballroom, this is the first time I've seen it illuminated by its chandeliers, hanging thirty feet above us, and reflected nine times in the great tainted mirrors which extend from the floor almost to the ceiling, on each wall except for the one which holds elongated windows looking out over Boar Lane. Every mirror's surface has its dense century-long history: jagged striations which zigzag or contort so that they conjure the forms of human bodies, impact-zones of drunkenly-thrown bottles, handprints and spurts of blood from long-forgotten gang-fights and lust-feuds, and nailfile-scratched graffiti of sexual obsession. Several mirrors are so tainted that they will barely reflect any longer. The walls alongside the mirrors are layered inches deep in nicotine tar-residues, along with accumulated strata of sweat and exhilarated body-fluids from the five-day non-stop dance marathons which became a legend in this city in the 1920s, together with innumerable other frenzied spectacles. The ballroom's stench is an intricate one, still infused with the residues of the performing-animal shows of the ballroom's first decades of operation, for which elephants were winched through the windows, and those of the conflagrations of the early magic-lantern, bioskop and cinematograph projections undertaken with dangerously unstable equipment in the 1890s. Farhad and Jim have arranged our instruments and amplifiers on the low platform by the windows, alongside the ash dance-floor, which is inscribed with a dense network of stiletto incisions, violent boot-scuffs and discolouring inundations of sweat from hot summer-night dances of decades ago, as though it were conceivable to read an embedded language of that ballroom's entire history in its dancefloor.

An elderly man in a bowtie and shabby black suit has been heatedly discussing the admission prices with the promoter, but he notices me gazing at the ballroom's walls and immediately walks over. 'I see you're admiring our ballroom,' he says. 'It's always for hire, for any occasion, and we're eager to offer incentives and to strike deals.' He offers me his hand and as I take it, I realise that his suit is emanating an identical stench to that of the ballroom itself, as though he hasn't left this space for decades. I point to the inch-wide crack which traverses the entire ceiling from corner to corner, crossing the mouldings of ivy leaves which surround the chandeliers. 'Are you sure the roof is going to hold for tonight?' I ask him. 'When the tramshed demolition starts in an hour or so, the whole hotel will start to shake.' He gestures dismissively at the ceiling. 'It's totally stable. An incendiary bomb landed directly overhead in 1941 and its weight caused that crack. But for some reason it didn't explode. If it had, this hotel would have been obliterated—all of the other great railway hotels of Boar Lane were destroyed, and only this one, the Scarborough Hotel and the Queen's Hotel survived.' He speaks the name of the last hotel with gritted teeth. 'It was before my time—I only started here in 1949—but I heard that a bomb-disposal team arrived a few days later, removed the bomb's timer and defused it, then left. For all I know, it's still up there. But nobody has ever complained about cracks. A few of the attic rooms are still occupied by our long-term residents.'

I can tell the proprietor is hitting his stride and is ready to extol his hotel for hours, but a fierce altercation abruptly erupts between Jim and the promoter over the sound-system hired for tonight. Four streamlined, brand-new cabinets are stacked on either side of our encircled instruments, small panels bearing the words 'AEG—Telefunken' attached to the meshing over the moulded black casings. Since the Griffin ballroom is almost square in design, I can tell that our cacophony's amplification will echo almost immediately from the mirrored back wall. Jim is berating the promoter: 'That's a top-range Telefunken system you've installed.' The promoter, usually so adept and confident in his misshapen body, appears crestfallen and confused: 'I don't know what you're fucking on about. It cost me a fortune to get that hired. I even got in touch with the company's head office in Frankfurt—they guaranteed you definitely won't be able to set it on fire. And it's equipped with the cutting-edge High Lom noise-reduction system that was only introduced last month.' Jim has now grabbed the promoter's shirt and is seething with fury: 'We don't want a noise-reduction system—we're after maximum white-noise fucking excess, you cretin. That's the first big problem. Second—the sound-system is manufactured by Telefunken. I doubt it's going to be compatible with my prototype synthesisers. You must know that Telefunken is the same German company that manufactured the radio directional indicator system which enabled the precision aerial bombing and destruction of much of this city in 1941. That technology was so accurate that when the pilots fire-bombed the air-raid shelters down there in City Square, they hit them full-on, their roofs collapsed and everyone inside was incinerated. And now you want us to perform through your fucking Nazi sound-system... You deformed bastard—you should have been drowned at fucking birth.' Jim stalks out of the ballroom.

I walk over to placate the promoter, but he's already composed again and grimaces: 'I've heard worse. I've been insulted all my life. And what counts is that there's now a queue outside that stretches down the entire staircase and out into Boar Lane—two hundred people. That's all I fucking care about.' Farhad is already soundchecking every instrument with professional zeal, and it's clear he's been watching Jim's operation of his experimental synthesisers so closely that he knows exactly how even the most opaque and mysterious of the prototypes works. After ten minutes, he's checked everything through the sound-system and gestures to the promoter, who will soon admit the audience.

Veronika has been sitting alone by the ballroom's back mirrors, on a gilt chair, retying her bandages as they seep blood down her wrists, oblivious to the argument. She still looks fragile, and I ask the proprietor if he has a dressing-room for us to wait in during the half-hour before the cacophony is due to begin. He looks at me in bewilderment: 'A dressing-room? No, we've never had one. This is the North. You're the first performer to ask that in a century.' I ask him instead if we can go up on the roof to wait. He doubts anybody's been up there since the wartime bomb was defused—the hatch could be locked or corroded, but we can try taking the staircase at the end of the corridor which leads past the attic rooms. Farhad will remain in the ballroom to watch over the instruments, but Veronika and I slip through the door and along the corridor. I'm not surprised to see the rusted hatch to the roof is already wide open, and we pass though.

Jim is sitting directly on the hotel's slate roof, leaning against the defused bomb casing and looking out across the line of adjacent roofs, beyond the Griffin's immense chimney stacks: the Royal Exchange Chambers directly alongside this one, then the Queen's Hotel and the Majestic cinema. The enormous grey projectile has rusted over the decades, and was evidently eviscerated and rendered harmless by the disposal team, but the outer casing appears still solid and the stencilled inscription of its manufacturing data remains legible. Jim tells me: 'I'm just calming down, don't worry... It's almost silent up here, at least—I think I can hear the people whispering in the attic rooms. And everything's quietened down over at the tramshed too—they must be making the final preparations for the demolition's main phase.' He points to the post-office's clock tower: 'It's due to begin in half an hour. We'll go back down then.' Veronika is standing beside one of the sculpted figures at the roof's edge. From the street below, it's impossible to tell if those figures are humans, animals or demons. She laughs in delight, and gestures for me to come over: 'Look at this guy.' We're right on the roof's edge, caught in a split-second vertiginous elation. An immense Purbeck-marble bearded figure with a muscled body, the chest part-covered by a robe that also encircles his right arm, is holding a furnace hammer in his left hand, poised over an anvil. His feet are bare, and this city's dirt has blackened them to ankle level, but the span of his legs from the ankles to the lower edge of his robe appears pristine. In his right hand, he holds a strange weapon of subjugation and torture, pressing it down heavily upon the head and wings of a griffin, to shackle it around its throat and maintain it in incapacitated asphyxiation, and the beast's claws are outstretched as though it's at the very last moment of its endurance and will either now submit to the bearded figure, or turn in insurrection to attack him and claw out his eyes. But for that moment, the figure's eyes are intact, staring over the roof's edge with severity and concentration, to determine this city's future.

Jim is fixed in a stubborn disposition and I can tell he's ready to delay our departure for the ballroom until the promoter himself manoeuvres his clubbed feet through the roof hatch and pleads for him to come down. I hear him cursing the name of the sound-system under his breath and he pulls a half-bottle of vodka from the left-hand pocket of his ancient leather coat, takes a mouthful and then offers it to Veronika and I. Veronika's face is covered with a sheen of cold sweat, as though the wounds in her hands have become infected, and she's biting her lips from the pain, but the alcohol appears to relax her, and she leans against the edge of the bomb's casing and looks up at the stars. A half-hour goes by and suddenly, from the far side of the railway arches, a sequence of pounding collisions, along with the noise of several hundred drills, signals that the main phase of the tramshed's demolition is now beginning. Jim tells us: 'When we hear the audience below howling for us, that's the moment to go down. And they'll need to howl, to be heard above that racket.' I tell Jim that he's going to drive the promoter berserk. 'It doesn't matter—it's the last time we'll perform anyway,' Jim replies, finishes the bottle and takes an identical one out of his coat's right-hand pocket. At 1am, we begin to hear a rumbling noise from below, as though replicating the in-progress demolition. Farhad appears, evidently dispatched by the promoter, but he's immediately distracted by the sound of the demolition, and stands in awe at the hotel roof's edge to listen. 'They'll clear an enormous area,' he says. 'They'll be able to build Thatcher's Northern palace in its place.' Jim shakes his head: 'More likely an internment camp, for when the miners and steelworkers unions are crushed, and Elland Road is full. Or maybe they'll just be battered to death in pitched battles where they stand. But it's going to be a wasteland, whatever it is.' I can hear the tramshed's roof-gantries snapping under the wrecking-balls, and I remember the building on its Futura nights of last October, inhabited by the frenzied cries of its audience's sleep-deprivation induced psychosis.

Jim realises that, since Farhad has been dispatched to the roof, his prototype synthesisers are unguarded in the ballroom below, and this finally convinces him that it's the moment to descend. He heads through the hatch and pushes aside the clientele who are overspilling the ballroom to wander the Griffin Hotel's corridors, battering in exasperation at the locked doors of the guestrooms. The ballroom is now packed with an expectant clientele of around two hundred overheated bodies, cigarette smoke swirling up to the chandeliers. Many of the audience are standing in isolation, propped against the tainted mirrors, but the bodies pressed into one another on the dancefloor form an adhered, impacted mass of sweat-soaked skin and gaping mouths. The ongoing tramshed demolition is audible in the ballroom and the roof is shaking, the crack across the ceiling visibly widening. As I pass the promoter's plywood table, he stops me with a strong grip on my shoulder and hisses: 'I'm not paying you, so you know that even before you start.' I push him aside and Jim has already activated his synthesisers, propelling their aberrant beats at maximum velocity as though in a punitive attempt to overrule the capacities of the sound-system, and I see the audience recoil from the cacophony's transmission directly through their skeletal and neural networks. For the first time, Veronika's drumming follows on from the synthesisers, and she is playing far more slowly than usual so that her arms' muscles anticipate the demolition's arrhythmic thuds. But Farhad's *tar*-playing, now so adept that he can accelerate effortlessly to seven times his habitual speed, accentuates the cacophony, impeded by my discordant Burns-guitar drone and expectorated vocal fragments of this devil's city at night.

For the first ten minutes, the cacophony is soaring, projected back towards us in intensified echo-variants after only a fraction of an instant by the abbreviated interval between the sound-system and the mirrored, nicotine-encrusted back wall, so it feels that the wide-eyed, convulsing bodies in the intervening space are being concertinaed by multiple, near-simultaneous strata of noise. When I look at those exhilarated bodies, I see only ghosts whose restlessness drives them into even more unhinged contortions. Beyond them, the promoter is standing on one of his chairs, overseeing the furore, and he's evidently placated, making hand-signals as though inciting us to push still harder into our cacophony's extreme zones.

I hear a cry from behind me, and turn to see Veronika with her palms laid flat against the skin of the snare-drum, the sticks flailing to the ground. She sees me looking at her, and shows me her palms, the furrowed wounds in them so deep that the crepe of her bandages has slipped inside them, and both of her wrists are now running with blood. She stares into my eyes, panicking—she cannot continue for another instant, but we are immersed in our cacophony. The microphone above her snare-drum picks up the minuscule sounds of her long fingernails involuntarily battering against the skin, and through some anomaly of the Telefunken sound-system, that amplified noise of fear and desperation abruptly subsumes and annuls all of the other sources of the cacophony—Jim's prototypes, Farhad's *tar*, my wild-dog thrash—so that the ballroom is solely animated by Veronika's fingertip spasms. Then she abandons her performance, knocks aside Farhad who is trying to retrieve her drumsticks from the ground as she flees, and runs blindly towards the ballroom's door, upending the promoter from his chair so that he crashes to the ground.

Jim re-sets the mixing-desk levels and attempts to continue, but some fundamental incompatibility is developing between his synthesisers' hardwiring and that of the sound-system, and all that emerges are stuttering noises of debilitating detonation that bleed into the seismic demolition drone, more prominent now that our cacophony is eroding into malfunction. Instead of the sound-system being set-alight by our cacophony, as at High Royds and the F Club, I can see it's Jim's synthesisers which are in danger of meltdown this time, filaments of noxious smoke emerging from their casings. Finally, he glares at the audience and snaps off the switches of his prototypes, unplugs them from the sound-system, and carries them from the ballroom in his arms. Only Farhad and I are now left, and I can tell that the wild-dog setting on the Burns guitar is no longer functioning: after a few moments of amplified feral sawing, it cuts out entirely. I turn the dial to the other settings, but those are fused too, and the microphone has also cut out. I position myself at the edge of the dancefloor, with my back to the audience, and watch Farhad performing. From time to time, over the coming moments, I feel fists striking my back, and bodies jostle and almost overturn me, but I'm so focused on keeping my eyes fixed on Farhad that I retain my balance.

From time to time, Farhad glances upwards from his *tar* strings, aware that he's now performing alone. The audience are situated on a knife-edge, between elated captivation and the onset of incensed rioting. But Farhad maintains a shy smile on his lips and he knows that a performance must never be abandoned or even suspended for an instant. I can tell he's exhausted, wrenched almost to the point of hallucination, as though it were a disembodied spectre playing the *tar*, and the speed of his playing, usually so adroit, is fluctuating in speed from that forcibly demanded of him for our cacophony to that of his recitals as a seven-year-old virtuoso in the Khak-i Marmar palace in Tehran. When we reach the twenty-minute limit of our contractual obligation, I gesture to Farhad and he sets aside his *tar*, reaches for his clarinet as he did at the High Royds ballroom, and exhales into it ecstatically, only once, as though with his last breath. Then he stands and gives a deep bow, one hand pressed against his chest, the other holding his *tar*. I can tell that the audience are only momentarily caught in silent suspension before their act of rioting, and we will need to leave fast. I walk over to Farhad and guide him into the crowd who miraculously part to let us pass, my left arm around his waist, to the far wall of the ballroom and through the doors, then along the corridor and down the flights of stairs, across the decrepit foyer with the somnolent clerks until we are out on Boar Lane. Jim and Veronika are nowhere to be seen—it's clear that Jim has already returned to his workshop by Le Prince's bridge to begin the repair work on his prototypes, and Veronika has started her long walk back up to Francis Street to staunch and bind her palms. Farhad and I cross to the far side of Boar Lane, my arm still around his waist. When I look upwards towards the fifth-storey hotel ballroom, the riot has already started, in a furore of screams, projectiles hurled through the windows under the concentrated gaze of the robed marble figure holding down the griffin with his weapon of subjugation.

At 7pm the next evening, I descend the stairs of the Ukrainian restaurant under the Roots Club for the last time. I promised Veronika's uncle that I will be present when he breaks the news of their expulsion to her, but the entire synagogue building feels silenced and emptied as though it's already been vacated and will soon be demolished as utterly as the tramshed which I passed on my way up to Francis Street, that immense assignment completed by 5am as scheduled, the amassed debris already carried away in hundreds of trucks to be landfilled in the flatlands adjacent to the Drax power-station, leaving behind only a jagged wasteland of tramline shards and steaming pools of indelible chemical residue. The Roots Club will not open for several hours, if at all, and Veronika's uncle only has his diehard clientele of solitary, aged men who enter as soon as he opens and sit all night at the restaurant's far tables, listening to the subdued voices of the announcers on the transistor-radio affixed to the wall. Veronika's uncle shakes my hand gravely: 'I had to take Veronika to the St. James casualty room as soon as she arrived back last night. Those wounds on her hands were so deep, so infected. I saw those wounds before, but last night they were twice as deep, and she wouldn't say a word about what happened. After the cauterisation and stitching, they gave her injections, since she was delirious in her fever. And now I have to tell her that we'll be evicted on the 31st. That's her eighteenth birthday. I don't know how I'm going to have the courage to say it, so I'm grateful you're here—you're the only one she listens to. If you would only marry Veronika...'. He shows me to a table in the corner, and sets down a bottle of Chernihivske beer, which I drink so immediately that he hurries to fetch another.

I'm as unnerved as Veronika's uncle. I remember last night as a calamity—after the sudden departures of Veronika and Jim, Farhad and I had to abandon the amplifiers to be ransacked or destroyed by the rioting Griffin ballroom clientele, the Burns Split Sonic guitar, Farhad's clarinet and Veronika's snare-drum too. Farhad was still gripping his *tar* resolutely as I looked up at the marble figure over the ballroom windows, but he was weeping with desperate exhaustion, and positioned the *tar* on his truck's passenger-seat as though it were an endangered human body as he set off from Boar Lane for the first of his Drax pre-dawn runs. On my way to Francis Street this evening, I tried to call Jim at his workshop from the call-box in front of the main post-office in City Square but he didn't pick up, and when I crossed the road to the foyer of the Majestic to consult with the cinema's proprietor, he told me that Jim will not be working tonight and his nephew will deputise once again for the projections of *The Texas Chainsaw Massacre*—and if Jim misses a fourth night in succession, he will be summarily dismissed from his position as the Majestic's senior projectionist and replaced in that status by his nephew.

After half an hour, Veronika descends the stairs of the restaurant, but I can see she's still enduring the effects of the medication she was given at the St. James hospital for the pain of her stitching. She's wearing an elegant emerald-blue silk dress from the 1950s and has a large spiral-bound notebook in her hand. She walks over to the corner table, sits down and shows me her palms, which are professionally bandaged and no longer leaking blood: 'I had to get my hands seen-to last night,' she says. 'That's why I couldn't stay.' I tell her that she was certainly right to leave when she did, in view of the disreputable venue. She sees me looking at her dress: 'It was my mother's. I wish she was here tonight, since it's the anniversary of my half-brother Konrad's death, on Sheepscar Road. We had different fathers... Mine was from Lacovia, on the Black River in Jamaica. He's probably there now, if he's still alive. All I ever heard from him was a postcard he sent me for my fifth birthday, and I know it by heart: "Dearest child, This river beside me is black, blacker even than the river Aire beside you. Don't forget me, don't weep too often. Love always from your loving father." By that time, my mother had vanished too.' Veronika calls over to her uncle: 'Where was Konrad's father from?' Her uncle shouts from the kitchen: 'The city of Mariupol.' Veronika calls out again: 'And what's the name of the river there?' Her uncle appears by the table and concentrates hard, as though he were unfamiliar with the region, or once knew the exact information, but has forgotten it, decades ago, and needs to make a great effort to recall it: 'Two rivers, the Kalmius and the Kalchik—a great battle was once fought by the Kalchik, but that was long ago. And Mariupol is by the sea. One river flows into the other before they finally reach that sea.'

Veronika laughs as her uncle sets down a small bottle of Borjomi carbonated mineral-water in front of her: 'Stalin's favourite!' But I can see tears in each of her eyes. She's silent for a moment until her uncle is safely out of earshot, then asks me: 'You really don't remember what happened between us during those nights last summer when the F Club went on upstairs, do you? I know you were out of your head on amphetamines and alcohol, and anything else you could get your hands on, so I don't expect you to have any clear memory. But I kept a diary.' She opens the cover of the spiral-bound notebook, which is filled with inscriptions in green ink, each on a separate page. 'I'll read you one or two.... Tuesday May 30th, 1978: "F Club night. Noisy. I like him, but I'm angry at him at the same time. I took a half-hour away from the bar towards the end of the night and we went to the back of the building. He kissed my throat, I was flying. He took down my pants and licked me... Tuesday June 6th, 1978: Same thing as last week, heaven, flying again. This time I wrapped my legs around him, bit him, and he got inside me, shot.... Tuesday June 13th, 1978: And again, shot inside me and in my mouth too. I like him... Tuesday June 20th, 1978: He's not here tonight. Nothing... Tuesday June 27th: Tonight we just kissed, behind the building, a few minutes, he said nothing, could barely stand. That's enough. Every time, he doesn't remember the last time. Nothing."' On each occasion Veronika comes to the end of her reading of a page, she pulls it from the spiral notebook, by the top corner, the thin filaments of paper ripping in sequence, then crushes the detached page in her fist into a ball and scatters it on the table. I am looking over her shoulder, at the isolated, aged men who are listening to the radio.

Veronika is about to read one final page, but her uncle comes over at that moment, and takes the seat beside me, putting his hand on my shoulder for a moment to support himself and facing Veronika obliquely. I rapidly gather the five tightly-fisted balls of paper from the plywood table-top, and put them in my pocket. Inside that pocket, I find the two badly-printed tickets which the promoter gave me last night for his last-minute event at the Queen's Hotel ballroom, tonight at 9pm. Veronika's uncle is now telling her of the forcible dissolution of his lease on this building and their forthcoming eviction: she will need to leave the rabbi's rooms on the top floor by the end of the month. If he can, he will locate a suitable building and open another restaurant, on the far side of Chapeltown Road, and Veronika can work with him there, but it cannot be the same as here, and she will not have the space to herself for her drumming. 'But I don't have a drum anymore, anyway, and I'll never have one again,' Veronika murmurs. 'I left it in the ballroom last night, with the bodies going mad, and

I don't think it survived that unruly crowd. Even the last sticks are gone—all I've got left now are the scars on my hands. I'll have to decide what to do. Time is running out, now—we only have a few more weeks left before Thatcher comes. By the end of this month, she'll make her move.'

Veronika's father glances at me, clearly alarmed that she may be growing delirious again from her medication, but he's relieved to have told her of their imminent expulsion, and nods at me in gratitude, though I've done nothing, then heads back into his kitchen. Veronika has her face in her bandaged hands, but when she takes them away, she's smiling through her sedation and turmoil, and I can tell that she doesn't want to spend the evening with the morose clientele of her uncle's carp-reeking restaurant and now needs distraction. I show her the tickets which the F Club promoter gave to me last night—all I know is that it's a secret event, arranged at the last moment through the promoter's wily manoeuvres. Neither of us has ever been inside the Queen's Hotel, even as far as the foyer, or even dreamed of going inside, and have only ever heard myths of its glorious ballroom, the most luxurious in the cities of the North, constructed with extravagance, at untold expense, in the 1930s, when the palatial new hotel was built to replace its predecessor on the same site, and only ever used for special events. Veronika's eyes are wide: 'I'm dressed for it—let's go!' She's already taken her diary from the table and is heading for the restaurant stairs.

I wait on the synagogue's seven marble steps while Veron-ika ascends to the rabbi's room, and when she reappears, she's wearing a long black Aran-wool coat from the same era as her dress, her diary now jammed into one of the pockets. The sky darkens as we turn off Francis Street and start walking down Chapeltown Road, as though we were plummeting into an abyss, Veronika still vertiginous from her medication and pain, my memory shattered out of oblivion by Veronika's diary entries. By the time we reach the Queen's Hotel, the vertically directed spotlights positioned above the entrance are illuminated, searing the marble facade between the suites' windows, few of which appear to be occupied. We approach the revolving doors, over which the hotel's name is lettered in corroded gold leaf, and I'm seized with momentary unease. In an instant, we will enter the Queen's Hotel: the domain of the masters of the North. Occasionally, as a small child, my father would take me to the main post-office's staff entrance to meet my mother as her shift on the counters ended, and as we walked hand-in-hand back across the City Square plaza, my mother would point out the hotel's doorway to me and lean to whisper in my ear: 'That's where the devil lives.' Veronika now points too, towards the raised balcony above the revolving doorway, its glass embossed with the white roses and black daisies of Yorkshire: 'Maybe Thatcher will give a victory speech from that balcony, next month, or May at the latest, to announce her plans for the North's denudation and razing. A crowd of one hundred thousand will gather in this square to shout her down, but instead they will be beaten down.'

We enter the revolving doors and are propelled into the hotel's luxurious Swedish-granite interior, preserved intact from its construction. 'Fucking hell... This place is half art-deco, half Reich-Chancellery,' Veronika whispers to me. The elevators to the suites are directly ahead, and at the far end of the corridor to my right, under a succession of low-lit chandeliers, I can see the entrance to the hotel's lavish bar. It's still almost empty but, once its regular occupants are gathered, it will form the determining site for all deliberations on this city's corruptions and acts of killing. The foyer's uniformed concierge is walking towards us, and I scramble in my pocket for our tickets, extending my fingers between Veronika's fisted pages of heated dawn tonguings and ejaculations. I show the concierge the shoddy slips of grey paper and he explains that the ballroom has a special entrance at the side of the hotel, so we will need to exit again and go around the building. Scrutinising the tickets, he notes: 'That's a private event, by special invitation only.' I can see in his offhand eyes that we are not his clientele, and nor do we occupy the bodies he wishes to transact, from one zone to another of this hotel's palatial anatomy.

Veronika is unfazed, and she's already pulling me back through the revolving doors and around the far end of the hotel's facade. We pass under a short, pillared tunnel inscribed with this city's insignia, and on the far side, along the deserted road leading to the railway station's side-entrance, I realise that a discreet set of three opaque doors, which I've seen a thousand times before but never identified, forms the ballroom's entrance. Veronika climbs the stairway and pushes open one of the glass doors. In an echoing vestibule with a thick blood-red carpet, the F Club promoter is sitting alone beside an empty mahogany table, his clubbed feet reclining on a cushioned gilt chair. I'm momentarily concerned he will disbar us from entrance as a consequence of last night's riot, and he has a bandage around his head from his violent upending by Veronika as she fled the Griffin ballroom last night, but it's clear he's now in his element: 'Look at this fucking place! Wait until you see the anteroom, and the ballroom itself. This venue hasn't been in regular use for years.' He appears so elated that I ask him if he's concussed. 'Yes,' he confirms. 'I had to go to the Infirmary last night once the Griffin's proprietor dispersed that bit of unrest. He did it effortlessly, that old bastard, in a matter of seconds, along with his bar-staff—he told me it was nothing compared to the riots they had there in the 1950s. He's seen it all.'

He takes an envelope from his pocket and offers it to me: 'I forgot to give you your fee last night. I've made a small deduction for the windows, and for my concussion.' I glare at him: 'You expect us to pay for our own riot? And that concussion's your own fucking doing—we didn't ask you to stand on a chair.' The promoter smiles magnanimously as though he were indulging a child, reaches back into his pocket to restore the deduction, then hands me the envelope: 'Whenever you want more bookings, let me know—I can always market an extreme, top-range cacophony, anywhere in the North. I know you lost a bit of equipment last night, but that's easily replaced. I'll even hire a certified non-Nazi sound-system next time to placate that excitable friend of yours.'

Several patrons pass by, and the promoter gestures them through to the anteroom with a near-imperceptible wave of his hand, evidently unconcerned about admission fees. I ask him if he's seen the Futura tramshed demolition-site, but he grimaces in disdain: 'That's the past, all those polluted, reeking venues—the F Club by the Aire, that tramshed, even the Griffin. Punk-rock is finished too, after that Futura fiasco.' His eyes are illuminated with hallucinations of grandeur: 'If it all goes well tonight, I'll have this ballroom five times a week, starting on the 28th. Tonight's a secret show. You must have heard that the concert scheduled for the ice-rink at the far end of Wellington Street was cancelled because of safety concerns. Two thousand tickets had been sold, but the fire-brigade decided the floor would crack open and everyone would be tipped into the ice reservoirs. You know I think fast—I contacted the management company and proposed this alternative... A covert, dead-secret, word-of-mouth, invitation-only evening. So you can be sure it'll be huge news tomorrow and I'll have sell-outs here for the rest of the year. I'm paying for everything, but I'll get it back a hundred times over. Don't expect a long show—it'll probably be even shorter than yours, last night. You'd better go inside now, if you want a seat—I've only invited a hundred people.'

I look into the promoter's face and wonder if his combination of right-orbital cerebral concussion and megalomaniacal psychosis will see him transported to High Royds by the end of the evening. I know that the decrepit ice-rink which I occasionally visited as a child was demolished at least five years ago, and that the Queen's Hotel ballroom is solely in the hands of the glacial masters and arbiters of the North, not of a wretched, misshapen promoter. I can only assume that the share of his up-front money seized by the hotel management will fund an immense gala occasion to celebrate Thatcher's forthcoming accession to power.

Veronika thanks the promoter for inviting us and he blithely waves us on, his eyes darting to see who will come through the doors next. We descend a deep stairway: the ballroom is located in a subterranean space below the hotel. Veronika grips my arm in excitement as we enter the circular anteroom with its pristine mirrors, domed ceiling and black-and-gold hooped columns. Around one hundred figures are waiting, lounging on black leather sofas, or eagerly eyeing the doorway inscribed in curved silver letters with the words 'Queen's Ballroom' and guarded by thickset men. I recognise two or three of those figures from F Club nights, or television transmissions, but the remainder are unknown to me. I feel wary to be embedded so deep in the heart of the North's palace of corruption, but I can tell that Veronika is captivated, leaning over to laugh into my mouth, and for the moment she's forgotten the laceration of her palms and the imminence of her eviction.

The guards are communicating to one another in whispers through handheld crackling radio-transmitters, and at a sudden signal, they unlock the ballroom doorway and the audience presses inside. Ten lines of ten gilt chairs, identical to the one currently supporting the promoter's clubbed feet, are arranged at one end of the ballroom in front of a small synthesiser—I recognise it as the model Jim owns, an EMS Synthi AKS—connected via a range of distortion devices into an already illuminated Vox amplifier. The synthesiser's casing is open and angled so that I glimpse the multi-coloured dials and pins, along with the blue and black keyboard. There is no platform or stage—the synthesiser is positioned directly on the thick silk carpet, with its woven design of roses and daisies. The ballroom's expanse and luxury are astonishing, and Veronika and I revolve to take it all in. Each wall holds seven side doors, which appear tiny against the immense dimensions of the oak-panelled ballroom, and I imagine that each of those doors, now allocated its own attentive black-suited guard, leads into a separate, sound-proofed room intended to enable the North's masters to momentarily interrupt their nights' habitual entertainment—magicians, Sinatra-interpreters, impressionists—to confer in spat-out maledictions with their co-conspirators as they determine this city's future. Seven rows of thick marble pillars transect the ballroom's space, as though reinforced to hold up the entire leaden weight and volume of corruption of the hotel above them.

Veronika and I are almost the last to take our seats, on the edge of a row, and we examine the programmes that have been carefully placed on each seat, their four-word content printed in discreet black letters on thick grey postcard-sized paper that contrasts with that of the shoddy tickets: *'Warszawa/Moss Garden/Neuköln'*. I see Veronika take her diary from her pocket and slip the programme inside its pages.

Ten minutes pass, and suddenly one of the side doors opens and an emaciated figure slips through into the ballroom, wearing a 1920s central-European suit but no shirt beneath it, and sweeping tendrils of dyed red hair from his blanched face. I involuntarily remember an image from the first of the films projected at the Futura festival, of a man sliding down a slope of coal residue. The figure crossing the ballroom's carpet on bare feet carries a child's miniaturised thirteen-stringed *koto*, and sits cross-legged in front of the audience with the synthesiser. He sets the *koto* to one side for the moment, resting it on the carpet. A space of twenty feet or so separates the front row of the audience from that figure, and the inviolable interval-space is intently scrutinised by the guards. The audience have not applauded, and at most I heard minuscule intakes of breath at the figure's appearance. He places the fingers of his left hand to his upper lip, as though unsure what to do, re-positions the synthesiser directly in front of him so that all we can now see is the back of the black case, then begins, but evidently mis-starts—a disconnected wail is ejected into the ballroom from the amplifier—and pauses for several seconds before beginning again.

Instantly, in the low-volume noise that occupies it, the Queen's Hotel ballroom is inhabited by the obsessions of a distant city, through which an eye is travelling, propelled by a body on foot or else looking through the window of a train's carriage: that city's disintegrations, erasings and conflagrations, and the woundings and subjugated elations of its bodies, many decades ago, and now. Once that city's conjuration in sound disperses into the ballroom's altitudes, the emaciated figure takes the *koto* from the carpet and begins to manipulate its strings as though on a tightrope between adept and inept gestures, envisioning another barely-there city or ghosts' site, while the synthesiser, even momentarily abandoned, still emits white-noise pulses as though it cannot be entirely silenced. Finally, he sets the *koto* aside and focuses again on the synthesiser, so that another riven city is embodied in the space of the ballroom, this one insistent and raw even as the noise that sustains it is collapsing, echoing against the ballroom's back wall. After the three pieces have been performed, the figure stands upright from his cross-legged position, crookedly smiling at the audience without a word, uncertain on his bare feet, and shaking his head slightly as though the last twelve minutes have been materialised by hallucination. As he starts to walk haphazardly towards one of the ballroom's twenty-eight side doors, three or four of his entourage surround him and re-direct him, while others collect the *koto* and synthesiser, and the door he's entered closes after him.

The Vox amplifier still hisses and drones intermittently, as though the performance is not entirely over. I now feel stilled in this city, and simultaneously propelled out from it. For several minutes, the audience appear unable to move and unready to disperse, and I glance at Veronika, who is still staring at the point on the ballroom carpet where the emaciated figure positioned himself, as though she were in shock, her bandaged hands over her face directly below her blue eyes. Then the head-bandaged promoter limps in front of the audience, evidently intent on announcing his acquisition of the ballroom for events from the 28th, but when he attempts to connect the microphone in his hand to the Vox amplifier, I see his body convulse as though it's receiving a punitive shock. His lips are positioned against the microphone, but he either cannot speak or his words are unamplified, and his disinterested audience are now animated and beginning to scatter, so he throws the microphone to the silk carpet in exasperation.

We will not need to leave the ballroom via the anteroom. The hotel's staff are opening the doorway that directly faces the one we entered by. We are the last to leave and I look back at the ballroom—the *koto*, synthesiser and amplifier now gone, the faint noise-residues hovering in the ceiling-level altitudes, the gilt chairs being stacked as though only ghosts momentarily occupied them, and the promoter remonstrating with the hotel proprietor who appears to be dismissing him in contempt. The opened doorway leads through a marble-lined subterranean corridor and then up a lavish stairway into the hotel's foyer. Many of the audience have already exited the hotel via its revolving doors, but I still have the envelope for the Griffin-ballroom cacophony's fee in my hand, and I ask Veronika if she would like to have a drink in the Queen's Hotel bar. She looks momentarily alarmed, but we descend the steps from the corridor and are submerged in the elegant room with its central chandelier and art-deco mirrors. The tables in the far corners are the most crowded ones, and I can see the devil already enthroned there, conferring with his associates, but I know he will not expel us, and would even welcome us, if he were not preoccupied with the intricate itinerary of his imminent acts, which will only accelerate and multiply, with the coming of Thatcher.

The waiter takes Veronika's coat and shows us to the only available table, which looks out through the window's black-tinted glass over City Square. The main post-office is darkened, but crowds are streaming out of the Majestic foyer after the final projection of *The Texas Chainsaw Massacre*. Veronika and I each order a bottle of Stolichnaya. We sit and drink several shots in silence. Then Veronika looks me in the eyes, and says: 'Thank you for taking me out tonight. I needed to get out. My uncle will never believe I've spent the evening at the Queen's Hotel.' She laughs and extends her bandaged hands over the table. 'I know he's given you hell all winter with his talk of you marrying me… I'd like to make him happy, but I know what's left of those moments in your pocket are just fragments of lust and oblivion.' The noise in the bar abruptly increases—the devil is gesturing with his cigar and has just finished telling a story to his acolytes, who are crying with laughter. Veronika and I can barely hear one another, but I ask her: 'You're going away…?' She looks puzzled: 'No, I'm staying here, for a moment…'. Her last words are scrambled. I tell her: 'But *I'm* going away.'

Veronika appears not to have heard what I've just said, and continues: 'I know I should leave, but I've decided to stay here until the Summer, to help my uncle establish his new restaurant and drinking-club, then I'll maybe make a journey to the Black River in Jamaica and see if my father is still there… I wish I could see my mother too, but she's so vanished that it's impossible to know where to look—even my uncle always says he has no idea, no trace.' Veronika is looking at me intently now, as though she believes I may have some inside information, perhaps let slip by her uncle in one of our many telephone conversations of this last winter, and the Queen's Hotel bar is the one place in this city in which secrets cannot be withheld. Her uncle has said nothing, but I can easily imagine how this city's rigid, self-enclosed Ukrainian community of the early 1960s could have excluded Veronika's mother, and exiled her even from her exile, after her dark-skinned child's birth. Veronika is looking still more searchingly at me, and I know I will have to reply in the next few seconds, or she will grow furious. The noise-level in the bar has dropped again, in the sudden silence of the devil, and I gesture for Veronika to lean forward so that I can whisper in her ear: 'You need to go to the confluence of those two rivers your uncle spoke about, the Kalmius and the Kalchik, on the edge of that city he mentioned—the city of Mariupol. You'll find a few plywood shacks there, among the cypress trees, alongside a stall selling bottles of beer. Children are playing games there. There's a little jetty from which a rowing-boat takes travellers across the rivers' confluence, for a few small coins. That's where I think you'll find her.' Veronika's left hand grips me tightly by the side of the throat and she leans her forehead on my shoulder for an instant, then sits bolt-upright while a succession of unstoppable tears pour down her face, over her lips and onto the front of her mother's emerald-blue dress, her own throat convulsing, and she mouths in silence: 'Thank you.'

Once Veronika drains her last shot, she tells me that she doesn't want to worry her uncle any longer, having left his restaurant this evening without warning, and is ready now to take a taxi back to Chapeltown. She will not walk. The waiter brings her coat, and we go outside to the hotel's taxi-rank. The aged driver at the front of the line of taxis is initially unwilling to drive to Francis Street, aware he will then have nobody to transport on the way back, and will need to drive an empty taxi. But when I reach inside the cacophony-fee's envelope and offer him four times the habitual fare in advance, he immediately consents, and even gets out of the taxi to open the rear door for Veronika. After she says goodbye, she runs a bandaged palm over my trousers to locate the five fisted pages and murmurs: 'Don't remember so much—it's too painful.' Once the taxi disappears from sight—Veronika's face looking at me through the rear window—I re-enter the Queen's Hotel bar, sit back down and order another bottle.

6.

THE BERLIN VOIDS,
MARCH 1979

By the time I'm ready to leave the Queen's Hotel bar, the sky over City Square outside is starting to lighten, and even the devil has abandoned his work for the night and slipped away, surrounded by his associates. I try to hear what he's saying as he passes my table but the words are expelled so rapidly, his cigar still lodged between his lips, that it seems to me he is talking in glossolalia, or in an unknown language, though his rapt acolytes appear to understand every word. I walk to the public call-box outside the main post-office and call Farhad's number, and he answers immediately, only just awake, ready to begin the first of his Drax runs for the day. I ask him if he can take me to the port on the northern bank of the estuary that serves to spill the river Aire's naphthalene flow into the North Sea, by the time the ferry leaves at 7pm this evening, and he agrees—it's only an additional half-hour beyond Drax, and he already took Lily that way, a month or so ago—but I know the extra journey there and back will consume the entire span of his working-day's allocated break. He will take a diversion from the M62 sliproad and pick me up from the Town Hall steps at 9am.

I walk back past the entrance to the Queen's Hotel, then the entrance to the Griffin Hotel, then enter the foyer of the Scarborough Hotel, concealed in an alley between the railway station's side entrance and the dark arches, and take the stairs to the top-storey room where I have stayed since last summer, following the sale of my parents' house. I put everything I own, and all of my remaining money, into an old leather suitcase, and leave the hotel. Then I walk back across City Square, through to St. Paul's House. The old cloth warehouse building with its terracotta minarets at each corner is dilapidated and awaiting demolition, its subdivided interior occupied on provisional short-term leases by the Northern consulates of countries too impoverished to rent office-space in the district of glass-facaded corporate towers between here and the Town Hall. I read the plaque on the door: 'Consulate of the German Democratic Republic, open Tuesdays and Fridays, 8-10am.' I still have an hour to wait, and I sit on the warehouse's steps with my suitcase. At 8am, a man in a grey polyvinyl-chloride raincoat with some kind of rubberised sheen unlocks the door, looks at me warily, and starts to climb the porphyry staircase to one of the upper levels. I follow him, and knock on the door of the office he's just entered.

The windowless office is minuscule and airless, and on the nicotine-coated walls, alongside the East German state insignia and photographic portraits of its leaders, I see an immense map of the city of Berlin, its eastern half as intricately annotated as the map of the Pennine town which Rita Rytka and the director of the Ripper police examined together, the western half voided and unnamed, as though after suffering an irreparable razing. I tell the consul: 'I need to apply for a visa, for immediate use.' He gestures for me to sit down: 'And for what purpose?' I think over the matter for a moment, and tell him: 'Cultural activities in East Berlin, architectural viewings and so on.' He nods, asks for my passport and examines the date of birth, then observes: 'Such a shame you'll still be too young to vote. Do you have any connections to the mining and steel-working unions of the North? Are you affiliated to any protest groups or radical organisations?' I shake my head and he rapidly loses interest: 'I can issue a short-term cultural visa, with a validity of twenty days. If you're taking the ferry tonight, then the overnight express train, your date of entry will be the 8th and your visa will expire at midnight on the 27th.' I hand him the fee. He winds the visa into his typewriter and inscribes a sequence of numbers onto it, then signs it and stamps it four or five times, before pasting it onto a page of my passport and handing it back.

I walk to the Town Hall and sit on the steps. After an hour, Farhad sounds his horn on the roadside by the subterranean police-station's entrance and I climb into the truck's passenger seat. I can hardly believe I'm escaping this city so easily. All of this last winter's obsessions and entanglements are being erased into a moment as voided as that map of Berlin's western zones on the consulate's walls, as Farhad accelerates towards the M62 sliproad. He's already made two runs this morning, and I can see he's exhausted already. I try to keep him awake by relating last night's event at the Queen's Hotel ballroom, but I see his eyes flash only when I evoke the child's *koto*. We pass by the Drax power-station and the river Aire is widening up ahead at its confluence with the river Wharfe. Then the motorway soars onto a bridge over the ochre river and I look down into the boiling morass of silt, waste and chemicals as it heaves the North's detrita towards the sea. It appears barely to be moving at this point, its aberrant currents almost turning back upon itself, but as it gradually expands into an estuary, it gathers velocity. After another twenty minutes, Farhad delivers me to the quayside. I hand him his Griffin-ballroom cut and Jim's fee too, asking him to deliver it when he can. I want Farhad to stay, but he must leave, and he passes my suitcase down to me and roars away.

I sit on a bench in the gaping estuary light and wait for the ferry. After a few hours, I take Veronika's balled diary-pages from my pocket, flatten them with the side of my hand against the wood of the bench and order them in sequence to read them later, then slide them into one of the compartments of my suitcase. At 6pm, I see the ferry slowly approach the quayside from the North Sea, and once I've bought my ticket and climbed to the open deck, it laboriously pivots in the estuary, its rivets screaming with the effort, and heads back out to sea, the last visible traces of the North—the illuminated Drax cooling towers and the grand century-old hotels of the Yorkshire coast resort towns—vanishing into darkness.

At 7am the next morning, we arrive at a near-identical quayside, beside the Breeddiep estuary whose waters flow westwards from the port of Rotterdam. But the ferry goes no further than the first spit of land, and the few passengers descend to disperse or wait on the forlorn railway platform. Every few hours, a train leaves for Amsterdam, but it's almost 6pm when the Trans Europe Express finally pulls into the platform, the 'TEE' logo prominent on the streamlined red and cream diesel engines propelling it from both ends, after completing its long journey from Warsaw. I sit by the window in a compartment of white leather seating, and at 7pm, the express begins its return journey, twelve hours until it will reach East Berlin's Friedrichstrasse station, hurtling over the flatlands. Nobody is travelling across Europe in this petrified end-of-winter interval, and the compartment never fills. Once the express reaches the border with East Germany at Marienborn, guards wordlessly inspect the visa in my passport, the train's engines are replaced with metallic-grey East German locomotives for the next stage of the journey, and an ancient Mitropa dining car with its insignia of a huge red 'M' surmounting a carriage wheel is brought out of an adjacent turning-shed and attached to the train.

As the express traverses East Germany at the dead of night, I see its cities revealed by acetylene floodlights: detention camps and barbed-wire boundaried prisons at those cities' peripheries, still-ruined cathedral domes and blackened firestorm wastelands even at their hearts. We cross rattling causeways over great rivers under moonlight, pass flame-expectorating furnaces and foundries which are working through the night, and—as we approach Berlin from the south-west, the dawn breaking now—enter immense lakeside pine-forests under which are amassed the bodies of hundreds of thousands of soldiers killed in the last-stand battles between invading Soviet battalions and desperate German units, thirty-four years ago. I keep my eyes fixed to the window, driven on by the adrenaline of the journey in restless gazing into the depths of catastrophic time. For a brief sliver of that time, the express transits West Berlin on tracks elevated above the city and I look out at the ornate apartment facades of the Charlottenburg district, the zoo-gardens and the winding course of the Spree river, then it abruptly leaves West Berlin behind and we're entering the Friedrichstrasse station. The express will remain under the glass canopy only for a moment, so I have to seize my suitcase and jump down to the platform—it will go on now, following the raised track alongside the Alexanderplatz to East Berlin's main Ostbahnhof station, then onwards, out beyond East Germany to the border with Poland and on to Warsaw.

The express-train platform is barriered from the other platforms of the Friedrichstrasse station, and the guards direct the few emerging passengers downwards into the passageways of an immense subterranea, constructed to channel those entering or leaving East Berlin. Opaque glass partitions divide the passageway I occupy from others, and I can make out spectral figures heading in the opposite direction, expelled or fleeing from the city I'm entering. I pass several frozen or bewildered figures who appear neither to be entering nor exiting, and have become stranded, as though propelled into this infernal subterranea to wander there unendingly. Finally, the passageways converge into a high-ceilinged pavilion, windows at roof-level channelling the early-morning light from outside. Later, I will hear that this hallway is named the 'palace of tears' since most of its space is occupied by the processing areas for those who intend to depart East Berlin without the possibility to return, carrying almost nothing, and who leave their friends and families at the palace's doorway, weeping. Only one channel at the edge of the pavilion is allocated for those who are infiltrating East Berlin, and the scattered figures walking ahead of me appear to be almost entirely elderly, carrying shopping bags. The border-guard looks at the visa issued to me two morning ago at St. Paul's House but all that concerns him is the glaring name of the city in which I was born, and its evocation for him of a football team of such violent malevolence that their ill-repute resonates throughout Europe. He notes: 'Twenty days, no longer', as he adds a stamp to those already imprinted by the Northern consul.

I reach the doorway of the palace of tears, inscribed above its apertures in Russian, German and French solely with the word 'exit'. The bodies disgorged here enter a wasteland of boot-pounded red earth and debris directly alongside the embankment of the river Spree, with the roof-canopy of the railway station behind them. The still air is cold, as though I've been propelled back in time by a month or more through this last winter, and a thick haze of amber coal-smoke hangs everywhere, beginning at a level just above my head, so that my capacity to view the city I've entered appears refracted by that choking medium. I walk eastwards along the river embankment, unsure which way to head. The Friedrichstrasse avenue crosses the river close to the palace of tears, but many of its buildings on either side of the river appear to have been destroyed decades ago and are still in ruins, with what were evidently once-grand hotels, entertainment halls and department stores left abandoned, zigzags of intact storeys alongside collapsed or vanished storeys, their interiors exposed to the corrosive elements. Further along the course of the river, I can see the towering stalk of a television transmitter, with a silver globe at its pinnacle, and alongside it, extending almost to the same altitude, the summit of a vast concrete building, its uppermost storey inscribed: 'Hotel Stadt-Berlin'. Along the deserted embankment, the river divides into two channels and a curved, pollution-blackened building occupies the interval between them. From the embankment, I cross an ornate bridge over the first channel, and poised between the two channels, I look back along the course of the river towards the palace of tears from which I emerged. The original bridge over the second channel was clearly obliterated with explosives long ago—the marble-faced bank of the far side of the river channel has been struck with such dense impacts of bullets, shrapnel and rockets that an intense battle between desperate combatants must have raged at this point—and only an improvised cause-way connects the island-zone to the northern bank.

I realise I am at the heart of what was once a colossal, thriving city—the wrecked golden dome of a vast synagogue to my left, the explosion-fissured facade of a grandiose church to my right—but that city was destroyed in a catastrophic battle, three decades or more ago, and its ruins have been left almost intact in their dereliction and exposure, as the barely-touched residue of that moment of conflict, too raw and torn-open to be sutured. But these streets' facades are simultaneously those of a capital city: excoriated, unskinned, striated, scarred: a disintegrated metropolis of ruins, inhabited almost solely by its wrenched ghosts. Many of the buildings' surfaces are multiply marked with the residual handpainted century-old lettering of their evanesced existences—as printing-works, or factories, or tailors' workshops—together with the split-second immediate incisions of machine-gun and shrapnel fire, concentrated around their windows, and finally the erosions and abrasures of the subsequent three decades of fierce winters during which those facades and their interiors have been open to the elements.

I turn right into a long street which runs almost parallel to the river, and read the street-sign: Auguststrasse. Children are playing all along the street, with only occasional cars. To the right, beyond a wasteground which appears to have once been occupied by a building that abruptly disappeared almost without trace in a pinpoint-aimed firestorm—only the wall-outlines of bedrooms in which intimate lives were led are still projected as shadows onto adjacent walls—I notice a sign announcing 'Ballhaus' and cross the wasteground. If that ballroom still operates, its last nocturnal clientele must have dispersed an hour or two ago, in the dawn light. I enter the unlocked building and climb the staircase to the first storey, open the ballroom's oak door and look inside. It's a decrepit, high-ceilinged ballroom from the final decades of the nineteenth century, built for the workers of this district. I'm immediately seized with memories of the Griffin Hotel ballroom, four nights ago, as I look around the cracked ceiling-to-floor mirrors surrounding the stiletto-indented dancefloor under two enormous chandeliers. Something frantic and wild has taken place here, and the velocity of the elated cacophony only elapsed a short time ago, leaving behind its detritus of bodies. A few young but worn-out figures are passed-out on the broken plywood chairs, their shirts and dresses still soaked in sweat, their faces reflected in the tainted mirrors, or else are collapsed in convulsions directly on the dancefloor itself, and the ballroom exudes a compacted stench of alcohol, semen, decay and frenzied dance-exertion into the stairway outside. I close the ball-room doorway and descend the echoing staircase.

At the end of the street, I head towards the vast and empty plaza into which the base of the television transmitter's tower is embedded. All around the summits of the new-ly-constructed apartment-blocks surrounding the plaza, swathes of neon lettering have been installed, currently unilluminated, but they will be activated again with the fall of darkness. In the concrete-coated centre of the plaza, fountains are spouting water. I enter the foyer of the hotel and take a room. The juddering elevator transports me to its highest level, and I step into the corridor and set down my suitcase on the carpet of the room of laminated fix-tures. Then I feel in the suitcase's compartment for Veron-ika's diary pages, which I spread out on the estuary port bench from their balled and pocketed constriction. I leave the room and keep heading upwards—the elevator goes no higher, but a narrow staircase extends further, circling around in its enclosure for several storeys, until it emerges onto a roof-terrace spanning the entire western side of the hotel's summit. The inscription 'Hotel Stadt-Berlin' is now directly beside me, each thirty-feet-high neon let-ter trailing electric wires. I look out over East Berlin: the wastelands and voids, the avenues of just-built apartment-blocks, the winding course of the westerly-flowing river Spree, and beyond that near-depopulated city, that of West Berlin, barely visible as a ghost-mirage in the rust-tinged coal-haze and boundaried by mountains of accumulated debris—bombed-apart apartment-buildings, their infinite stones and shards collected by innumerable hands across a decade or more from 1945, to be amassed into those sum-mits—at its western periphery. The air up here is sunlit but still cold, and apart from a few tables occupied by over-coated elderly men drinking slivovitz and speaking heatedly in a distant eastern European language, the terrace is deserted. I inhale a deep breath of the polluted but elating air, and I feel as though I were a sanatorium convalescent, after the rigours of this last winter. I take a table at the terrace's edge, Veronika's diary pages still in my hand, and once the waiter has brought me a glass of strong black coffee, I'm ready to begin reading those curtailed fragments of our lives in the devil's city.

Darkness fall abruptly in this city, and I'm still holding Veronika's diary pages in my hands, having read them a hundred times or more, when the waiter comes to tell me the roof-cafe is closing. The neon letters of the hotel's name alongside the tables have now been illuminated, and I could continue to read, through the coming night. I look around the Alexanderplatz and all of the neon inscriptions—on the summits of the newly-constructed apartment-towers and affixed to each storey of the department stores—are now being activated in the dusk air, in glaring colours, lauding the chemical industries and plastic production of the German Democratic Republic. In the plaza down below, I can hear screams and curses, and see erratic movements of bodies that interrupt more linear transits beside the fountains. Across the plaza, in the upper storeys of the department store by the Alexanderplatz railway station, I watch two or three figures with film cameras tracking the movements of those aberrant bodies in the plaza below.

I take the elevator down into the hotel foyer, and walk out towards the plaza's central fountain. Four or five figures in leather jackets and torn t-shirts are wading in the fountain's water, screaming up at the plaza's towers in fury and exultation. Another ten or more are fighting with one another, climbing on each other's backs and veering around the plaza, or semi-collapsed around the fountain's tiled edge. Some of them must be only twelve or thirteen years of age, none older than seventeen. All of them carry large bottles of beer or transparent spirits in their hands, and it's clear they are only beginning their night's drinking and provocation, and will continue relentlessly, until they lose consciousness in the plaza or are arrested. As I approach them, one of them curses me in anger, his left hand gripping a bottle of near-drunk spirits, his right hand running his pale fingers through razored, bleached hair. I point upwards to the cameras which are filming their uproar from the adjacent department-store tower, and he laughs in derision at my naivety. At first, it's impossible for me to understand his expectorated words, but gradually I realise that he's cursing the geriatric director of the state security agency which oppresses this city's punk-rock faction, and who has announced on state television, in a speech slurred and sent awry by dementia, that all of the German Democratic Republic's young enemies, especially its punk-rock dissidents, will now be expelled from its cities, conscripted into the army, or imprisoned for two years of cultural reorientation.

Once he realises that I'm evidently not myself an agent of the security police, his suspicion eases, and he tells me of the punk-rock resistance-cells of East Berlin, officially prohibited from performing in any venue of this city, or gathering at all, so that they group together only on its edges, in the grounds of insane asylums or in abandoned villas and factories, always under threat of being violently dispersed by plain-clothes security agents. But tonight, here in the Alexanderplatz, they will provoke the security agents, and with luck, there will be bloodshed. I ask him if any recordings exist of East Berlin punk-rock cacophonies, but he shakes his head in exasperation, his eyes rolling into semi-consciousness as he gulps from his bottle, drains it and collects another, cooled by the fountain's glacial water. They have no recording equipment, no clubs, no bars, nothing, and can only impel themselves into drunken frenzies under surveillance-camera regimes of imminent arrest. He laughs in despair, and tells me that the only way in which they have access to recordings is when they can persuade their grandmothers—too aged any longer to be subject to restrictions on access to West Berlin—to cross the border to the vinyl record-shops of the Goltzstrasse district of West Berlin, then bring the records back through the Friedrichstrasse crossing under the disabused eyes of the East Berlin border-guards. He's starting to sink into a still-standing alcoholic coma, but his eyes illuminate momentarily and he tells me he's heard a performance will take place tonight, in an abandoned gasometer to the north of here, in the district of Prenzlauerberg—he gestures vaguely with a razor-sliced arm northwards towards the avenue that heads out of the Alexanderplatz—and I ask him if he and his friends will go, and he nods his head, but it's clear they're already too incapacitated by alcohol, and more concerned to anticipate the imminent violent confrontation to come, with the security agents who will be sent to disperse or arrest them.

I turn away—I can tell that the punk-rock gang is veering out of control, I'm being scrutinised with hostile eyes, and if I stay for a moment longer, asking questions, I will be attacked. On the far side of the hotel tower, an avenue—Greifswalderstrasse—emerges from the plaza between two cemeteries, one on either side. It's almost dark now, but through the gates and railings of the cemetery on the avenue's westerly side, I can see that many of the ornate century-old tombs inside have been razed by aerial bombing or incised and blown-apart by shrapnel impacts, as though to open apertures for this city's ghosts to enter and inhabit its streets: ghosts more living than the living. I walk uphill for half an hour through a district of disintegrated tenement buildings until I reach a vast terrain which appears to have once held many chemical-industry installations and warehouses. The striated facades of tenements surround that terrain on every side. I enter the industrial lands between the two tapering red-brick pillars of a gatehouse, their tips still illuminated with gas-burning lights. The entire terrain exudes a dense stench of multiple gas and chemical residues, but it's clear from the great accumulations of debris that most of the site has recently been demolished.

I pass by the ruins of a freight railway station which evidently formed the loading-point for the cylinders and vats of gas distilled here, and see three immense five-storey circular gasometers up ahead in the far north-western corner of the terrain. They are almost the last intact structures still standing, but they're disused, gutted and awaiting demolition—the ironwork construction at their summit used for pressurising the gas inside has already been dismantled to its skeletal core. At their top storey, decades-old lettering in flaked white paint enumerates the products generated by the gasometers, as though to convince the occupants of the surrounding tenements of the essential work being done there, vital to the life of the city. A few figures are moving around in the wreckage and debris alongside the gasometers, and a splintered sound of guitar feedback is emerging from the nearest of them. I approach it, open the reinforced iron door at ground-level and look inside. The voided space is colossal, with steel inspection walkways installed at each of its five levels and ventilation openings pierced in the brick walls behind those walkways. Stars are visible in the night sky above the roof's shredded carapace. Inside, in the exact centre of the stained concrete floor, four young figures, two male and two female, are wildly thrashing at guitars, facing inwards towards one another as though to combat their own vulnerable exposure, their hand-built amplifiers and speakers powered by a small generator which itself emits an overloaded noise of imminent malfunction that threatens to engulf the guitar thrash. But they're clearly only testing the limits of the sound-system for now and the performance is not ready to start yet—a figure by the door takes my arm and tells me to return in an hour, at midnight.

I walk back to the gatehouse and gaze up at the undemolished warehouse building directly alongside it, constructed in layers of yellow and red glazed brick, the roof surmounted by a clock-face which recalls for me the one on the warehouse beside Le Prince's bridge. The gatehouse keeper sees me outside, emerges from his hatch and gestures me over, so that we stand together in the illumination of one of the gas-lit pillars. He is shaven-headed and aged, his collarless shirt stiff with chemical residues. As soon as he begins to speak, I can tell his lungs are destroyed. He asks me: 'You're interested?—Nobody is interested anymore in this site. We're obsolete, surpassed... All gas production is now centralised at the Bitterfeld plant. I'm the last person still employed here. I worked here all my life. You're from another country?' I say nothing. He's wary, but it's irresistible for him to share his passion: 'The site was developed from 1872, as the city expanded and demand for gas soared, for lighting, heating, cooking, transportation. At that time, there were no residential buildings in this area... Prenzlauerberg. Only after the entire installation had been built, these tenements surrounded it, in the 1890s—to house the workers, or those for the breweries over there.' He points towards distant, darkened streets. 'All closed too now. This district has been almost abandoned—just a few enemies of the state left,' he grimaces, but his face lights up when he begins to incant the products once manufactured here: 'Coal tar, benzene, naphthalene, ammonia—household and industrial-grade gas—nowhere in this city achieved such levels of production, especially in the 1900s. And in the heart of an inner-city district,' he adds, as though this were a source of special pride to him. 'The gasometers still standing were built in 1908, but we had three more, right here, alongside this gatehouse: beautiful ones, sisters, supreme quality brickwork, the most beautiful ever built. People travelled from all over Berlin to see the "beauties of Danzigerstrasse". And then they were blown apart, by terror-bombers, from the USA and England. Are you an Englishman?'

I still say nothing, and he continues: 'We don't know yet when the remaining gasometers will be detonated—soon, it may be this month. Then a wonderful park with new apartment-blocks will be built here, after the land is cleansed of chemicals—and they lie deep, so it will take many years to eradicate them. I've heard that a great bronze monument to Ernst Thälmann will be erected, beyond that warehouse.' All I know of Thälmann is that he was an opponent of Hitler, arrested along with other German Communist leaders at Hitler's accession to power in 1933 and then interned for many years in a concentration camp before being killed shortly before the camp's liberation.

'Was Thälmann murdered at Sachsenhausen?' I ask the gatehouse keeper. He strains to understand my German words, then realises what I've said: 'Sachsenhausen!' He gestures towards a location which is intimate to him—the site of the Sachsenhausen camp is only a short northwards distance away. 'Ne, Junger. Buchenwald. You know nothing.' He turns in contempt and returns to his gatehouse.

I walk back to the gasometer and enter the reinforced iron door. There appears to be no admission fee, and only around fifty figures form the audience, many of them leaning in solitary silence against the rough concave brickwork of the gasometer's interior wall. I scan the faces for that of Lily, but if she is here, I no longer recognise her. The space is lit by two or three bare lightbulbs hanging from the first-storey walkway. The performers are grouped together by their generator, evidently nervous and unsure whether to perform. But after a further half-hour, they abruptly pick up their instruments and begin to thrash at them, so that the generator screams in protest and the shreds of noise ricochet around the gasometer walls. Some of the audience move closer, as though to protect the performers, while others remain affixed to the gasometer's walls. One of the performers has a microphone but no stand, and she has to stop thrashing her guitar to pick up the microphone from the ground and hold it to her lips, her eyes closed, then she begins to exclaim rapidly into it, as though urgently pressed for time.

At that moment, eight of the spectators—dressed no differently from the rest, and around the same age—detach themselves from the outer and inner strata, propel all four performers to the ground with adept gestures, holding their faces to the concrete, then seize the microphone and pound it into the ground, until its wire mesh is crushed and it wails away into silence. Four of the young security agents remain with their hands on the necks of the performers on the ground, while the other four turn towards the audience they've infiltrated and seize two of them, the targeted faces evidently memorised from surveillance film or photographs. A figure in a uniform by the gasometer's door yells into a handheld loudspeaker: 'Leave now! Disperse now! Otherwise there will be more arrests!', and the remaining audience hunch their shoulders and melt away into the darkness outside. I leave too. A few minutes later, I pass again through the pillars by the industrial lands' gatehouse on my way back towards the hotel, the watchman's eyes inside the gatehouse fixed upon me.

When I return early the next morning, drawn to that site so that I pace up Greifswalderstrasse at a speed beyond my own volition, the watchman is still there, inside the gatehouse, bare-chested and shaving his head with a cut-throat razor over a metal bowl of water. I realise that he lives in the little cubicle behind the window from which his eyes track the bodies entering the space between the gas-lit pillars, still burning in the dawn mist. He's just finished using the razor, and is rinsing his head, dripping water over it. He looks up at me and immediately acknowledges my presence with a movement between a salute and a fist-clenched dismissal, as though I were now already a regular patron of the industrial lands. He comes out of his hatch, holding an official notice: 'You should know that the time of the gasometers' detonation was set earlier this morning,' he tells me. 'The 27th, 4pm. Last night, a fascist cell infiltrated one of the gasometers. The sooner the park is built, and we have our bronze statue of Thälmann, the better. It should be a beautiful time.'

He still has his shirt off, his chest muscled from relentless work and covered in improvised ink-tattoos, and I can tell he's impervious to the dawn cold, as though he's only recently been consigned to his sedentary status in the gatehouse. I ask him if he worked in the gasometers himself, but he shakes his head—that was specialised work, he was only a coke-shoveller, the lowest grade, almost fifty years. I tell him I will take a look at the gasometers, but he's oblivious and simply waves in their direction. He turns away, but abruptly returns and grips my arm: 'On your way, keep away from the Palm House.' I realise he's speaking about an imposing, pollution-blackened building I passed last night, now voided and abandoned, on the periphery of the industrial lands. Above the oak doors of the entryway, I saw a carved palm leaf. I look in horror as the watchman's collapsing lungs appear to convulse inside the inked wall of his chest, but he's still determined to speak: 'I spent the winter of 1928 in there, in room 33, with a hundred others. We were the destitute. In that *Jahrhundertwinter*, twenty below-zero every night for four months, the beginning of November to the end of February. The destitute queued outside for hours in the ice, five thousand every night. Only one night's stay allowed, but you could queue again, from scratch, the next night. I got all my tattoos there, I was all ready to die. Then I was assigned work here...'. His voice diminishes to silence and he disappears inside his cubicle.

I cross the industrial lands to the north-western corner and see the three gasometers up ahead, astonishing in their beauty, even in their dereliction and imminent extinction. I approach the one in which last night's curtailed furore took place. The reinforced iron door is already open, and my feet echo as they traverse the fissured concrete floor to the central space. Among the ineradicable chemical spillages, I see four small pools of fresh blood alongside scraped-skin fragments: the traces from the instant when the performers' faces were pressed-down with such velocity into the serrated concrete that blood seeped from their noses or mouths and their skin tore away. The instruments and amplifiers are gone, but the generator is still there in isolation, illuminated and droning, using up its last reserves of power. I look upwards, beyond the successive steel walkways towards the skeletal remnants of the roof. As I walk back towards the hotel, I see that printed demolition notices have already been affixed to the gasometers' walls, to the facades of the surrounding tenements, and all along Greifswalderstrasse, but those notices are already overlayered by mimeographed sheets of paper, protesting and opposing the operation.

For the next eighteen days, as I convalesce from my winter in the devil's city, time becomes petrified, as though I were now inhabiting a city whose engrained ruination and punitive regime freeze and incapacitate the bodies populating it, even before their birth. Those bodies are corralled by their police and security agents, by eyes and cameras, but if this city falls, and is renovated or rebuilt, an entity still more brutal will control it. The immense apartment-towers constructed in the last few years around the Alexanderplatz and along the avenues heading westward from it appear already consigned to new ruinations and depopulations, glacial space expanding around their occupants. I spend the days sitting in winter sun on the roof-terrace of the Interhotel Stadt-Berlin, trade delegates from Sofia and Yerevan bartering deals on adjacent tables. The expresses and local trains incessantly cross the city on the elevated tracks far below, following the winding course of the river Spree.

At night, I wander through the streets of the inner-city, along Auguststrasse and north into the district of Prenzlauerberg. I see almost nobody except the children who play games in the gas-lit streets until late into the night, under the excoriated, bullet-raked buildings whose walls' plaster has desiccated to fallen dust and whose balconies are lost or unstable. From time to time, I come across the wreckage of a just-fallen balcony on the pavement, flowers and soil mixed with the shattered plaster and corroded metalwork. The danger of being caught under the fall of plummeting balconies terrifies the children of these districts more than anything else, so they always walk along the streets' dead centres unless compelled—demonstrating their daring, or taunting their own terror—to stand directly beneath the balconies. From what the children tell me, when I sit on the steps of buildings to rest, almost all of the tenements still standing between the firestorm wastelands will be razed soon, and their families will be moved to new homes on the peripheries of East Berlin. They enumerate the new districts' names with excitement: Marzahn, Hellersdorf, Ahrensfelde. Often, the tenements extend off the street in the form of three or four successive courtyards, each more eroded than the last. Except for the Auguststrasse ballroom, there are almost no nightclubs or bars in these streets, only rooms pierced into the tenement facades in which alcohol is drunk with addicted speed. Whenever I see adult bodies, they are overwhelmingly those of the aged and maimed, the insane and those still traumatised after decades by firestorms or sieges, along with the dissidents and punk-rock factions who choose to inhabit these unowned streets since their space is so disintegrated and awry that security agents cannot readily identify them here.

From time to time, I feel I need to record images of this city, which appears to be dissolving as I traverse it, and I think about buying a super-8 film-camera. If I can film the vanishing memories of this city of ghosts, they will help me to preserve the fragile inscription of last summer's ghost-gestures of lust in Veronika's diary pages. One day, I walk all the way along the monumental avenue of East Berlin, the Karl-Marx-Allee, whose 1950s marble-clad apartment-blocks were modelled on those of the USSR's cities and were among the first to be constructed after this city's razing. I pass two cinemas allocated prominent sites along the avenue, the International Kino and the Sputnik Kino, and when I reach the avenue's end, I find a small shop on the ground-floor of an apartment-block, below a neon film-camera icon. The solicitous proprietor is dressed in an immaculate suit, and he has second-hand film-cameras ready to show. He is especially keen to demonstrate the mechanism of a Praktica camera, manufactured in 1973 in Dresden, and already six years old. He has colour cartridges for it, and it's inexpensive, since he has a surplus—1973 was the year of an international youth-festival in East Berlin, and choreographed parades and motorcades passed along the Karl-Marx-Allee on their way to assemble at the Alexanderplatz. The occupants of the apartment-block above our heads bought cameras to film the occasion, but those cameras are now already obsolete.

On the 27th, I walk back along Greifswalderstrasse towards the industrial lands and pass by the gatehouse, but the watchman is preoccupied—the entire terrain he supervises is saturated with figures who are here to witness the detonation or to protest against it. As I approach the gasometers, I can see that four or five hundred people have assembled, many of them balanced on the parapet of a railway bridge on the far side of the industrial lands or else standing on the roofs and chimney stacks of the tenements that surround them. Closer to the explosive-wired gasometers, this city's distraught punk-rock gangs—for whom this site was a rare zone of refuge from subjugation—are protesting. And the bodies that habitually dissolve from sight in this city—the transsexuals, the outlandish, the dissidents—are now exposed in broad daylight and chant in anger against the East German regime, its security agents, its collaborators and infiltrators. I hear the reviled names of the regime: 'Honecker, Stoph, Mielke…'. But over two thousand police officers have encircled the gasometers, their number far in excess of the protestors, and it's clear that the detonation teams are now completing their preparations. I walk to the back wall of the Palm House in order to have the entirety of one gasometer in shot. Two uniformed police officers see the film-camera and approach me, asking for my identity card. I have only my passport, and they scrutinise the visa, unsure whether to confiscate the camera. But the crowd beside the gasometers is growing increasingly unruly as 4pm approaches, and they lose interest in me and turn away. One of them tells me: 'Your visa expires today. You must leave the German Democratic Republic immediately, then you will not be arrested.'

At exactly 4pm, with the police still holding back the crowd, the detonation is activated, and one gasometer after another ignites, two or three seconds apart, with the gasometer of the thrashed cacophony the last to be destroyed. For a moment, I hear nothing, then the noise of the detonation abruptly insurges, convulsing the air. I remember the cacophony of the Futura tramshed's arduous demolition, which I heard from the roof of the Griffin Hotel, but this noise is far more sudden and engulfing. All of the surrounding tenements are shaking. The gasometers hold upright for another instant. Through their ventilation openings, I can see the split-second balls of fire rising inside each one, emerging in a projectile of flame through the roofs. Immediately afterwards, that fire is transformed into virulent orange smoke and as the three gasometers crumple and fall in sequence, a momentary white-heat mirage of the atmosphere splitting-apart is conjured directly above each of their roofs. All of the gasometers are now reduced to great mounds of debris, apart from one obstinate sliver of the last-detonated building, wrenched askew but still towering above the industrial lands.

I see the line of police and the detonation crews begin to back away from the gasometer ruins in panic. They've evidently not anticipated that the explosions are now unleashing a vast cloud of toxic smoke, rising up from the century-layered compacted detrita of the industrial lands, and it will choke anyone who does not immediately leave Prenzlauerberg, its residues set to permeate the district's facades and interiors for many years to come. I pass by the gatehouse but the watchman appears unconcerned, remaining at his post, his lungs already too maximally seared to sustain any further damage, when the cloud imminently envelops the gatehouse. I take a tram down to Alexanderplatz, place the Praktica camera inside my suitcase, then leave the hotel to return to the palace of tears. Before I enter the glass-ceilinged hallway, and pass beyond the weeping figures at its threshold, I look back in the direction of Prenzlauerberg, and the dense cloud of smoke and debris now covers that entire district and is rising high into the sky above East Berlin.

An ice-driven wind is propelled from the east directly into my face and eyes, as though concentrated by its recent traversal of an aperture designed to augment its raw velocity sufficiently to awaken and render-lucid all those walking lost through the streets of West Berlin at the dead of night, near-comatose with alcohol or narcotic abuse but enduringly standing upright, and even somehow still in fragile movement, their bodies irresistibly projected through the city's darkened streets. I realise I've been in a near-blackout state for the past four or five hours, a hair's breadth from crumpling with the finality of those three gasometers in the industrial lands, and falling unconscious, mirages uncoiling above my head.

I stop for a moment and attempt to orientate myself. First, I remember arriving at the Zoologischer Garten railway station after leaving East Berlin and taking a train on its elevated course until I could see animals in their enclosures as the zoo beside the station closed for the evening. I studied the departure timetable in that station's grey tiled hallway, addicts and the mad reeling across its space and eyeing my suitcase. No Trans Europe Express is crossing the great rivers and furnace-lands of East Germany tonight on its way to the Hook of Holland ferry-port, but tomorrow night, at 2am, an express will leave the Zoologischer Garten station for that quayside, and if I take it, I will be back in the devil's city by the end of the month. I left my suitcase in a locker, and the key and ticket, valid for a thirty-six hour duration, are still in my pocket. Then, I remember the all-night elation of the many nightclubs and punk-rock bars of the Goltzstrasse and the Winterfeldtplatz—the Mitropa and Niemandsland bars, the Dschungel and Exil clubs—inhabited by bodies dancing and driven against one another in noise-compelled ecstasy. Those bodies possessed a different configuration to those of East Berlin: desperate too, but beguiling and lithe, ready to survive. At each club, I took another drink... And I remember crimson lips telling me that all those transiting the bars and clubs of West Berlin are only momentary, restless passengers who will move on to another venue in an instant, and so I now need to see the clubs—those lips speak the name of one opened only this last winter, the SO36, installed in the shell of a former slaughterhouse building—of the adjacent district, Kreuzberg, reached solely by an avenue which passes under forty-four ruined railway bridges. It's not far—I can take a taxi, or I can walk. But the taxis' windows in the Goltzstrasse all emit the heartbroken voice of Googoosh and that makes me think of Farhad's exiled sadness, so I will walk, though I've been drinking and am almost falling.

I've just turned off the main artery of Schöneberg, the Hauptstrasse, and at the crossroad it's the iced-serrated wind that drives directly east to west along Yorckstrasse—the avenue binding the districts of Schöneberg and Kreuzberg—that is making me lucid again. Ahead, I can see the avenue descend into a near-unlit subterranea under an immense swathe of derelict railway tracks and marshalling yards. From what those crimson lips in the Mitropa bar told me, the forty-four bridges crossing Yorck-strasse carried all northbound and southbound bodies and goods into and out of Berlin for almost a century until the firestorm destruction and razing of the railway sta-tions those tracks served: the Potsdamerplatz and Anhal-ter stations. Now I'm starting to enter the subterranea, and my memory transports me for an instant back to the dark arches under the railway tracks in the devil's city and the exhilarated run I made between their water-streaming walls, alongside the exhaling bodies of Iris and Lily, on the night of the Futura festival, a winter ago. The west-facing sides of the bridges over my head are saturated by graffiti lettering promising imminent riots and demon-strations, and they are so narrow that they were evidently each designed to carry only one railway track, its bed now grass-grown and sprouting slender birch-tree trunks over the parapet. The ornate ironwork pillars supporting those bridges are delicate too, as though grown frail and exposed in the thirty-four years of their dereliction, and those stalks have been embedded in buckets of cement to prevent them buckling and collapsing into the avenue below.

The gas-lit street-illumination here is weaker still than that of East Berlin, and almost no vehicles are making the journey between the two districts in this exhausted end of the night. As I cross the bridges' intervals, I look up at the stars now starting to fade above the railway wasteland. At the subterranea's mid-point, I see a decades-closed station's entrance, sealed with bricks, the peeled paint of its name's lettering illegible now. Once I've passed by it, I begin to hear insistent whispered voices interrogating me from the shadows cast by the bridges' pillars: *'Willst du ficken?'*, *'Hast du Lust?'*... For an instant, in my disorientation, I believe that it must be the ghosts of the dead of Berlin who now want to fuck: the dead who died young in this city, in wartime aerial bombing or firestorms, their lungs burning-up and desiccating in the de-oxygenated white-hot air. But when I glance into the shadows, I can see the teenaged eyes of the addicted and the abandoned—faces of emaciated girls and boys in amalgams—still pursuing their work at the night's final moment, in the diminishing darkness before dawn, and their voices keep questioning me from every bridge's pillars until I leave the last one behind, and emerge into Kreuzberg.

I soon see that the Kreuzberg district's buildings are barely less damaged and eroded than those in the centre of East Berlin, whose terrain almost surrounds this district so that its early-morning air already has the rusted taste of the amber coal-smoke blown across the river Spree from the chimneys on the far side, and those striated buildings hold obsolete century-old inscriptions of former existences that are identical to those of the Prenzlauerberg district: breweries, furniture workshops, long-gone ballrooms, disinfection halls... But this district is still alive, animated by its population of exiles, many of them only now returning—their voices yelling in caustic uproar—from all-night bar and club excursions: punk-rock gangs and activist cells, as well as solitary figures, eyes directed down in obsession, alongside the melancholy Turkish and Iranian workers heading towards factories. All of those figures, even those most alive, appear in danger of being engulfed at any moment into this district's unpeeled and overlayered facades, to vanish into their fissures and join the teeming spectres already embedded there. Those facades are dense with graffiti and posters, their content pitched in fury, denouncing riot-police actions, property speculation, compulsory demolitions. I walk past the SO36 club, the narrow lettering of the neon sign above its entrance still burning in broad daylight but that entrance shuttered now, so I walk on, past smoke-filled Turkish cafes in which men sit resolutely alone at plywood tables. And I walk all day. At one point, I reach the canal which separates Kreuzberg from the adjoining Neukölln district, and I follow the edge of the canal all the way until its slow-moving waters pour into the river Spree. It's impossible to turn eastwards along the river here—the watch-towers of the East Berlin border block the avenue that crosses the canal just before its confluence with the Spree—so I turn in the opposite direction, the river on my right now, its West Berlin bank lined with a succession of derelict warehouses.

An elevated railway appears ahead, and I enter a wasteland of black earth and weeds in which only scattered tenement-houses still survive in obstinate isolation. To my left, I see a domed railway station and a yellow subway-train on the platform, and to my right, an immense bridge crosses the river. I walk over and read the plaque at its edge—'Oberbaumbrücke, erbaut 1894–96'—and it appears deserted at this side, but it's immediately clear that it cannot be crossed. A sign alongside razorwire and stacked concrete blocks indicates that the bridge is the territory of the German Democratic Republic and citizens of West Berlin must not approach. The course of the elevated railway continues across the bridge, above its roadway level, but the trains' journeys evidently end at the station behind me. The bridge's two sandstone towers appear to have had their upper levels violently sheared-away, and the granite pillars that once supported its brick-built span are now detached, eroded to jagged steles. Beside that blackened bridge's threshold, a railed promenade runs beside the river and a group of children, around seven years of age, are chasing one another along it, chiding those closest to the railing not to go near to the water. But once I've passed the children and look back, I see they've already ducked beneath the railing onto the bank in order to reach out over the water for floating detrita and fallen branches for their games. From the warning-signs along the bank, I know the entire river belongs to the German Democratic Republic and if a child falls in and rescuers follow, they will be shot by the border-patrols, so any child that falls and cannot swim must be left to drown. But the West Berlin children cannot resist going close to the river's edge, just as the East Berlin children are drawn to stand beneath the tenements' unhinged balconies that will imminently collapse.

At the far end of the promenade, another avenue begins, heading north-westwards, eroded buildings at each side. In the distance, I can see the border with East Berlin that will soon curtail this avenue, but here at this end, a few decrepit shops occupy the tenements' street-level windows. A shop is selling second-hand televisions and I'm startled to see one malfunctioning monochrome screen showing the face of Thatcher, speaking into an interviewer's microphone as she leaves her house and enters a car in the street outside, the broad-daylight over-illumination of the television lights burning out her face's features to a molten silver mask. The obsolete warehouses still extend along the river's bank at my right, but the tenements to my left abruptly end and a voided zone appears, bordered by the grey-brick windowless firewalls of buildings still awaiting demolition. Over that terrain, children are playing in burnt-out stolen cars. Beyond it, I reach the plaza in front of what appears to be a vast hospital building, a belltower and clock-face between its two intact, pointed towers, brick outbuildings stretching away on either side. Debris from recently elapsed confrontations is still scattered over that plaza—bloodied bandages, shards from shattered riot-shields, flame-blackened bottles filled with rags—and the facades around the plaza are saturated with the same posters and graffiti I saw earlier, denouncing property speculation and riot-police operations. I enter the hospital's oak door. The foyer extends vertically upwards through the building's three storeys, with circular plaster medallions surrounding each level and showing figures in religious dress caring for the ill or dying. But the building is clearly no longer a hospital—from the many handwritten notices taped to the walls, I can tell that the wards in the storeys above are now occupied by activists' meeting-rooms or artists' studios.

I walk along the bare wooden boards of the ground-floor corridors, then ascend the stairs to the first floor. I enter a bar located in what was evidently once the hospital's pharmacy, with hundreds of hand-labelled oak drawers, cabinets and medicine-bottles extending up to the ceiling behind the counter. Three elongated windows look out over the plaza in front of the hospital, stretching up almost to the level of the chandeliers whose light barely reaches the twenty or so tables far below. On the walls, tiled friezes again show bodies being cared for in their last moments, their wounds bound, their overheated foreheads cooled. Although I've heard the sounds of instruments playing through the doors of the wards I've passed, it's quiet in here, with only the murmured voices of the clientele, most of them dressed in 1920s black suits and dresses, or in long leather boots and ripped silk or latex that reveals skin never exposed to the sun. The bartender has short, brilliantined black hair and is wearing sunglasses, and as though I were myself in a terminal condition and in need of urgent ministration, she assesses me with what appears to be a compassion so deep that it traverses the dark lenses. She sees me looking up at the bar's name, hand-painted in black letters directly on the cabinets over her head: 3 Schwestern. As she hands me a glass of vodka, she tells me in a low voice: 'There were once three beautiful sisters, on Danzigerstrasse, in the district of Prenzlauerberg, in East Berlin...'. I grip the glass and sit at a small table beside one of the windows that look out over the plaza.

I've only taken the first frozen sip from the glass when I sense that a figure has appeared on the chair facing me, and is gazing at me. I focus, and see Lily's face. I wonder for a moment if I'm hallucinating with exhaustion, since her long near-white hair is now cut short, but she's still wearing the same alpaca and silk coat as when I last saw her, as Farhad drove her away towards the estuary port. And Lily still holds the adept spectral power of self-conjuration to be simultaneously there and to be disappearing. She's not smiling, and her face looks grave and concerned, as though I've been pitched into an in-extremis state. She appears unsurprised to see me, as though it were duly inevitable that I would become stranded in West Berlin. As ever, I can tell that Lily would prefer to remain utterly silent, and simply gaze into my face. But I ask her when she left East Berlin. She looks around the pharmacy and out of the window, in her own time, then finally begins to speak: 'I never went there at all. When the train arrived at the Zoologischer Garten station, I couldn't help myself. I walked directly into the zoo.'

She falls silent again and is still looking out of the window into the evening air. I know not to interrupt her. After a few minutes, she continues: 'Since then, I've been danc-ing.' At first, I assume she's spent her nights at the bars and clubs that I visited last night, but she points to the small leather satchel suspended over her left shoulder: 'Here are my dancing shoes. I've been taking classes, in the studios on the top floor. My class just ended. Do you know Anita Berber, the 1920s naked addict dancer?... Her dances at the Eldorado ballroom scandalised Berlin. She died here at the Bethanien hospital, in 1928, aged twenty-nine, from tuberculosis and exhaustion, in the ward right next to this pharmacy, the ward for the dying, after abandoning a dance tour, spitting blood... Her lungs destroyed, her body destroyed... Morphine, alcohol, cocaine... Beirut, Damas-cus, Tehran. How is the Iranian boy?—the one scared to die.'

She's silent again for several minutes, then points to the plaza outside: 'There have been riots here all this last month. The hospital was closed nine years ago and was all set to be razed by speculators, and replaced with apartment blocks. It's been here since the 1840s. The city authorities are corrupt. But they're all scared of the rioters. The activists, the militants, the punk-rock gangs... I never saw such enraged eyes. They kept on charging against the riot-shields, even with their faces already split-open. Now we'll see if this place survives.' I ask Lily if she's visited the SO36 Club and would like to go there tonight, but she shakes her head as though she hasn't understood my words. Finally, she whispers: 'Another time. This evening, I'll take you right across the city, across West Berlin. To the Kant Kino.' As we leave the pharmacy and descend the steps to the Bethanien foyer, she tells me that she listened to the radio news from England before leaving for her dance class. Tonight, Thatcher will take power. She's pro-voked a vote of no-confidence in Callaghan's government, and it will take place tonight. It's the end of the winter, and Callaghan will fall.

I walk back along the avenue towards the domed station, Lily silent beside me, but once we've climbed the steps to the elevated platform level, she laughs for the first time as she looks out over the twisting course of the elevated railway that obstinately extends beyond the trains' stopping-point at this station, above the firestorm-seared ground towards the river-bridge with its two sheared-off towers: 'I'd like to take a train in the opposite direction, that way...'. Then she points to the metal sign with the station's name, Schlesisches Tor, written in black letters on a white expanse: 'This is the line's end-station. West Berlin end-station... People here call it the end-of-the-world station for everyone stranded on this island.' On this narrow strip of last-ditch land between the river and the canal that tapers out towards the bridge, we're surrounded by East Berlin, and beyond East Berlin, by East Germany. A yellow train approaches and once its driver has walked from one end of its carriages to the other, it takes us most of the way across West Berlin on its raised course, but as it approaches the Zoologischer Garten station, it abruptly dips into a subterranea.

All I know is that we are going to a cinema, and once we're up at street-level, Lily leads me past two immense film-palaces, the Zoo Kino and the Delphi Kino, but we're going further, walking westwards, along a rundown avenue of old hotels and restaurants. After fifteen minutes or so, I see a vertical neon-sign ahead, only one word of red letters: 'Kino'. A queue of two hundred or so figures extends from the entrance, animated groups alongside bodies in solitude adhered to the cinema's facade of poster display-cases above which the words 'Kant Lichtspiele' are inscribed. The queue then zigzags down the avenue on the far side of the cinema. It's clear this is a dilapidated neighbourhood-cinema dating from the first years of film projection in Berlin, far different from the palaces Lily and I left behind by the Zoologischer Garten station—the hoarding above the entrance has a board for detachable letters to be assembled into the names of films, but the letters are haywire, illegible, or have fallen into the street below. The audience are entering now and we're almost the last inside, stepping into the mahogany-panelled foyer where Lily hands ten-mark notes for each of our admissions into the promoter's hand, then we climb a flight of stairs under a dome evidently constructed to hold a long-gone chandelier, and we're inside the blue walls of the auditorium of battered seats, a thick curtain in front of the screen. Glass wall-mounted gas-lit obelisks illuminate one side of the auditorium, and the street-side holds three emergency exits. Everyone is seated and Lily and I take the last places. From the haywire restlessness of that audience, I realise we're not going to be watching a film.

At 10pm, the promoter appears in the aisle by the emergency exits, turns down the lights and heaves on a lever to open the curtain. In the narrow raised space between the spectators and the screen, several amplifiers and instruments are scattered between the piled-up cabinets of a sound-system. Lily laughs and whispers in my ear: 'I wonder if you can remember the Futura nights...'. Four figures appear from the edges of the screen and enter the space, and I recognise the epileptic singer in his C&A shirt and work-trousers from the first tramshed night as the cacophony abruptly erupts and he puts his lips to the microphone: 'This is the hour when the mysteries emerge...'. But something irreparable has happened to his body and movements in the six months since that Futura night—he appears exhausted now to a far-gone point of sclerosis, as though he's traversed the most intense zone of his fits and emerged at the far side into a reconciled stasis of quietude, no longer convulsing or spasming, barely moving at all as he supports himself upright by gripping his microphone stand, while the cacophony swallows him. The spectators in the broken-down seats are subdued, remaining almost silent whenever that cacophony is suspended for a few seconds, and the singer's eyes gaze out in those intervals as though searching for the aperture in the auditorium's back wall from which the projector will emit its beam of images.

After thirty minutes or so, two of the figures alongside the singer have already disappeared behind the screen, and only the cacophony's percussion still propels itself through the singer's body in aberrant bursts, until the singer's sclerosis is extinguished in a final cried-out exhalation and he disappears too into darkness. A moment later, the promoter re-ignites the lights to their maximum radiance and pushes opens the emergency doors, inciting the audience to leave immediately. A film will start soon—the promoter incants the name: *'Nosferatu'*—so the auditorium has to be emptied. The disappeared figures have re-emerged already from behind the screen to carry away their amplifiers and to help push the sound-system cabinets against each wall to allow the screen to be fully visible again. Lily and I are propelled out into a decrepit moonlight-filled courtyard that appears only ever traversed by those leaving the cinema, its walls as striated and bullet-raked as those of East Berlin, then we pass through an iron gateway onto the avenue and head back to the Zoologischer Garten station.

As the train re-emerges from the subterranean level on its journey back to the Kreuzberg end-station, I see the East Berlin television transmitter and the illuminated sign of the Interhotel Stadt-Berlin appear far ahead in the distance. On this elevated stretch, we've left the streets of tenements behind and are immersed within an unlit terrain. I realise we're now crossing the immense railway-zone between the Schöneberg and Kreuzberg districts, somewhere to the north of the Yorckstrasse avenue with its forty-four bridges. The train jolts to a stop in the empty Gleisdreieck station. Lily turns to me: 'I'm changing here', and suddenly stands to leave the train, her satchel already over her shoulder. I was expecting her to return to the Kreuzberg end-station and now I'm lost—the entire area around this station appears darkened and depopulated. There's nowhere to live in this void. I look at Lily's face: Is she going into the wasteland to change into her dancing shoes to dance naked on the black earth, among the debris? The signal is already sounding for the train's doors to close again. Lily is now extending her delicate hand in a formal gesture, and when I put out my own, she rapidly grips and releases it as though terminating all negotiations between our bodies. But seeing my bewilderment, she whispers that she will meet me tomorrow evening, if I want, in the Bethanien pharmacy, after her class, then she slips away and I turn to see her figure through the window, walking fast along the platform.

The train comes to a stop at the Kreuzberg end-station, and I walk back across the firestorm terrain to the end of the promenade by the river Spree. An abandoned century-old warehouse marks the limit of the promenade's course, and I look up at the pitted facade to the still-functioning clock-tower on its top storey: 11pm. At the other end of the promenade, I can see the barriered entrance to the impassable bridge, but a commotion is underway at the promenade's mid-point, and as I approach, I see a policewoman lifting a drowned black-haired girl of around seven years of age from the river's bank, her mouth open, leaking water from her lungs, a sodden emerald-blue and yellow sportswear-top still zipped to her throat for warmth, above a long daisy-flowered dress. An approaching ambulance's siren wails from the direction of the station, and the policewoman has already ducked under the railings with the child's body in her arms, and is waiting at the promenade's edge. A small crowd are gathered, including what appear to be the girl's parents or relatives, their voices lamenting in Persian. They seem terrified to enter the ambulance, and it drives away without them. I hear voices in the crowd saying that she was the seventh child this winter drowned here, and it took an age as always for the East Berlin border-patrol to cross the river, fish the body out of the water and leave it on the bank for the West Berlin police to collect.

The crowd soon disperse, except for the weeping relatives. By the end of the promenade alongside the beginning of the bridge's razorwired parapet, I see a public call-box, the yellow door still ajar as though left-open in the panic of an emergency call, and I enter. Two sides of the glass within the call-box's casing are shattered and opaque, but the sides looking out over the river and along the promenade to the warehouse are intact. Without knowing exactly what I'm doing, I take all the coins from my pockets and call Jim's number from memory, reading the international dial-code from the information glued above the receiver. I listen to the ring-tone for four or five minutes, but then Jim picks up, and says his name in full. In the interval that follows, I can hear voices in his workshop and I realise he's listening to the radio. Finally, I ask him what he's projected tonight and he recognises my voice. '*Nosferatu*', he says, 'but the cinema was empty, everyone's listening to the radio or watching television tonight for the result—it's due in a few minutes.' He asks where I am and I tell him, but all he says is that he assumed I was somewhere, on the Trans Europe Express network. Then he begins talking in detail about the damage to his synthesisers sustained at the Griffin Hotel ballroom—the malfunctions so severe he's had to rewire the prototypes from zero, it took such intricate work that he almost lost his job, but now the work is done.

He's silent for a moment, then I hear his voice again: 'You won't know. Farhad was killed in a crash, it's already weeks ago, the day after you vanished. He was driving exhausted on Sheepscar Road, heading here, to hand over my Griffin ballroom cut... He swerved to avoid someone running across the road, out of nowhere. He still had the *tar* in the seat beside him—he got so paranoid in the end, that someone would steal it—but it was crushed too.' It takes me a while to speak, then I ask Jim if he's seen Veronika, but no, he's seen nothing of Veronika, she didn't come to Farhad's funeral, neither did I, there was almost nobody there, just Farhad's father, and Jim, and the promoter: 'Every night, he comes to the cinema to ask when he can announce another cacophony. He lost the Queen's Hotel ballroom, now his club's back by the river.'

It's 11.19pm, and I slip my last coins into the call-box slot. Jim tells me that one of Callaghan's oldest MPs, a close friend, is ill, dying, and an ambulance was sent to Yorkshire this evening to collect him from hospital and bring him to vote, but Callaghan called him on the ward and told him not to come, he could still beat Thatcher... Then, at the last moment, an hour or so ago, Callaghan panicked, changed his mind, and told his aides to get hold of the ambulance driver and instruct him to transport the dying MP at maximum speed down the M1, siren wailing, but the aides realised it was too late, and so the ambulance remains in the hospital's grounds beside the confluence of the Calder and Aire rivers. The vote's result is read out on the radio: 310/311. Callaghan has fallen, and England has fallen, the North has fallen, to Thatcher. The election date will be announced tomorrow. Jim transmits the news in resignation, as though it were a foregone conclusion: 'Thatcher is coming...'. But the no-confidence vote was lost only by a hair's breadth margin, as precarious as that between glaring lucidity and blackout unconsciousness. Now, by a hair's narrowest breadth or the widest of abysses, Thatcher is coming.

The last coins run out and Jim's voice is cut, but he's silent already, engulfed there in the devil's city. I walk past the child's lamenting relatives who are still gazing into the black river's waters, and stand with my hand against the bridge's shrapnel-gouged sandstone parapet, beside the razorwire and stacked concrete blocks. I cannot cross and I cannot return.

7·

CODA

Decades passed. As foretold, Thatcher came to power that Spring, 1979, and destroyed the North, and its cities, and its people, but was usurped by her own minions after only a decade, and died, in embitterment and dementia, her ashes interred in the Chelsea Royal Hospital's grounds. Although he appeared immortal, the devil died too, his body exhibited in the Queen's Hotel bar and buried in the Woodlands cemetery in Scarborough, but once his crimes—always known—were archived, his headstone was pulled out from the black earth of Yorkshire and ground to landfill. The Ripper, finally captured in 1980, still lives, his eyes blinded, in the asylum of Broadmoor—not that of High Royds, now closed—but he will die soon, too. When the history of that winter—the winter of discontent—is known, the ashes of Thatcher, the devil and the Ripper will be unearthed, mixed, and poured from Le Prince's bridge, into the river Aire waters, no longer running with naphthalene, to be carried out into the North Sea.

Many years after that winter, standing in the Berghain nightclub, a former electricity generating-station that once served the Karl-Marx-Allee in East Berlin, I looked up at the striated, chemical-encrusted and disintegrated walls of the abandoned turbine room, blurring and insurging with the nightclub's cacophony, and started to remember the walls of the Futura tramshed, and that city of the North, in that desperate winter of ecstasy and exhilaration, consigned to oblivion.

© DIAPHANES 2018
ISBN 978-3-0358-0030-2

DIAPHANES
HARDSTR. 69 | CH-8004 ZURICH
DRESDENER STR. 118 | D-10999 BERLIN

PRINTED IN GERMANY
LAYOUT: 2EDIT, ZURICH

WWW.DIAPHANES.COM